Back in School

The American Campus

Series editor, Harold S. Wechsler

The books in the American Campus series explore recent developments and public policy issues in higher education in the United States. Topics of interest include access to college, and college affordability; college retention, tenure and academic freedom; campus labor; the expansion and evolution of administrative posts and salaries; the crisis in the humanities and the arts; the corporate university and for-profit colleges; online education; controversy in sport programs; and gender, ethnic, racial, religious, and class dynamics and diversity. Books feature scholarship from a variety of disciplines in the humanities and social sciences.

Vicki L. Baker, Laura Gail Lunsford, and Meghan J. Pifer, *Developing Faculty in Liberal Arts Colleges: Aligning Individual Needs and Organizational Goals*

Derrick R. Brooms, Jelisa Clark, and Matthew Smith, *Empowering Men of Color on Campus: Building Student Community in Higher Education*

W. Carson Byrd, *Poison in the Ivy: Race Relations and the Reproduction of Inequality on Elite College Campuses*

Nolan L. Cabrera, *White Guys on Campus: Racism, White Immunity, and the Myth of "Post-Racial" Higher Education*

Jillian M. Duquaine-Watson, *Mothering by Degrees: Single Mothers and the Pursuit of Postsecondary Education*

Scott Frickel, Mathieu Albert, and Barbara Prainsack, eds., *Investigating Interdisciplinary Collaboration: Theory and Practice across Disciplines*

Gordon Hutner and Feisal G. Mohamed, eds., *A New Deal for the Humanities: Liberal Arts and the Future of Public Higher Education*

Adrianna Kezar and Daniel Maxey, eds., *Envisioning the Faculty for the Twenty-First Century: Moving to a Mission-Oriented and Learner-Centered Model*

Ryan King-White, ed., *Sport and the Neoliberal University: Profit, Politics, and Pedagogy*

Dana M. Malone, *From Single to Serious: Relationships, Gender, and Sexuality on American Evangelical Campuses*

A. Fiona Pearson, *Back in School: How Student Parents Are Transforming College and Family*

Barrett J. Taylor and Brendan Cantwell, *Unequal Higher Education: Wealth, Status, and Student Opportunity*

Back in School

How Student Parents Are Transforming College and Family

A. FIONA PEARSON

RUTGERS UNIVERSITY PRESS

NEW BRUNSWICK, CAMDEN, AND NEWARK, NEW JERSEY, AND LONDON

Library of Congress Cataloging-in-Publication Data

Names: Pearson, A. Fiona, 1966– author.
Title: Back in school : how student parents are transforming college and family /
A. Fiona Pearson.
Description: New Brunswick : Rutgers University Press, [2019] | Series: The American
campus | Includes bibliographical references and index.
Identifiers: LCCN 2018045030 | ISBN 9781978801882 (cloth) | ISBN 9781978801875
(pbk.) | ISBN 9781978801899 (epub) | ISBN 9781978801912 (web pdf)
Subjects: LCSH: Adult college students—Family relationships—United States. |
Public universities and colleges—United States. | Adult education—United States. |
Educational change—United States. | Educational equalization—United States.
Classification: LCC LC5251 .P33 2019 | DDC 378.1/98—dc23
LC record available at https://lccn.loc.gov/2018045030

A British Cataloging-in-Publication record for this book is available
from the British Library.

♾ The paper used in this publication meets the requirements of the American
National Standard for Information Sciences—Permanence of Paper for
Printed Library Materials, ANSI Z39.48-1992.

www.rutgersuniversitypress.org

Manufactured in the United States of America

To Mom, Dad, and Scott with love.
You are parents who inspire.

CONTENTS

Back in School

1

"We're Not Living in the Old School Anymore"

Student Parents on Campus

Marta entered my office, set down her bags, and began pressing me for advice regarding her schedule for the spring term. She had graduated over twenty years earlier from a local community college with an associate's degree in business administration and was now ready to resume her college career by pursing a bachelor's degree in sociology. Her educational career had been temporarily postponed in the early 1990s by the birth of her daughter, which was followed soon after by the birth of her son. She initially put off her education to focus on caring for her children, and later used her associate's degree to leverage a job to pay household bills. Now that her daughter is enrolled in graduate school and her son is preparing to receive his bachelor's degree, she feels it is "her time"— she is ready to go back to school. Within five minutes of our meeting I knew Marta's family's educational history, and within ten minutes she was sharing pictures of her daughter, son, and cousins, describing each family member and listing their educational accomplishments. Marta was incredibly proud of her children and excited to be "back on track," in college, once again pursuing her dream of completing her bachelor's degree.

Yet, as we talked more, Marta expressed concerns regarding the costs of a college degree, not just in terms of money but also in terms of time. She did not need this degree for her job—she was working for the state of Connecticut and had what she described to be "a decent salary and benefits." She was still helping out her daughter, paying for her graduate school tuition. Also, with a full-time job, she was limited as to when she could enroll in classes—anything offered during the day would be impossible for her. Most of the core curriculum that she would eventually need was offered only between 9:00 A.M. and 4:00 P.M., Monday through Friday. She would be an ideal candidate for online programs, which cater to busy working adults, but she was not interested in that kind of educational experience, preferring instead a traditional classroom with teachers and classmates. She wanted to engage face-to-face, eye-to-eye. Pursuing a degree at this particular state university did not seem to me to be a practical option for Marta. Nevertheless, she wanted back in.

Although she didn't explain in any detail why finishing up her degree was so important to her, I understood her desire. As she flipped from one picture to the next on the screen of her phone and described her family members' educational accomplishments, I was reminded of other women in my life who were not expected to go to college. My mother and my mother-in-law were driven by the same desire in the mid-1970s and 1980s, when the passing of Title IX increased college access and resources for women. At that time feminist activists were demanding that the "personal was political," and I saw that mantra lived out on the home front as my mother went to work, bought her first car, and went to class. Neither my mother in California nor my mother-in-law in New York had been expected by their families to attend college, but with public college systems in both of these states expanding, both women found opportunity on opposite sides of the country. They attended classes in between their hours working government jobs and tending to their families, eventually receiving baccalaureate degrees that enabled them to identify as college graduates. My mother, my mother-in-law, and the parents interviewed for this study understand that we live in a world where a college degree confers not only economic advantage but also respect. My mother and mother-in-law, like Marta, wanted in.

Marta's children are grown, and so she has moved into a stage of her family life that fundamentally differs from the student parents in this study who are actively parenting infants, young children, or adolescents. However, I share her story here because it so clearly exemplifies the complex interplay of interactional, cultural, and institutional dimensions guiding students' decision to attend college, particularly those students who have familial obligations or are returning to school after a multiyear absence. Marta's current job status and the fact that her children are older and will soon be self-sufficient free her from having to consider how her education might shape her job opportunities, and so she differs from most of the student parents in this study in that she is not overly concerned about how this degree might influence her career. However, like many of these student parents, Marta yearns for the respect of her children. When she discusses her educational hopes and dreams, she describes herself as excited to learn, to read Shakespeare, to take advantage of what she believes is an educational opportunity and not just a job requirement. This collegiate "club" that Marta, like so many others before and after her, seeks to join will provide her with a level of social prestige that has so far eluded her and cannot be conferred by her middle-class job alone.

My conversation with Marta reveals that students choose to go to college for a mix of reasons that are not all directly career related and that are not explicitly addressed in much public discourse about the purpose or value of college.

It is no surprise that Marta and the student parents interviewed for this study believe a college degree to be both possible and necessary. As I highlight in the following pages, possibility is revealed in the relatively open admission policies of many public universities and community colleges, their geographical accessibility, the rise of for-profit educational institutions that target working adults, the rise in distance learning through online programs, and the widespread availability of financial assistance.

However, as I continued to advise Marta, I began to feel conflicted; as much as I believe in helping students to advance educationally, I held reservations about encouraging her to pursue this degree. As far as I could tell, she didn't want or need this credential in order to advance in her job. Also, it soon became clear that she was going to have to make some significant sacrifices that would disrupt the current balance of her life. She worked full time and so stated that she could take only evening classes. Further, she is still helping her children to pay for college. This would be the third college tuition bill that she would be paying. Mesmerized by her energy, I wanted to support her as she planned for her educational future. I wanted her to get the degree that she desired, but the reality of her current situation made me question both her and my motivations. Why *should* she invest her time, energy, and dollars in this way at this time? What does Marta stand to gain from this experience?

Every one of the forty stories by student parents that I share in these pages is unique, but the narratives reveal struggles, motivations, aspirations, and successes comprising similar threads. Most of the parents I interviewed for this book confess to having very little, if any, time to consider the value of their college experiences as they shuffle between caregivers and classes. Instead, they are concerned with ensuring that laundry baskets contain clean clothes and with carving out hours to complete college homework. Children need feeding, and rides between home and campus need to be arranged. These student parents' day-to-day routines are frequently mundane yet complicated by the many external forces—people, homes, schools, jobs—requiring constant attention. Tending to these various obligations leaves them with very few opportunities to leisurely reflect upon what they want out of their education.

Although parents' lives are rife with competing obligations, fulfilling daily tasks doesn't in every case and at all times produce conflict or tension. When student parents feel themselves being stretched, as they inevitably do, they often respond with creativity, challenging traditional conceptualizations of what it means to be a mother, father, provider, and college student. Rou, at fifty-four years old, never thought he would have the opportunity to be a father, but that changed four years ago when his daughter was born. When I ask him if his wife is supportive of his educational goals, he responds that because she is the breadwinner and because his college schedule is flexible, he can devote time to fathering in a way that previous generations could not, and so she appreciates that he can be a "Mr. Mom." That said, not everyone in his family has been so supportive—his in-laws have explicitly challenged his masculinity, questioning his choice to return to school after having been laid off a year ago. And Rou has had a tough go of it, moving from job to job over the years, in part due to a medical condition that impairs his ability to take on more physical work. But Rou relishes both his fathering and his student roles and brushes off their criticism, asserting, "We are not living in the old school anymore. We're living in an entirely different mode of society."

No doubt, some student parents have it easier than others. Some, like Rou, have supportive partners, dependable *and* affordable caregivers, and sympathetic professors and mentors. These reinforcements ease the demands of the day and allow them to focus their attention as needed. A mother who knows that her child is well cared for in a comfortable and safe setting can better concentrate on an in-class review for midterm exams. Others, however, run into overwhelming obstacles, like Rose, who is battling an oppressive husband with a gambling addiction, or Lucille, who regularly navigates labyrinthine medical and state bureaucracies to address her autistic son's educational and mental health needs. Student parents facing such barriers are likely to receive lower grades or to experience internalized feelings of inadequacy and bouts of depression. Nevertheless, all the students in this study share stories of survival. Whether they are motivated by economic or social mobility, a love for learning, or a feeling of recognized accomplishment, these students are actively working toward their academic goal of earning a college degree. They are moving forward as they strive to weave together their various identities, aspirations, and expectations.

Back in School celebrates these students' achievements. It also examines their educational aspirations and highlights the social processes and institutional resources that facilitate their successes or obstruct their long-term goals. Because these students are attending community colleges and regional comprehensive state universities, this study addresses public institutions, which are locally focused and educating the majority of our nation's college students (NCES 2016). I ask, how do policymakers, professors, college administrators, counselors, or social workers provide or deny access to child care, tutoring, financial aid, or other campus- or community-based resources? How do social norms and governmental and organizational policies influence access to these resources and influence student parents' experiences on campus? More broadly, I seek to understand the cultural, economic, and political forces that shape contemporary conceptualizations of education and work as we venture forward in the twenty-first century. What do we expect from a college education, particularly in our public colleges and universities? And how are our educational expectations and opportunities shaped by public policies, the economy, and cultural beliefs regarding the perceived function of higher education?

At the state university in central Connecticut where I teach, I am no longer surprised by the sight of baby strollers on the pathways and children playing by the center court fish pond. And our campus is far from unique in this regard. Campus administrators, faculty, and staff—particularly those working for public universities or two-year community colleges—are ever more likely to encounter in their offices and classrooms students who are parents negotiating the multiple demands of work, family, and school. These changes are in part due to increasing numbers of older students returning to college, eager to attain a degree that they may have deferred in order to start a family, engage in paid work, or enter the military (NCES 2018). Many of these older students are returning to school with the hopes of redirecting their career paths or, like Marta, finishing up degrees that they started years ago but never finished.

With access to college and the perceived need for a college degree steadily rising, the number of older and returning students on postsecondary campuses has reached historic highs over the past few decades, a trend reflected across the United States and in other industrialized nations around the world (OECD 2015). According to the U.S. Department of Education, approximately 25 percent of undergraduate students in the United States are raising children under the age of eighteen, and over half of those students are single parents (NCES 2015a). The largest percentage of these student parents are found on community college campuses; just over 30 percent of the students attending two-year public colleges report caring for dependents as compared to nearly 15 percent who attend four-year, baccalaureate-granting public institutions (Gault et al. 2014; Noll, Reichlin, and Gault 2017). Although it is clear that student parents are more likely to be found enrolled in two-year associate- or graduate-level programs, over the past thirty years *all* categories of postsecondary institutions (two-year, four-year, private, public, for-profit, and nonprofit) have experienced record levels in their enrollment of student parents (Choy 2002; NCES 2018).

In response to this rising demographic, many postsecondary institutions have increased their distance learning opportunities, providing flexible learning options that would appeal to many student parents (Mettler 2014). Advertisements on late-night television and via various internet searches explicitly acknowledge the perceived needs of student parents and older, returning adults desiring a college degree. For-profit programs, such as the University of Phoenix, compete with public state schools, such as Arizona State University, which in 2017 offered over seventy baccalaureate degrees online in majors ranging from art history to technical entrepreneurship and management. In 2011 *U.S. News and World Report* added a new category, "Best Online Programs," to its annual inventory of best colleges, indicating the increased presence, relevance, and institutional acceptance of online learning in higher education (Haynie 2014).

For those student parents who prefer a traditional campus experience and can afford the often higher tuition, a small number of private, liberal arts colleges have long offered comprehensive academic support programs to facilitate the success of student parents on their respective campuses. Several of these programs have historically catered to mothers returning to school. The founders and directors of programs such as Smith College's Ada Comstock Program, Tufts University's REAL Program, and Endicott College's Keys to Degrees program focus on the needs of nontraditional students and caregivers. These programs have helped student parents in various ways, with some providing access to affordable, high-quality child care and others offering family residential living opportunities.[1]

However, comprehensive residential programs for students with children are the exception rather than the norm. According to analysts at the Institute for Women's Policy Research, over 90 percent of private, nonprofit colleges did not provide any on-campus child care, undeniably the most important institutional resource for student parents with young children (Miller, Gault, and Thorman 2011: 17). The lack of child care can be partially explained by the rise in number of private, for-profit colleges, which is the least likely type of postsecondary institution to provide on-site child care—less than 1 percent offers such a resource. Many private, for-profit colleges don't have to offer child care because they are more likely than all other types of postsecondary institutions to offer distance learning options so that students can pursue their degrees from home (Aud et al. 2012). In emphasizing distance learning options, these colleges are freed from having to provide a number of on-ground student services, including counseling offices, student activities, and resources such as child care.

Public colleges have been significantly more likely to offer such care—in 2003, 55 percent of four-year and 53 percent of two-year colleges provided some form of on-site, early child care program (Gault et al. 2014). However, in recent years, students attending public colleges have seen their on-site, campus child care options dwindling, as college administrators wrestle with the enduring effects of the 2008 economic recession on their campus budgets. A report from the Institute for Women's Policy Research reveals that 32 of 572 child care centers located on a community college campus closed between the years 2007 and 2009 (Miller, Gault, and Thorman 2011: 18). As the economies of many states continue to suffer and as public colleges struggle to balance their budgets in the wake of austerity and diminished state funding, it is highly likely that the proportion of campuses offering on-site child care will continue to decrease in the years to come (Mitchell and Leachman 2015).

Clearly the responses of postsecondary institutions to this emerging student demographic group of older students are mixed. Over the past four decades, colleges have responded in varying ways to the needs of students with disabilities or those who are first-generation students, athletes, or veterans, providing necessary institutional supports to address their distinctive situations and facilitate their success on campus (Hamrick, Evans, and Schuh 2002; Long 2012). These resources—including tutoring, mentoring, targeted counseling, and learning and testing accommodations—serve these students in important ways that ultimately increase their long-term likelihood of academic success. Unlike these various student constituencies, however, student parents remain a largely invisible group and are often left to figure out campus life by themselves, particularly when it comes to arranging for child care, weaving domestic and student obligations, and "coming out" as a parent to their professors and student peers. They are very much aware that as students, they are not perceived to be the "norm," particularly in bachelor's and graduate programs, and that the academic road ahead of them will likely be filled with obstacles that traditional students do not face.

In these pages are the words of student parents who are forging a way to weave together their student and parent identities at work, at home, and on campus. Some are young parents and so blend in with the general student body, and others are returning to campus after many years of working, military service, or raising families. Some qualify for public assistance and others are comfortably middle or upper-middle class. All of them have decided to attend public regional universities or community colleges that are geographically accessible and less expensive than most private nonprofit or for-profit alternatives. All of them believe that in going to college, they are improving their lives and the lives of their family members. Through their experiences, we gain insight as to how these students define success and strive to attain dignity within the various social spheres in which they travel. Through their experiences, we also gain a deeper understanding of the role of public higher education in the twenty-first century.

The Twenty-First-Century Student

Although the experiences that I describe in *Back in School* are specific to the student parents interviewed, anyone who is or has been a student will recognize many of the interactional, institutional, and cultural influences analyzed. Most students understand the difficulties of managing their time and negotiating the competing demands of various professors, family members, friends, or employers. And, of course, most students are challenged with managing their campus identities and responsibilities, all while maintaining strong personal relationships and tending to their physical health. Friends and family members may push and pull, hoping to wield some influence over students' demanding study schedules. Professors may slip in additional assignments with only a week's or even a day's notice, and employers may request additional hours during finals week to accommodate the needs of their businesses. All-night cramming sessions before an exam are both a cultural cliché and an all-too-real experience, revealing the pressures and stressors that often mark the college years.

In recent years, many students, not just student parents, additionally share a heightened awareness of the economic implications of their day-to-day educational choices. College has never been more expensive. The College Board, which annually tracks college and university tuition trends, reported that the cost of college has steadily increased over the past three decades, outpacing general inflation and levels of state funding and financial assistance (Baum and Ma 2013). It is therefore not surprising that instrumentalist logic, which defines the value of a college degree in terms of its practicality and the likelihood of procuring a specific job, dominates both public and private discourse. In an era of growing inequality, stagnant wages, increasing educational costs and student debt, and a culture in which branding and commodification are norms rather than exceptions, politicians, policymakers, and students are today more likely than past generations to talk about the value of their degrees in economic terms.

Instrumentalist discourse and logic, however, have not gone completely unchallenged in the public sphere. In *The Knowledge Factory*, Stanley Aronowitz (2000) laments the steady rise of "corporate universities" and the ways that they are shaping education and ultimately failing "to prepare students for a world of great complexity" (p. 158). More recently, sociologist Gaye Tuchman (2009), university president Michael Roth (2014), and journalist Fareed Zakaria (2015) join a chorus of critics who argue that too many twenty-first-century postsecondary institutions have deferred to the whims and needs of a fickle marketplace. When university administrators appropriate the language of corporations, we become accustomed to hearing educational objectives discussed in the context of customer service and returns on investment. These critics are fearful when colleges use such language and emphasize training over critical inquiry and sacrifice a broad education to narrow job preparation. The ostensible goal of such an educational system is to develop malleable employees rather than an educated citizenry. Instead, critics like Tuchman, Roth, and Zakaria advocate for a postsecondary liberal arts education that promotes clear and creative thinking, debate, democracy, and freedom.

Yet it's near impossible to forgo the language of the marketplace and a narrow focus on skills and jobs when the cost of college increases faster than the rate of inflation and shows no sign of slowing down. As the price of college tuition and student debt increases, anyone who has a stake in the issue is discussing the role of higher education in regard to how it shapes personal lives and contemporary society. What do we expect from a college education? What kinds of classroom learning do we value? Perhaps most importantly, how do we imagine students' lives will be improved by their college or university experience?

Past research has clearly revealed that how we come to value a college education is very much determined by our access to particular kinds of educational institutions, our understanding of the purpose of college, and our expectations regarding the kind of learning that takes place in college classrooms (McDonough

1997; Mullen 2010; Rose 2012; Stuber 2011). In very important ways these beliefs are influenced by not just a student's academic capabilities but also a student's resources—economic, social, and cultural—that collectively influence the student's position in the larger social sphere. That is, an individual's educational access and views regarding the purpose of college and the value of learning are all very much shaped by the kinds of postsecondary institutions that others in a student's social milieu are likewise attending. Their perspectives and college access are also affected by their familiarity with and adherence to the cultural norms and values that are reflected in an institution's mission, curriculum, organizations, and resources. And educational researchers have repeatedly affirmed that students' cultural and social capital are highly correlated with their economic status (Armstrong and Hamilton 2013; Mullen 2010; Stuber 2011). As wealth increases, so does one's knowledge of the college game and how to access selective colleges, lucrative internships, and promising entry-level jobs.

Further, an examination of life course experiences paints a more complicated picture than is often revealed in contemporary debates regarding the purpose of college. Even those students enrolled in applied career and technical programs, particularly in for-profit colleges, are far from assured a job that they might consider to be a career upon graduating (McMillan Cottom 2017; Mettler 2014). This is not to say that short-term or skill-based degrees are of no value; associate degrees or vocational and technical certifications can most certainly provide the necessary skills training or credentials that allow for personal opportunity or upward mobility (Rose 2012). However, most of the student parents in this study have found those short-term degrees or vocational certifications to be insufficient to attain either the standard of living or the type of job that they desire at this point in their lives.

For some of these college students, acquiring specific skills in order to succeed in a particular job is their primary expressed goal. Other students are less concerned with skill building and instead seek a credential in the form of a degree that they believe will provide them with a competitive edge over other uncredentialed job applicants. Many of these students also reflect upon their gain of social status once they are able to refer to themselves as college graduates. And yet, others talk about the desire to learn about themselves and their world in order to share that knowledge with their children.

Jeffrey J. Selingo (2013), editor at large for the *Chronicle of Higher Education*, maintains that college in the twenty-first century is "no longer a one-size-fits-all experience" (p. xv). Although we may think of "American higher education as a cohesive system," he contends that "there is nothing uniform about it" (p. xvi). My findings in this study confirm that what we expect from and experience in college in the twenty-first century has never been more varied and complex. Particularly in public community colleges and universities, whose budgets are significantly affected by local and national legislators and who serve highly diverse student bodies, the purpose of higher education is fiercely debated and contested.

These issues regarding the role of higher education in the twenty-first century concern all students as they prepare to devote precious energy, emotion, time, and financial resources to their postsecondary educational experience. Those student parents who lack financial resources or whose emotions and time are stretched thin due to their obligations to family are most likely to have their commitment to a college education tested. All college students, particularly those who are caregivers, are asking what sacrifices—in regard to not just money but also time and emotion—are acceptable in their lives? In short, just how much is a college education worth?

The "Good Parent"

Not only will students, even those who are not parents, recognize some of the interactional, cultural, and institutional processes examined in *Back in School*, but most parents, even if they are not now in school, will likely understand the external pressures and demands described in the pages that follow. Most parents have dealt with the stress and concern that come along with caring for an ill child, making frantic phone calls to doctors or caregivers, and rearranging daily schedules to accommodate a child's immediate needs. They have struggled to coordinate the scheduling demands of various household members, and they have found themselves seeking creative solutions when caregiving programs or schools are closed for national holidays or, in colder climates, unexpected snow days. Further, all parents are challenged with negotiating relationships with other adults—partners, siblings, their own parents, cousins, friends—who either aid in this complex process of parenting or compete for attention and assistance. Some of these family members and friends make parenting easier, providing child care at a moment's notice or chauffeuring children between school and soccer. Others add to the demands of parents' already complicated daily schedules, requiring counseling, transporting, or general caregiving.

And for all parents these responsibilities and relationships are often very much shaped by gender. Many mothers feel pressure to live up to mythical expectations imposed by what Susan J. Douglas and Meredith W. Michaels (2004) describe in *The Mommy Myth: The Idealization of Motherhood and How It Has Undermined Women* as the "new momism," or what Sharon Hays (1996) defines in *Cultural Contradictions of Motherhood* as "intensive mothering." Such expectations dominate public discourse regarding what it means to a *good* mother in an age of increasing economic inequality. A good mother not only provides food, clothing, and shelter for her children but also invests an extraordinary amount of time, emotion, and money to ensure that her children are personally and relationally successful. Within the neoliberal political and economic spheres, the children of a good mother are financially independent from the state and are expected, as a result of her careful guidance and self-sacrifice, to become successful in their careers and active contributors to the economy. These "good mothers" are not "takers" from welfare, relying on public assistance to provide food, shelter, or child care. They are instead altruistic providers, who—in the words of Sarah Palin, the 2008 Republican vice presidential candidate—are "mama grizzlies," doing anything and everything to defend and provide for the needs of their young.

Most mothers, particularly single mothers, fully realize the impossibility and impracticality of such ideological and politicized social constructions of motherhood. Despite knowing this, most mothers find it difficult to ward off feelings of inadequacy when falling short of such idealizations. The student mothers interviewed for this book were no exception. Many student mothers talked at length about feeling overwhelmed by the many demands of the roles they were juggling and the moral pressure to live up to contemporary conceptualizations of the "good mother." They rarely felt that they were doing enough at home, at school, or at work and nearly always felt that their energies were divided and insufficient. Joy, a fifty-two-year-old mother of three, describes the quandary many parents, particularly mothers, experience when faced with an ill child on a school or work day. Joy exasperatingly confesses, "There's just worlds colliding."

Although ideologies surrounding fatherhood likewise exert constraining moral pressures on fathers, the historical context producing that pressure and its effects are significantly different. Most fathers have not been exposed in the media or in public policy discourse to the same level of cultural monitoring and critique as have been mothers. This is not to say that all fathers escape public critique—low-income African American and Latino fathers have been frequent targets in public discourse regarding the problems of teen motherhood and the plight of the urban poor (Connor and White 2006; Hamer 2001). However, fathers in general and active fathers in particular have benefited from a shift in public perception that has redefined masculinity to encompass hands-on fathering. As a result, fathers may receive praise for engaging in mundane caregiving or household work that mothers are simply expected to perform.[2]

The double standard is even more glaring when the case of single parenthood is considered. Desyre, a social work student, has been raising her two-year-old daughter by herself, with little to no assistance from her daughter's father. When I ask Desyre whether or not she believes parenting is generally valued in our culture, she immediately describes how perceptions of single parents vary along gender lines, lamenting, "If you see a father . . . a single father, it's like 'Oh, he's the greatest thing in the world.' But you see single mothers all the time, and it's just like, 'Yeah,' you know?" Adding further sting to this painful double standard, low-income women are often blamed for their single-parent status. Whereas single fathers are presumed to have been abandoned and left on their own to raise their children, single mothers find themselves stigmatized as promiscuous or lacking in control (Duquaine-Watson 2017; Roberts 1997). In both cases, women are perceived as primarily responsible for creating the problem of low-income, single-parent households.

Fathers do not have it uniformly easy though. Many more men have begun to take on traditionally feminine or womanly activities in the household as conceptualizations of masculinity and femininity evolve; however, such changes are not unconditionally accepted, much less celebrated, in all communities or homes. Several fathers in this study speak candidly about the skepticism they face when expressing their desire to forgo the traditional role of breadwinner in order to pursue a college degree—they face their masculinity being questioned and their sense of self being challenged. In regard to going back to school, prioritizing education over job can be an emasculating experience for many student fathers, particularly in families or communities in which traditional gender roles prevail. These men, like the fathers interviewed by Andrea Doucet (2005), author of *Do Men Mother?*, find that fathering is a complex, identity-forming activity that is very much influenced by the social contexts in which it is performed. Their fathering behaviors are as much shaped by the immediate demands and structuring of their day as they are by cultural norms reflected in their immediate family and in society at large.

Both mothers and fathers are trekking new ground as they reconceptualize their familial roles in the twenty-first century. When a mother feels guilt as she leaves her infant with a caregiver so that she can go to class, she psychologically engages in a war between competing, morally infused ideologies regarding the best way to parent. Should she be devoting time and energy to address the present needs of her child? Or should she attend to her academic self-development, for which the outcomes are abstract, long-term, and, as a result, far from clear? Such contradictory feelings are exacerbated when it is so difficult to find and retain affordable, high-quality child care, when concerned family members question her devotion to their needs, or when professors question her dedication to their courses. When student parents' experiences do not match the expectations that they and others have regularly relied upon for meaning making, they reveal the sometimes deep tensions between their individual actions and the social systems in which they are enmeshed. But so too is created an opportunity for alternative meanings and, ultimately, the possibility for transformative cultural and social change.

Sociological Lenses: Linking the Particular with the Structural

In the mid-1980s, I entered college as an eighteen-year-old with no family members dependent on my income or time. I never really thought about not going to college, having watched my mother struggle over the years as she pursued her own college degree, first at the local community college and then at a nearby state university. I abstractly believed in the value of college, even if I only vaguely knew what I wanted out of my education beyond a credential. I worked off campus to earn money to pay for my car and leisure activities, but my parents could afford the then-reasonable state school tuition fees, and my hours for the most part belonged to me.

Jumping ahead twenty years, my familial and educational experiences were vastly different—I was then six years into a doctoral program, all while teaching full time and raising two young girls. I was intellectually invigorated by my studies, which provided me with an opportunity to engage in multidisciplinary analyses of key issues that personally and socially resonated, and I loved teaching in the college classroom. Nevertheless, I felt profoundly different from most of my graduate student peers as I plodded around campus in my pregnancy pants with my schoolbag stuffed with emergency diapers. I watched cohorts of students come and go as they moved through the program more quickly than I because of my part-time student status. I had chosen to attend this particular university because it was the only institution nearby that would allow for me to enroll in graduate school part time. Within a few months of my daughter being born, I found other graduate students who shared my experiences, nursing babies while leafing through tomes from our respective disciplines. We shared strategies for tending to fussy eaters while voicing our concerns regarding whether or not we would actually make it through to graduation. Many a day, I wondered why I felt such guilt when I went to the zoo in lieu of the university library. I would chastise myself for not being able to stop obsessing about a project on my desk back home while at the park with my daughter.

This is not to say that all moments during those years were wracked by contradictions—there were plenty of times when I felt my identities as student and parent blended harmoniously. For one, I was fortunate to have an incredibly supportive, if equally busy, partner whose academic schedule similarly provided him with flexible work hours. We were able to schedule our teaching obligations so that one of us was nearly always available for our daughters, and we actively attempted to share as equally as possible the work of caregiving, cleaning, and cooking. I also had supportive professors, several of whom had young children of their own, who invited my daughters into their offices and homes and encouraged me to share rather than hide my needs as a mother and an academic. Further, my experience as a parent significantly influenced my teaching and scholarship as I began to direct my intellectual energy into research on education and parenting. In the late 1990s, just before the birth of my first daughter in 2000, I became interested in exploring the effects of the U.S. 1996 welfare reform law on students' educational opportunities. By 2003, I was conducting interviews with student parents while visibly pregnant with my second daughter. My large belly during those months served as an unusually successful icebreaker as I met with students, who, in addition to sharing their experiences managing school and home, were sometimes eager to provide me with advice about how to best manage my impending labor and delivery.

Three years later, I began a tenure-track position while my daughters were then three and six years old. My office mate, a new hire in a different department, was pregnant and concerned about how she was going to manage her spring teaching load—her baby was due at the end of December, right in the middle of a month-long break between fall and spring classes. Unlike my experience in graduate school, which I've come to learn was more atypical than that of most of my peers in academia, she was not encouraged to share her parenting needs on campus. I'm still not quite sure how she survived that spring term, negotiating class preps, grading, and committee meetings with a newborn's erratic sleeping and feeding schedule. Before the semester started, we had no lactation rooms on campus—at least by the end of January after the birth of her son, we had one (although it was hardly ideal, located in an old faculty bathroom with cold tile floors, no windows, and a practical steel chair circa 1970s). Parents on campus had no paid maternity leave (unless of course one was eligible to purchase short-term disability insurance—such insurance generally considers pregnancy a "disability"), no infant care, and no parent support group. Although twelve years later, our university still has no paid maternity leave and no infant care, we at least have two groups and our faculty union advocating for such resources and actively working to change the culture on campus for all parents.

Collectively, these personal experiences have deeply informed *Back in School* and shape the perspective that I bring to this project. As a sociologist, I am practiced in exploring the connections between what C. Wright Mills, over half a century ago in *The Sociological Imagination* (1959), described as "personal troubles" and "public issues." Mills maintained that to make full sense of our individual experiences, we must turn to history while simultaneously examining how social structures have influenced our comprehension of the past and present. Further we must interrogate power and explore its functioning in our biographies and social world as these histories are constructed. Our biographies, Mills contended, are very much constrained by social and historical realities and the limited choices that those realities make available to us. Mills nonetheless advocated for transformative action, positing that we "by the fact of this living," can contribute "however minutely, to the shaping of this society and to the course of its history" even as we are borne of and subject to its "historical push and shove" (p. 6).

Most sociologists concede that the "push and shove" of history and social structure upon our lived biographies is strong. Attempting to bridge the gulf between agency and social structures, sociological theorists have examined the powerful influence of culture as a structurally embedded yet potentially transformative mediating force shaping social action (Bourdieu 1990; DiMaggio 1997; Hays 1994; Sewell 1992). One highly influential theory of culture is provided by Pierre Bourdieu (1977, 1984), who explores the dynamics shaping the relationships between culture, structure, and agency in his theoretical construction of habitus. It is one's habitus, a set of "systems of durable, transposable dispositions" (1977: 72) that guides individual action and increases a person's likelihood of responding in a particular way within historically situated social contexts. As Bourdieu so artfully describes, even though we may perceive ourselves as individual actors in our social world, each one of us is like a "train bringing along its own rails" (p. 79). We may lay the track, but we are also wedded to its materials and sources in complex ways.[3] Importantly for Bourdieu, one's habitus is clearly informed by and influences one's position in the social class structure. For these reasons, a number of educational researchers have come to identify habitus as a key site for examining the role of culture in the process of reproducing inequality in schools and society (Dumais 2002; Lareau 2003; Mullen 2010).

Although Bourdieu is duly credited for shedding light on complex social processes that help us to understand how inequalities are reproduced, his theory of habitus is criticized for its near exclusive emphasis on "signals of socioeconomic and cultural status" (Lamont 1992: 181) and its fixed "determinism that makes significant social transformation seem impossible" (Sewell 1992: 15). In addressing the limitations of any theory that diminishes or even erases the interconnections between structure and agency, sociologist Sharon Hays (1994) calls for a more integrated and dynamic conceptualization of culture. She advocates for "a conception of structure as more than a pattern of material, objective, and external constraints engendering human passivity; for a conception of agency as more than action that is un-structured, individual, subjective, random and implying absolute freedom; and for a conception of culture as a part of social structure" (p. 58). Such a theory of culture would acknowledge the prevalence and durability of social structure while allowing for transformative, albeit limited, agency.

With this objective in mind, Hays defines culture as systems of meaning that transcend the individual yet influence and are influenced by individual action and are an integral part of social structure. These systems of meaning include "not only the beliefs and values of social groups, but also their language, forms of knowledge and common sense, as well as the material products, interactional practices, rituals, and ways of life established by these" (p. 65). Hays highlights here the various dimensions of culture that guide action, drawing much needed attention to the complex process of meaning making. In this way, Hays reminds us that culture influences "not only what we think about, but *how* we think about it" (p. 68), leaving sociologists of culture to explore the vast intricacies of these social processes.

One of the more provocative turns in the sociology of culture that examines "how we think" is advanced by Ann Swidler (1986, 2001), who shifts our gaze
to this messy process of meaning making. Swidler encourages analysts to explore
both the "what," the cultured capacities—the skills, habits, and styles—that constitute social actors' cultural "toolkits" and the "how," the ways that social actors,
singularly and in the aggregate, nurture, select, and use their capacities in the
context of social institutions and interactions.[4] In line with many contemporary
theorists of culture, Swidler maintains that culture is embedded and reflected
in ourselves, our actions, and our environments and is therefore ultimately frag-
mentary and dynamic, not existing "out there" in any stable and unified fashion (DiMaggio 1997; Hays 1994; Sewell 1992). Instead, culture's influence lies in
strategies of action and so is "*facilitative* rather than determinative" (p. 105).[5]
Swidler acknowledges the complex and varied ways cultural theorists, going back
as far as Max Weber ([1958] 2003), have used the concept of logics to elucidate
processes of meaning making and action. She herself advocates for an understanding that conceives of such logics as "tools or resources that cultivate skills
and capacities that people integrate into larger more stable 'strategies of
action'" (Swidler 2001: 187). The task for social analysts, then, is to research how
competing cultural logics emerge at particular historical moments and how
social actors turn to and use such logics, or not, in the dual processes of meaning making and the shaping of dispositions toward action.

Anita Ilta Garey (1999), in her book *Weaving Work and Motherhood*, provides
a compelling example of a potential path forward for exploring these cultural
social processes, specifically as they shape contemporary parenting. Garey's
interview study examines how women hospital workers with children use what
she refers to as "strategies of being" to "reconcile their identities as mothers and
as workers" (p. 13). In doing so, Garey focuses her analysis on a strand of strategies or dispositions that refer to ways of thinking that "reconcile actions with a
sense of self" (p. 23).[6] While so much work and life balance research focuses on
conflict between parenting and worker roles, Garey instead relies on the meta-
phor of weaving to illuminate both the process of merging mothering and worker
identities and the product of having woven a coherent sense of self in the context of otherwise constraining cultural and institutional structures.[7]

In the pages that follow, I explore the various ways these student parents
negotiate the "push and shove" of history, culture, and various social institutions as they forge tracks that they hope will lead them to fulfilling their educational and familial goals.[8] Along the way, these student parents encounter
obstacles that halt their progress. At other times, they gain access to resources
and ways of meaning that fuel them forward. Here I not only highlight the effects
on student parents of organizational structures and public policy but also explore
how they embrace, reject, or modify competing cultural logics. Collectively, these
social processes shape and are shaped by these students parents' strategies of

being as they make sense of parenting and the purpose of higher education—fifty years prior, most of these students would not likely have attended college at all. At the beginning of the twenty-first century, however, these students can now choose to pursue a college degree, and, just as importantly, they feel the pressure to attain such credentials. Their perspectives provide insight into the various ways individual identities, social institutions, and culture are reproduced or are challenged and changed.

Learning from Student Parents

To better understand these social processes, I interviewed forty students—twenty-nine mothers and eleven fathers—between the years 2007 and 2014 in the state of Connecticut. Finding these student parents was not easy. Most college campuses do not collect data that allow for the distinct identification of students who are parents, a problem that has hindered researchers hoping to better understand student parents' needs (Goldrick-Rab and Sorenson 2011; Miller et al. 2011).

For one, not all student parents define their parental status in ways that might be represented in various campus-based surveys. Although students who are applying for financial aid—including grants and loans—will provide information regarding dependents, not all student parents apply for financial aid. Just over 14 percent of the students in my sample reported not relying on any loans or grants to pay for their education. Even when student parents do answer questions regarding their dependents, either on financial aid or other surveys, their answers may not reflect their home situations in ways that allow us to identify them as student parents. For example, young student parents living with their own parents may not claim their own children on their tax returns. Instead grandparents who are claiming their own children (as long as those children are full-time students, they may be claimed as dependents until they reach the age of twenty-four) may also claim their grandchildren. Or parents who are not married but live together with their children or who are divorced and share partial custody may very well not claim their children as dependents on financial aid applications because their partner instead claims them. In short, the term *dependents* denotes a tax status and not the lived caregiving experience of many of these parents, shaping their responses in such surveys in sometimes unpredictable ways.

Given these existing limitations, I relied on purposive, nonrandom sampling methods to identify potential participants. Student parents responded to posters that I distributed around campuses of two public universities and two public community colleges, all four of which were located in the northeastern U.S. region. These colleges and universities primarily serve students from within the state, with less than 5 percent of admitted full-time university students coming from outside the state. In 2013, the average annual cost of in-state tuition, room, and board for an undergraduate student was almost $20,000 at the four-year state universities, and tuition was just under $4,000 at the community colleges. Most students in this study responded to the posters, which were placed on student center billboards, on cafeteria walls, in the stairwells of classroom buildings, and outside library entryways. At least six parents stated that they learned of my study from a parent whom I had previously interviewed—at the end of my interviews, I provided participants with a small business card–sized flier that briefly described the study and encouraged them to pass on the information to other potentially interested parents.

All forty parents interviewed are raising children under the age of fourteen years, with twenty-nine students raising children ages five years and younger (see the appendix for more information about the sample). I paid student parents $25 for participating in the study—a nominal fee that I hoped would aid in their paying for child care while they met with me. Full interviews lasted from one to four hours, with most interviews averaging two hours. At the beginning of the interview, student parents completed a brief written questionnaire, covering basic demographic information regarding themselves, their family, and their work and educational history. After they completed the questionnaire, I utilized a semistructured interview format, asking them a series of questions regarding their familial and educational experiences. I asked them to share the story of their transition to college and to explain their reasons for pursuing a college degree at this particular juncture of their lives. I also asked them to share the stories of the birth of their children and to describe their approaches to parenting. Finally, I asked them to voice their perceptions of cultural beliefs pertaining to education and parenting and to explain how their beliefs correlated with or diverged from those beliefs promulgated in popular discourse.

In addition to talking with student parents, I informally interviewed over twenty-five various campus and community representatives—faculty, program directors, and administrators. Some of these people have worked with student parents, and others have actually advocated for increased student parent resources on college and university campuses over the years. Directors of campus-based women's centers have long argued for child care services and counseling support, particularly given the past and still present reality that woman more often than men are primarily responsible for family caregiving responsibilities. In response to prevailing popular discourse regarding caregiving demands and the workplace, many campuses in the past few decades have hired work life coordinators to address the unique needs of faculty, staff, and, in some cases, students who are tending to the caregiving of family members, including spouses, children, and elderly parents. The public colleges attended by these student parents did not have work life or student parent coordinators, but in talking to administrators from other private and public colleges and universities, I came to understand how campuses can work to create family-friendly cultures for students, faculty, and staff. These supplemental interviews in conjunction with analyses of higher educational history, public policy, and national data—all of which allow me to contextualize these findings—complement the stories and perspectives shared by student parents, providing culturally and institutionally based counterpoints to students' stated beliefs regarding what it means and what it takes to be a student parent in the twenty-first century.

The Shape of This Book

I begin chapter 2 by historically situating this analysis, providing an overview of higher education that helps us to understand how a seat in a college classroom came to be both open to and expected by these student parents. The contemporary social institutions and cultural logics that currently influence these student parents' educational opportunities and strategies of being are profoundly shaped by this history. A review of the emergence of higher education reveals an ever expanding network of colleges and universities over the past two hundred years. As access to postsecondary institutions increased, in part due to changes in funding sources providing aid not only to colleges but also to college students themselves, so did the expectation that one would attend college after high school. I also explore debates regarding the purpose and function of college at the beginning of the twenty-first century. I review various cultural narratives that inform higher educational policymaking and influence the ways in which many students have come to articulate the purpose of a college education, particularly as it is connected to future employment As the price of college tuition and student debt increases and as varied critics, including Florida governor Rick Scott and CNN journalist Fareed Zakaria, present competing views about the purpose and role of public colleges and universities, anyone who has a stake in the issue is discussing the role of higher education as it shapes personal lives and contemporary society.

Chapter 3 examines the specific college-going experiences of these student parents, with an emphasis on the ways that institutional and organizational social norms, resources, and processes shape those experiences. By examining their choices to attend public colleges and universities, their access to financial aid, the availability of on-campus child care, and their interactions with faculty and peers, we gain insight as to how students enact their cultured capacities in the context of a particular campus culture. The culture that a campus develops may or may not recognize and address the unique skills, habits, and styles of particular student subgroups. Students' experiences with programs and with the professors, coaches, and case managers who represent those programs collectively impact student parents' educational trajectories, fundamentally influencing their sense of belonging on campus and their success in an academic environment.

In chapter 4, I shift the focus from macro-oriented frames exploring educational history and organizational culture to examine the cultural logics that students draw upon to make sense of the role of higher education in their lives. Student parents have decided that pursuing a college degree is worthy of their investment of money, time, and energy, but what is it that they expect to gain? In an age of rising tuition and indeterminate job opportunities, just what do students want from their college experience? As I explore student parents' descriptions of their educational expectations and aspirations, three distinct dispositions emerge—job seekers, practical explorers, and self-reflective learners. In this chapter, I trace the ways that students draw upon sometimes competing and sometimes complementary cultural logics that reflect distinct educational dispositions. These dispositions possess the potential to shape their college experience and influence their likelihood of educational success. The tensions that exist in public debates about the value of higher education are very much at play in how these students discuss their expectations of college and reveal their strategies of being.

Chapters 5 and 6 explore the potential implications of students' strategies of being as revealed in their home lives and career trajectories. To facilitate this exploration, I focus on two ideologically common cultural logics that strongly influence contemporary narratives of parenting, work, and education: gendered separate spheres and instrumentalist framings of schooling, jobs, and the economy. In chapter 5, I turn to the home front and analyze how students align with or challenge cultural ideals of gender, parenting, and work. I examine how student parents conceptualize their student and parent identities, engaging in strategies and interpreting their effects in ways that bolster their sense of well-being and worth. This section reveals how students negotiate their household, caregiving, and educational labor at home in the context of a gendered separate spheres logic. I also explore morally infused cultural idealizations of parenting and how student parents come to understand and sometimes challenge what it means to be a "good" mother or father (Hays 1996; Moen and Yu 2000). As these student parents seek to affirm their parenting and student identities, they encourage those around them to likewise value their caregiving, domestic, and educational labor. This analysis provides a glimpse into the struggles that students experience at home, struggles that some days weigh them down but other days free them from social constraints and stretch their imaginations.

In chapter 6, I examine how students' past experiences and aspirations align with or challenge dominant cultural framings that emphasize the positive relationship between education, job skills, and the economy. Tracing the job and educational histories of three students—a job seeker, a practical explorer, and a self-reflective learner—I analyze the connections and disconnects between these student parents' prior educational credentials, past jobs, and future educational and career aspirations. Public and political discourse tends to portray higher education as a cure-all for the shortcomings or failures of individuals within the contemporary economy. However, a close examination of these students' histories reveals that such a message oversimplifies the complexities of a twenty-first-century capitalist economy in which declining real wages, increasing income inequality, gendered jobs, outsourcing, quickly evolving technology, and a weakening influence of labor are collectively shaping individuals' career trajectories.

In the final chapter, I conclude by reviewing the various ways these student parents' experiences reinforce or challenge dominant cultural logics regarding parenting and the role of public higher education in the twenty-first century. A majority of these student parents have chosen to be a part of a traditional campus culture where they can grow, learn, and prepare themselves for not just a job but a life in which they are empowered to become better mothers and fathers. Such growth is evidenced in the ways that many of them feel their lives have changed for the better as a result of their educational learning and accomplishments. Further, in advocating for caregivers' rights and resources, these students are also, not always consciously, calling for changes that will produce greater gender equity both on college campuses and in their lives. However, their experiences also reveal stark problems with the landscape of higher education—a college degree does not promise economic stability or social mobility. We must face the fact that education alone cannot solve the problems of an economy that is grounded in rising inequality.

Ultimately, this study highlights the complex cultural, organizational, and institutional forces shaping student parents' interactions and experiences, providing a unique perspective that both draws upon and contributes to the sociological literature on education, social policy, gender, and culture. *Back in School* reveals that these student parents are challenged with addressing many of the same questions that other students and parents are facing at this historical moment. What do we expect of our institutions of higher learning? What makes for successful parenting? In an era when the answers to these questions are far from clear or straightforward, student parents are making sense of their lives each and every day and are negotiating contradictions when experiences and aspirations collide.

The stories shared in these pages reveal that most of these student parents expect and believe that they are improving their lives and doing the right thing by going to college. These stories also reveal how cultural logics and institutional resources facilitate or hinder their ability to weave together their student and parent identities. These student parents' perspectives and experiences help us to understand the tensions resulting from intersections between individuals and social structures and provide valuable insights regarding both parenting and the social role of higher education at the beginning of the twenty-first century.

2

The American Dream?

Expanding Opportunities and the Changing University

Student parents' college pathways are in many ways as diverse as the student parents themselves. Rou, a fifty-four-year-old Vietnam War–era veteran, became a father later in life and now has his "hands full" as he and his wife care for Honor, their four-year-old daughter. Rou is currently unemployed, but Rou's wife works at a local group home for adults with disabilities. Her job provides the family with health insurance, but her income is just high enough so that they do not qualify for most public assistance. Having been laid off from American Airlines and a local hospital, Rou is now taking advantage of his GI educational benefits, redirecting his career goals and working toward an associate's degree studying human services at a local public community college.

When I ask Rou why he is pursuing a college degree at this point in his life, he contends that "having jobs and having a career are entirely different." Rou possesses decades of work experience, but he believes that not having a college degree has held him back from advancing professionally and economically. "This whole credibility thing," Rou continues, "that's, to me, that's what it's all about. If you don't have a paper, how credible are you?" As far as Rou is concerned, his vast work experience means little to others. He is convinced that a college degree will legitimize the value of his knowledge and will set him above other job applicants without a degree.

Amber, who is twenty-five years old and recently divorced, has primary custody of her one-year-old son. She always expected to go to college and is now working to earn a bachelor's degree in English. The fall after graduating high school, Amber began studying education at a nearby state university. She opted to leave the campus dorms at the end of her first year to move in with her long-term boyfriend and, after commuting for a term, left school altogether to work and plan her wedding. After settling into her new marriage, she made the decision to return to school, this time enrolling in a local community college where she earned her associate's degree in general studies, a degree that would allow her to continue exploring possible disciplines and majors.

Soon after transferring back to the four-year public university, Amber discovered that she was pregnant. Suffering from severe morning sickness, she withdrew from her classes and focused on her health. However, her relationship with her husband was failing and by the time she reached her eighth month of pregnancy, they decided to divorce. Amber's former husband is still very much involved in her son's life, but she is his primary caregiver. Although the past two years did not flow as expected, Amber is keen to graduate with a degree in English, a subject she loves. She expects to teach high school writing and literature and is excited about the prospect of having a job that is intellectually stimulating, family friendly, and financially rewarding.

Carol, a thirty-nine-year-old mother of three, likewise intends to teach. She echoes Amber's desire to engage in paid work that is personally satisfying, and she is convinced that attaining such a job is possible only with a bachelor's degree. Carol grew up in Jamaica and, after graduating from high school, attended a business college where she received her associate's degree in accounting and management. Because she was never able to find a job using her two-year college degree, Carol ended up working in a hotel. She recalls putting in long days, making low wages, and rarely seeing her two children, who were being cared for by her aunt. To improve her job prospects, she moved to the United States, leaving her two children with their father and under the primary care of her aunt. First living in Miami, then New York, and finally in Hartford, Connecticut, Carol met her present husband while working in a cousin's restaurant. Four years ago, she felt stable for the first time in her job and relationship, and so brought her two children up from Jamaica. Not long afterward, she became pregnant with her third child.

Carol's story is full of movement and fresh starts. Now that she is committed to keeping her children with her in the United States, she is intent on building up her educational credentials to provide economic stability as well. After taking classes at a local community college in both child care and nursing, she decided to pursue a bachelor's degree in elementary education. Carol strongly believes that a college degree will inoculate her against employment uncertainties. As long as she is improving herself with education, she feels confident that she will survive any job changes that come her way. Carol confesses, "I was never afraid of moving on to another job because I was always in school and I was studying and I was learning more. . . . Education is key for you to have a comfortable life."

College: The American Dream

Although the specifics of their individual life trajectories differ, these three students do not provide any surprising answers when explaining why they are in college. In the United States, we've come to believe that earning a college degree is necessary for success. Parents in middle and upper-middle-class communities are bombarded with information regarding the costs of college and the importance of establishing college savings plans. For most of these families, attending college is assumed and so must be planned for. At the other end of the economic spectrum, parents in economically depressed or struggling communities are heralded with Horatio Alger–like stories that focus on self-initiative and the power of learning. In those cultural narratives, resilient individuals use a college degree to escape persistent rural poverty or urban plight.

All parents are aware of prevailing cultural narratives that extol the general value of education. If they and their children expect to claim middle or, better yet, upper class status, college credentials are required (Lazerson 1998). The influence of these cultural narratives is reflected in undergraduate college enrollments, which increased 28 percent between 2000 and 2016. During those same years, the percentage of young adults between the ages of twenty-five and twenty-nine possessing an associate's degree or higher increased from 38 to 46 percent (NCES 2018). Public attitude polls administered during the U.S. economic boom years of the 1990s revealed that 87 percent of respondents believed that a secondary school graduate should go on to college rather than taking a job after high school (Immerwahr 2004). A high school diploma is no longer enough to fulfill the American dream.

Rou's, Amber's, and Carol's beliefs regarding the need for postsecondary education are hardly irrational. Particularly in the latter part of the twentieth century, as manufacturing jobs slowly gave way to jobs in the service and information sector, many in the United States have come to perceive a college degree as necessary to land reasonably if not highly compensated jobs. A college-level degree, so the argument goes, ensures credibility and freedom in the workplace and hence long-term financial stability. Aggregate data that frequently make their way into popular news accounts and college recruitment presentations reinforce such perceptions—in 2016, full-time workers aged twenty-five to thirty-four who had earned a bachelor's degree earned a median salary of $50,000 a year, whereas those with a high school degree or its equivalent earned only $31,800 (NCES 2018: 249).

When these (less often reported) data are broken down by gender and race/ethnicity, the median salaries are significantly lower for black, Latinx, Native American, and women students of nearly all racial/ethnic groups, but in every category, those individuals with at least some postsecondary education outearn their counterparts who possess only a high school degree. According to a 2018 report issued by the U.S. Census Bureau, college attendance rates increased to historical highs in the wake of the 2008 recession, a time marked by high levels of unemployment. When jobs are scarce and competition is high, the unemployed or underemployed come to view a college degree as the best defense to remain viable job candidates. During that time, the number of students attending any kind of postsecondary institution increased from 17.2 million in 2006 to 20.4 million in 2011. Although the number of students subsequently decreased to 19.1 million in 2015, the current number of enrolled students is still significantly higher than in 2006 and continues to increase each year (Schmidt 2018).

Keenly aware of how globalization and technological change have forever changed the labor sector, most families today have drawn the conclusion, promoted in kind by employers and colleges, that a college degree is not an intellectual luxury but rather an absolute necessity if parents and their children are to survive in this modern economy. Rou, Amber, and Carol have learned this lesson well and so are earning their college degrees.

During the first part of the twentieth century, however, very few of the student parents described in these pages likely would have considered pursuing a degree past high school or, even more importantly, been eligible or able to attend college in the first place. Amber and Carol might have considered enrolling in a teaching program at a normal school, a form of college devoted to instructing mostly women for entry into the teaching profession. At that time, teaching was a rapidly growing career opportunity and one of the few jobs available to women. The career opportunities sought by Rou could have been attained in the early 1900s without a college degree at all. Both the economy and the prevalence of higher education—and just as importantly, the relationship between the two—have changed dramatically over the past century.

To understand the contemporary landscape of our nation's colleges and why so many of us have come to believe that a college degree is indispensable and possible, it is helpful to step back and place this moment in historical context. How is it that the opportunity to pursue a higher education emerged and evolved? How are these opportunities shaping the current experiences of all college students, not just the student parents in this study, but a vast majority of the nation's population who had previously been excluded from higher education? Why is it that a college degree has come to be deemed as both necessary and possible for anyone desiring to live the American Dream?

How Did We Get Here? The Emergence of Higher Education

Just as owning a house came to symbolize personal success in the years following World War II, possessing a college degree is believed by many to be a marker of having achieved the American dream in the twenty-first century. Such a belief has been shaped profoundly by transformations in U.S. cultural, economic, and political spheres during the late nineteenth and mid-twentieth centuries, defined in part by the shifting nature of work and educational institutions' deepening connection to the labor market (Aronowitz 2000; Brint 2002; Veblen [1918] 1993).

Most colleges that arose during colonial times primarily served young white men from socially or politically powerful families, versing them in religion and the classics with the purpose of promoting responsible, moral leadership. Rather than providing opportunity, colonial-era colleges were formed to provide a moral grounding for the emergent nation's future religious, business, and political leaders.[1] High tuitions and social mores ensured that a college education would be reserved for a select group of young men, ultimately preserving the status quo of the elite, religious, and governing social classes. In accordance with prevailing ideologies, college leaders' emphasis on liberty, not equality, masked the fact that a vast majority of people living in the new colonies—including rural farmers, slaves, free blacks, American Indians, and all women—were generally considered unfit for and hence were excluded from the college classroom.[2]

This began to change, however, at the beginning of the nineteenth century, a time when over seven hundred colleges in the United States closed their doors and the population of students steadily dwindled on many campuses. Recognizing the limitations of narrowly "preserving" the status quo, Francis Wayland, progressive educator and president of Brown from 1827 until 1852, contended that leaders in higher education needed to decide "between adopting a course of study that appealed to all classes or adhering to a course that appealed to one class" (qtd. in Rudolph 1962: 218). Wayland and others believed that unless colleges democratized education, making it available and relevant to all social classes, the college system would ultimately fail, a premonition that for a time seemed to be gaining hold in reality as college after college closed. In such a climate of diminishing college enrollments, educational progressives' ideas regarding the need to democratize higher education slowly took hold, evidenced most clearly when a number of postsecondary institutions began to either diversify their student populations or construct segregated campuses that addressed the needs of women and racial or ethnic minorities.

Oberlin College, which offered women an education from its founding in 1833, opened its doors to free black students beginning in 1835. The oldest historically black institution of higher education, Cheyney University in Pennsylvania, was founded two years later in 1837. By 1860, women could pursue a postsecondary degree in over forty-five schools.[3] In the following decades, a number of elite private colleges established annexes—including Harvard's Radcliffe and Columbia's Barnard colleges—to address the educational needs of women who qualified for entry into their exclusive institutions but had been denied entrance solely on the basis of their gender. Hampton University, alma mater of the young Booker T. Washington, in 1878 welcomed a group of formerly imprisoned American Indians, a move that marked the beginning of the University's expressed commitment to educating tribal members from across the nation. As educational leaders successfully promoted the idea that an educated citizenry ought to be the foundation of a strong nation, the number of primary schools and colleges steadily grew.

In addition to expanding the diversity of their student bodies, many colleges began to expand course subject matter to include emerging technological and scientific disciplines and to address the professionalization of occupations, including teaching and nursing. Curricula in many state institutions began to address farming, scientific, and manufacturing interests, and a general understanding began to take hold that these new technologies demanded new learning and hence training.[4] A fruitful merging of capitalism with science provided higher education with a fertile ground for growth.[5] And with belief in compulsory primary education gaining ideological ground, so also grew the need for more teachers and the construction of normal schools to educate those teachers.

Higher education had been steadily evolving for some time before Justin Morrill, a Vermont representative and later a senator in the U.S. Senate secured a place in history with his namesake legislation establishing land grant universities. Riding on this wave of change, Morrill put forth a congressional bill in 1857 advocating for federal investments to create a nationwide system of agricultural colleges that would offer a broad education while simultaneously imparting practical skills in farming, mining, mechanics, and the military. Congress passed and in 1862 President Abraham Lincoln signed the Morrill Act into law, promising loyal states 30,000 acres of federal land per each senator and representative with the expectation that this land would be sold to finance the construction of colleges that would offer agricultural and technology programs (U.S. Congress 1862). Nearly thirty years later, legislators reinforced the law by passing the Second Morrill Act in 1890, which further funded the program and required that states, in particular resistant southern states, either allow African Americans to enroll in already established white-only land grant colleges or develop separate colleges for black students.[6]

Although access to higher education did expand over the course of the nineteenth century, a college education was not necessarily open to all without discrimination—many colleges and universities continued to deny entry to women and racial or ethnic minorities. Even those institutions and states that pledged to provide "separate but equal" facilities for African American students, as required by the Second Morrill Act of 1890, too often fell far short of that promise. Educational opportunity may have been gradually increasing, but most students attended colleges in their immediate geographic vicinity and entered classrooms serving students who shared their gender, race/ethnicity, and social class background (Thelin 2004). At the beginning of the twentieth century, white middle- and upper-class women were just as likely as their male counterparts to reap the benefits offered by collegiate life; however, they were more often than not segregated by institution and discipline. For example, women vastly outnumbered men attending the nation's steadily growing number of normal schools that provided entrée into the teaching profession, one of the few professions open to women (Apple 1982; Sadker, Sadker, and Zittleman 2009). Further, even within ostensibly coed and racially diverse institutions, such as Oberlin College, women and racial/ethnic minorities experienced social isolation and discrimination (Baumann 2010; Thelin 2004). Opportunities in higher education existed, but in most cases they were not the same opportunities for all—segregation persisted.

College for All? Investing in Students

Not until the mid-twentieth century, following the humanitarian crises wrought by World War II and cultural shifts emphasizing civil rights that were later reflected in educational legislation and Supreme Court decisions, did the United States again see a significant expansion of access to higher education. In 1944, the Serviceman's Readjustment Act, or GI Bill, was passed to manage the millions of soldiers returning home from the war and facilitate their transition, both short and long term, into the workplace. The GI Bill provided low-interest loans to veterans for housing and postsecondary educational benefits, including tuition payments, book allowances, and living expense stipends (Aronowitz 2000). The program was incredibly successful; in 1947, approximately 49 percent of students admitted to colleges were Word War II veterans, and by 1956, when the program ended, nearly half of the sixteen million veterans had taken advantage of educational supports (U.S. Department of Veterans Affairs 2012).

The social benefits accrued from these educational opportunities, however, were not equitably experienced. White, male veterans were the primary beneficiaries of educational resources, and so racial inequities endured and the gender parity that previously defined the college student population at the beginning of the century temporarily disappeared. Of the almost eight million veterans who took advantage of the GI bill's educational benefits, only a very small number were women. In the postwar years men became one and a half times more likely than women to occupy a place in the college classroom, and many college doors remained closed to racial/ethnic minorities (Goldin et al. 2006; Greenberg 1997). Black veterans were shut out of segregated, white-only colleges and found few seats open to them in overcrowded historically black colleges.

These trends continued until the 1960s, when the passage of civil rights legislation and the Higher Education Act (HEA) of 1965 began to expand postsecondary opportunities for previously underrepresented groups, including women, racial/ethnic minorities and, later in the 1970s, individuals with disabilities. Women began to enroll in colleges in record numbers beginning in the late

1960s, when a changing economy, access to birth control, and second-wave feminist movements together challenged and redefined family dynamics and women's roles in the household and workplace (Moen and Yu 2000). Women's entry into colleges was further enabled in 1972, when colleges and universities receiving any form of public financing were legally required by the federal government to open their doors to women as a result of Title IX, a landmark amendment to the HEA of 1965. As a result of these cultural and legislative changes, the proportion of women earning bachelor's degrees began to steadily outpace men beginning in 1982, a gender shift that persists and has been reflected more recently in women's predominance in master's and PhD programs (Aud et al. 2012; Goldin, Katz, and Kuziemko 2006; Jacobs 1996).

Around the same time that Civil Rights legislation and Title IX expanded educational opportunities for women and racial/ethnic minorities, legislators also began to recognize the need to facilitate college access for low-income students. With the implementation of the federal Basic Educational Opportunity Grant (BEOG) program, students with limited economic resources were increasingly able to pursue a college degree in order to participate more fully in the then burgeoning informational economy. Rhode Island senator Claiborne Pell in the 1970s initiated the needs-based financial assistance program for postsecondary schooling—renamed the Pell Grant program in 1980—citing the post–World War II GI Bill as partial inspiration. Pell hoped to replicate the successes experienced by many U.S. veterans through the program's provision of financial assistance to men and women who desired a college education but had been denied such an opportunity due to their limited financial resources.

Around the same time that the BEOG program emerged, Senator Pell also worked actively with Vermont senator Robert T. Stafford to establish the Federal Guaranteed Student Loan Program, later renamed after Senator Stafford in 1988, which provided low-interest loans to college students. By 2016 just under half of all first-time, full-time undergraduates were awarded Stafford Loans as a means of funding their college education (McFarland et al. 2018: 217). The Pell Grant Program, along with the Stafford Loan Program and contemporary versions of the GI Bill, have enabled generations of low- and middle-income students to pursue postsecondary degrees and continue to provide financial assistance for eligible students today.

The New Economy: Investing in Colleges and Universities

The cultural shifts that expanded college access were also made possible due to a changing economy and a governmental focus on investing in science, technology, and national defense. With manufacturing jobs slowly being transformed by advancements in technology, the rise of the service sector, and the eroding power of labor unions, the likelihood of attaining a middle-class standard of living with no more than a high school degree became increasingly difficult. Factory jobs, including those in the powerful steel and automotive industries, had by midcentury reached their peak in regard to job opportunities and career potential. Companies began to move many of their operations overseas, or jobs in these industries were eliminated as machines took over, creating new jobs, albeit fewer of them, that required training and knowledge in the fields of technology. Wages in these industries also began to stagnate and even falter as the power of labor unions decreased, in part a result of the passage of the Taft-Hartley Act of 1947, which legalized right-to-work laws. These laws stunted the growth of unions, who could no longer require that all employees join their ranks, thereby limiting labor's power and influence in the workplace (Cohen and Kisker 2010). The jobs that emerged midcentury began to reflect a changing economic landscape where service and professional occupations increasingly dominated and educational expectations for employment intensified. Between 1967 and 2010, the earning power of a high school degree alone decreased by just over 17 percent, whereas the earning power of a college degree increased by almost 7 percent (Duncan and Murnane 2011).

Further, governmental decisions to invest in science, technology, and national defense projects were easily advanced in a post–World War II era marked by Cold War fears and a desire to assert scientific dominance in the wake of the Soviet Union's launching of the Sputnik satellite. Colleges and universities benefited from the influx of federal dollars directed toward their science and technology programs, two such examples being the National Defense Research Committee's investments in radar technologies at MIT and the Army Corps of Engineers' collaboration with university scientists in researching the atomic bomb (Cohen and Kisker 2010: 189). With the passage of the National Defense Education Act in 1958, the vast expansion of the National Institutes of Health, and the establishment of the National Science Foundation in the aftermath of World War II, colleges and universities could for a time rely on steady streams of funding from these federal organizations as their research functions expanded and their role in educating a scientific and technologically savvy workforce increased (Kerr 1963; Lucas 2006).

The increased access to and hence demand for a postsecondary education likewise paralleled the expansion of public college and university systems. Although an organizational structure of higher education had been emerging over the course of the century, the tiered system of community colleges and state colleges and universities that presently defines many of the nation's public institutions is in part a product of President Harry Truman's President's Commission on Higher Education, formed in 1946. The Commission's task, as outlined in Truman's appointment letters, was to facilitate access for World War II veterans returning from war and to assess "the functions of higher education in our democracy and of the means by which they can best be performed."

In 1948, Truman's Commission produced a plan of action that clarified the role of community colleges, a term that commission members introduced to refer to those postsecondary institutions "designed to serve chiefly local community education needs" (vol. 3: 5). As the proposed name suggests, community colleges were intended to serve local students, in particular older, "adult" students, who sought an education that focused on the thirteenth and fourteenth years of schooling. This community college education would be free and available to all "regardless of race, creed, color, sex, or economic status" (vol. 5: 3). For those students intending to pursue careers in teaching, journalism, art, or music, the system of public colleges of arts and sciences and teachers colleges were expected to provide two- and four-year programs encompassing a broad general education (vol. 3: 17). Finally, universities and professional schools would likewise provide a broad education with the addition of offering more applied programs in areas such as health, agriculture, and engineering, along with opportunities to pursue graduate degrees. To finance such developments, the Commission proposed that the government invest over $2.5 billion in facilities, salaries, and scholarships, a significant sum of money that was nonetheless argued to be a worthwhile investment, providing both short- and long-term benefits to the nation.

As more high school graduates sought a college education and as federal spending on higher education grew, individual states began to evaluate the structure and organization of their public institutions in an attempt to meet the needs of an ever-expanding student population. Building on the Truman Commission's vision of public higher education, former University of California president Clark Kerr in 1960 introduced his "Master Plan," which described a coordinated state-level system of community colleges, state colleges, and research universities that served as a model for many states that were, like the federal government, investing heavily in postsecondary education. The plan hierarchically ranked three tiers of postsecondary education, with community colleges providing either vocational degrees or entrée into the more selective state colleges or the even more selective public research universities.

With the government investing money into higher education and with Truman's Commission on Higher Education and Kerr's Master Plan providing blueprints for the development of a tiered public college system to accommodate the influx of students with varying academic abilities, economic resources, and educational goals, college enrollment in public institutions increased dramatically across the United States. At the turn of the twentieth century, postsecondary institutions awarded approximately twenty-nine thousand degrees. By 1950, that figure had increased to over half a million, and over 2.3 million students were enrolled in a college or university (Lucas 2006: 247). By 1990, approximately 10.5 million of the then 12.5 million postsecondary students attended public colleges or universities (Lucas 2006: 249). In 2010, approximately 76 percent of the over eighteen million students attending degree-granting postsecondary institutions were enrolled in public colleges or universities (Aud et al. 2012). The expansion of public colleges and universities transformed the educational landscape, and for a time, increased access to higher education as had been envisioned by Morrill, the Truman Commission, Kerr, and so many others who saw higher education as necessary to alleviate inequalities and provide for a thriving economy and democracy.

The Twenty-First-Century College Student

The myriad cultural, political, and economic changes described above have shaped current student demographics and in one way or another facilitated the growth on college campuses of the overall student population. As the system of higher education expanded and the economy shifted, adults who might have otherwise directly entered the military or job market upon graduating high school began to rethink their post–high school options. They both have the opportunity to attend college and have begun to feel the pressure to pursue two-year, four-year, or postgraduate degrees.

Today, of the over twenty million students enrolled in colleges or universities, almost nine million are over the age of twenty-five (NCES 2016). The National Center for Educational Statistics found that between the years 2000 and 2009, the enrollment of students over the age of twenty-five increased by 43 percent, and the center predicted an additional 23 percent increase during the next decade (NCES 2011). Importantly, a distinct majority of those students are women (see table 2.1). In 1970, 28 percent of the college student population consisted of students age twenty-five and over, and 63 percent of those students were men.

TABLE 2.1

Percent of Students Enrolled in Degree-Granting Institutions by Age and Gender, 1970–2010 (Percent)

	1970	1980	1990	2000	2010
Ages 24 and Under	72	63	58	61	61
≤ Age 24 Women	44	49	51	54	54
≤ Age 24 Men	56	51	49	46	46
Ages 25 and Older	28	37	42	39	39
≥ Age 25 Women	37	54	60	59	60
≥ Age 25 Men	63	46	40	41	40

Source: National Center for Education Statistics (2011: table 200).

By 1990 the total percent of the college student population age twenty-five and over had increased dramatically, and the gender proportions had reversed. In 2010, almost 40 percent of all college students were age twenty-five and over, and 60 percent of those older students were women. The gender disparity between men and women has consistently been higher for students age twenty-five and over than for those under the age of twenty-five. In 2010, approximately 8 percent more women than men under the age of twenty-five enrolled in college, whereas the gap between women and men age twenty-five and over was 20 percent, with women vastly outnumbering men.

It is true that possessing a college degree is likely to improve one's position in the labor market, and the rewards in terms of future income are on average higher for those with a college degree, particularly a graduate-level degree, than for those without. That is one important reason why more individuals are enrolling in college—enrollment increased by 28 percent between 2000 and 2016 and is predicted to increase another 3 percent between 2016 and 2027 (NCES 2018). Goldin and Katz (2007, 2009) find that the value of a college degree in terms of earning power is higher today than it was during the latter decades of the twentieth century. The economic value of a college degree actually decreased between the years of 1910 and 1980, but as the supply of college graduates has leveled out, the monetary return for possessing a degree has steadily risen since the 1980s.

Economists, however, cite concern for future college graduates because the proportion of middle-class jobs that can provide a sustainable living wage is decreasing. Recent studies reveal that job prospects are best for those individuals in the highest- and lowest-paid fields, with jobs in the middle sphere steadily being replaced or significantly altered by computerization (Autor and Dorn 2013; Autor, Katz, and Kearney 2006). Further, not every student who enters into the world of higher education ends up leaving with a degree, and those who are most likely to slip away are those with the fewest resources and the greatest needs. The six-year graduation rates for students pursuing a bachelor's degree, a typical bench mark for most bachelor's degree–granting institutions, reveal significant gaps along the lines of race, gender, and institutional selectivity (see table 2.2). College retention rates for all students pursuing baccalaureate degrees are highest in nonprofit private colleges, both selective and nonselective institutions, which are often smaller and more likely to have low student to faculty ratios than most public colleges and universities. Retention rates are lowest in for-profit private colleges, which are best known for providing online programs that are particularly attractive for working adults (Bound, Lovenheim, and Turner 2010; McMillan Cottom 2017). Finally, the low retention rates of black, Latinx, and Native American students have been a persistent problem facing many of our nation's colleges and universities of all levels and types over many decades (Harper and Reskin 2005; Ross et al. 2012).

TABLE 2.2

Six-Year Graduation Rate of Students Seeking Bachelor's Degrees Beginning in 2009 by Gender, Race, and Institutional Selectivity

	White	Black	Latinx	Asian/Pacific Islander	Native American
Public—All	62	40	53	71	39
Male	58	35	48	67	36
Female	65	44	57	74	42
Least Selective*	36	17	26	42	14
Most Selective	84	60	72	90	78
Nonprofit—All	69	44	61	78	52
Male	66	38	57	76	50
Female	71	48	64	80	54
Least Selective	46	29	31	38	25
Most Selective	91	79	90	95	83
For-Profit—All	29	16	29	40	17
Male	32	16	27	41	16
Female	27	15	30	39	17

* "Least Selective" refers to colleges that are open to all applicants due to their open admission policies and "Most Selective" refers to colleges that accept fewer than 25 percent of applicants.

Source: National Center for Education Statistics (2017: table 326-10).

Beginning in 2008, student enrollment levels in private institutions steadily outpaced enrollment in public colleges and universities, primarily a result of highly successful online programs offered by for-profit colleges. Between the years of 1998 and 2008, for-profit colleges increased the number of baccalaureate degrees awarded to students by over 400 percent (Staklis, Bersudskaya, and Horn 2011). Although the vast majority of students in the United States attend nonprofit or public colleges, nearly 10 percent of all postsecondary students are now enrolled in for-profit institutions, and since many of these students qualify for federal financial aid, some legislators who have become keen on either cutting college costs or federal assistance programs (although the two are not always mutually exclusive) have come to agree that for-profit universities warrant careful observation.[7]

The Meaning of a College Degree

As Clark Kerr watched his Master Plan come to life in the 1960s and access to college continuously increased, a number of scholars began to actively criticize the role that higher education had come to serve in our rapidly evolving civil society. These scholars were wary of the ways in which colleges and universities had come to legitimize their function in the social landscape.[8] They rejected instrumentalist framings and "human capital" theories put forth by economists that encouraged politicians and university administrators alike to view education narrowly as a means of investing in one's future occupation and as a vehicle for improving the economy.[9] Individuals who invest in a college degree, so goes the argument of human capital theorists, will gain the necessary skills and knowledge to reap the rewards of that investment in regard to higher earnings. Such a view was perceived to be not only shortsighted but disingenuous according to the critics of human capital framings.

Scholars criticizing instrumentalist, human capital framings argued two key points, offering up words of caution as college and university systems rapidly expanded. First, they expressed concern that colleges and universities were increasingly focusing their stated missions on job training and producing narrowly skilled employees at the expense of advocating for a broad-based education that allowed for the holistic intellectual development of a knowledgeable citizenry. Second, some of these scholars contended that most colleges, particularly baccalaureate-granting, elite institutions, were not and never had been particularly interested in the process of job and skill training anyway. They were instead concerned with credentialing and maintaining or increasing the value of the credentials they had to offer to students. Ivy League and highly selective small liberal arts institutions have traditionally emphasized and continue to promote general learning, not job-specific skills, within their baccalaureate curriculum (Mullen 2010). These institutions instead rely on the reputations of their institutions and prestigious networks of alumni to ensure the continued value of their credentials to provide access to jobs, successful careers, or graduate school, where students will acquire additional credentials and more job-specific knowledge. In sum, these scholars criticizing instrumentalist appeals highlight the disjunctures between discourses surrounding higher education and their reality. Whether colleges and universities were promoting job skills or credentials, institutions of higher education found instrumentalist appeals to be beneficial in that they ensured a steady increase in their student enrollment.

Certainly, instrumentalist framings continue to resonate with many twenty-first-century college students in various ways as I will elaborate in later chapters. The narrative that college is necessary for a successful career has firmly taken hold in the public imagination, and for many people it represents attainment of the American Dream. Most of the students whom I interviewed also recognize the credentialing function of higher education in the contemporary economy and culture. They may not consciously distinguish the difference between acquiring job skills and a credential, but they understand these distinct yet related educational objectives. We see this framing of higher education reflected in the opening of this chapter when Rou rhetorically asks, "If you don't have a paper, how credible are you?" Rou has held many jobs and possesses a number of skills, but he has never obtained a degree that validates his knowledge via an educational credential. Many younger students like Amber, who have less work experience than older students like Rou, explicitly address a desire to acquire both job skills and a credential. She expects to acquire practical knowledge regarding curriculum content, class management skills, and a degree that will credential her to teach high school students.

Just as students talk about the economic and cultural value of job skills and "a paper" or degree, most political discourse that addresses the purpose of public education in the twenty-first century also highlights and conflates the credentialing and job skill development functions of colleges and universities. Policymakers who otherwise occupy opposing positions on the political spectrum nevertheless tend to come together in the way that they articulate the value of public higher education in regard to skills, credentials, the economy, and jobs. Within the political sphere, the instrumentalist rhetoric of human capital reigns, and increasing job-skill development and credentialing are presumed to predict the future success of our contemporary economy.

In his 2014 State of the Union address, President Barack Obama reasserted his commitment to making college affordable for all and to strengthening a particular kind of education that leads to the development of human capital and employment. To reinforce the connection between college and jobs, he maintained, "We're working to redesign high schools and partner them with colleges and employers that offer the real-world education and hands-on training that can lead directly to a job and career." We are surrounded by public discourse that links going to college with getting a job, and so, unsurprisingly, such discourse shapes the way many individuals have come to conceptualize not only the purpose of pursuing a degree but also, as Obama's statement suggests, the *kind of education* that should be provided in our institutions of higher education.

When politicians express these perspectives, their words are often tied to policy-based initiatives and funding that can ultimately influence the educational opportunities that are available in the public sphere. In 2012, Governor Rick Scott of Florida challenged his state's public colleges and universities to charge lower tuition for degree programs with high job-placement rates for their graduates. Governor Scott's call for change was not taken up by Florida's state colleges, but his proposal incited heated public discussion regarding the kind of programs and curricula that colleges ought to provide. Scott's challenge reflects the idea that college is intended to develop an educated workforce in this twenty-first-century economy and that the value of college programs that are not directly connected to identifiable jobs ought to be questioned.

Instrumentalist framings also informed debates over fifteen years earlier as legislators discussed reforming social welfare programs for low-income families. U.S. welfare reform in 1996 notoriously shifted the focus of the former entitlement program—which provided public assistance to low-income families—limiting access to higher education and instead emphasizing paid work. Thereafter, cash support was given only to parents, mostly mothers, who worked toward high school or short-term degree or certificate programs that were directly connected to the local job market. Little or no support was provided to parents seeking baccalaureate or graduate-level degrees. Such a dramatic shift was easy to make in a world in which the central function of higher education is perceived to be job preparation.[10]

Both Scott's and welfare reformers' proposals are grounded in the belief that the primary purpose of a college education is to provide students with the skills and training necessary to succeed in a specific job. When articulated in this way, any educational experience that is not directly related to a job is evaluated as less essential and hence, according to Scott's proposal, ought to cost more for the student desiring that educational experience, or, according to the drafters of the 1996 welfare reform, should not be a program-supported option for those mothers or fathers receiving public child-care or cash assistance. Such policy debates reveal that not all college programs are considered equal when job training is determined to be the foremost function of higher education.

According to current welfare policy in most states, a low-income mother will not receive public support if she pursues a baccalaureate degree in philosophy, but she may receive assistance if she instead enrolls in a short-term program to receive her certification as an electrical technician or early childhood educator. The logic guiding political discourse resulting in the construction of such policies works in part because it remains perfectly aligned with instrumentalist framings that narrowly define the value of an education as access to jobs. Who knows what access to jobs, if any, that a degree in philosophy from a state university may promise, but a certified electrical technician is likely to find work in construction or repairs, and there are plenty of positions available in the relatively low-paying but growing field of child care. In this way, politicians can argue convincingly that, for those individuals receiving public assistance, only certain kinds of degrees ought to be allowable and that linkages between degrees and specific jobs must be clear.

What we expect from a college education very much shapes the kind of education that is available in the twenty-first century. Educational initiatives and political discourse that reify the relationship between education and the economy have long come to shape the way that many Americans have come to articulate their perspectives regarding the purpose of higher education in their lives. Perhaps even more importantly, such instrumentalist discourse can substantially influence the educational opportunities available to public colleges and universities and segments of the population that are most dependent on local and state-provided funds and resources (Mitchell, Leachman, and Masterson 2017). And those students who are most dependent on needs-based financial aid are most likely to be targeted by for-profit colleges and universities that promise job skill development and upward social mobility but have been shown to have extraordinarily high dropout rates and credentials with questionable social value, particularly given their high price (McMillan Cottom 2017).

A symbiotic relationship between higher education and the marketplace has been growing for over 150 years, but as access to institutions of higher learning increased, students' expectations and college experiences became more diversified and stratified. How we conceive of and talk about the purpose of higher education, both in political venues and in our homes, absolutely matters in regard to access and opportunity.

Bringing "Heart" Back into the Conversation

Instrumentalist logic and framings, however, have been challenged in recent years. In 2013, the American Academy of Arts and Sciences (AAAS) published *The Heart of the Matter*, authored by the Commission on the Humanities and Social Sciences (CHSS), a diverse group of college administrators, politicians, company representatives, and artists, including the cellist Yo-Yo Ma, former Supreme Court justice David Souter, and Adobe Systems chairman of the board John E. Warnock. The Commission formed in 2010 at the behest of several members of the U.S. Congress to respond to political and popular discourse that had been targeting college degree programs and even specific courses, particularly those in the humanities and social sciences that were not perceived to be directly connected in any clear way to the economy. U.S. senators Lamar Alexander and Mark R. Warner expressed their concern quite clearly in a September 27, 2010, letter addressed to the AAAS: "Our strong tradition of research and scholarship in the humanities and social sciences—in history, jurisprudence, philosophy, foreign languages, cultural studies, sociology, and economics—is, in large part, responsible for our nation's unique ability to evolve with historical circumstances. We are concerned that this great tradition of humanistic teaching and research is at risk, and as a result, puts the unique American character at risk as well" (qtd. in CHSS 2013: 63). Just over two months later, representatives David Price and Thomas E. Petri likewise shared their apprehensions regarding the fate of a liberal arts education in college curriculum: "As other nations race to adopt the American system of liberal arts education as a foundation for economic growth and geopolitical competitiveness, our nation's own humanistic research enterprise is shrinking as a result of growing financial challenges as well as a diminished interest in our national history and shared values" (qtd. in CHSS 2013: 65). These letters expressed bipartisan support for the Commission to address the public assault by various political leaders on the humanities and social sciences within our nation's colleges and universities.

In addition to addressing the concerns conveyed by Republican and Democratic members of Congress, *The Heart of the Matter* was published to complement, if not in part to counter, reports produced in the last half century by organizations including the National Academy of Sciences, the National Academy of Engineering, and the Institute of Medicine. These reports have continuously emphasized the need to invest in science and technologies, including the National Academy's 2007 publication *Rising above the Gathering Storm*, which advocated the strengthening of research and education in science, technology, engineering, and math. In the same spirit as these prior publications, *The Heart of the Matter* seeks to clarify the need for a general education and for courses in the humanities and social sciences in order to "create a more civil public discourse, a more adaptable and creative workforce, and a more secure nation" as well as to provide "a source of national memory and civic vigor, cultural understanding and communication, individual fulfillment, and the ideals we hold in common" (CHSS 2013: 9).

The authors of *The Heart of the Matter* foresaw that in calling for general support of a liberal arts education—the kind of education that is not provided in most lower-prestige vocational programs but that continues to define the curriculum in the nation's most prestigious colleges and universities—they would likely be confronted with accusations of elitism. Their attempt to preserve interest in and support of the arts, humanities, and social sciences could be interpreted as a means of preserving the culture of the ivory tower status quo. In anticipation of such a condemnation, the Commission explicitly counters,

How do we understand and manage change if we have no notion of the past? How do we understand ourselves if we have no notion of a society, culture, or world different from the one in which we live? A fully balanced curriculum—including the humanities, social sciences, and natural sciences—provides opportunities for integrative thinking and imagination, for creativity and discovery, and for good citizenship. The humanities and social sciences are not merely elective, nor are they elite or elitist. They go beyond the immediate and instrumental to help us understand the past and future. They are necessary and they require our support in challenging times as well as in times of prosperity. They are critical to our pursuit of life, liberty, and happiness, as described by our nation's founders. They are *The Heart of the Matter.* (CHSS 2013:13)

The authors here invoke the phrase that ultimately became the title of the report, driving home their support for disciplines that do not serve explicitly utilitarian functions in the larger economy. They also reject the charge that integrating learning that is not job specific is elitist—quite the opposite, they argue that denying students the opportunity to engage in creative and integrative thought can limit them from fully understanding their world and engaging in it culturally, socially, and politically.

The spirit in which this report was conceived aligns with arguments presented by several contemporary critics who have expressed concern over the fact that so many students can only conceive of their education in economically utilitarian terms. In *College: What It Was, Is and Should Be*, Andrew Delbanco (2012) argues that at its essence, a college education ought to teach one "how to enjoy life" (p. 32). In making this point, Delbanco quotes another of his colleagues, Judith Shapiro, former president of Barnard College, who, in advising her students regarding their college expectations, tells them, "You want the inside of your head to be an interesting place to spend the rest of your life" (p. 33). Ken Bain (2012), in *What the Best College Students Do*, similarly describes a liberal arts education as providing students with the opportunity to expand their experience of living. Bain writes, "What is life after all? It is experiencing reality over time, but if you can take any moment and enhance it, know it in historical context, explore its social context, dissect it and all its many voices, and integrate it into your experience, you can derive far more out of any one time and place. You can extend your life" (p. 204). CNN host and best-selling author Fareed Zakaria (2015) argues that "a liberal education gives us greater capacity to be good workers, but it will also give us the capacity to be good partners, friends, parents, and citizens" (p. 151). All these ideas very much reflect traditional arguments regarding the role of a general education and the liberal arts in contemporary universities. According to these lines of thought, a general education provides students with exposure to diverse disciplinary perspectives, enabling creative connections and thereby enhancing their understanding of the world and themselves. These debates regarding the purpose of higher education have existed in the United States since its founding but have become even more pervasive as both the availability and the cost of higher education have increased in recent decades.[11]

When I asked student parents to explain their educational motivations, all of them at some point resort to discourse that emphasizes their job and career goals; in other words, they readily turn to instrumentalist framings and logics. Yet, as I describe later in chapter 4, all but fourteen of these student parents additionally rely, with varying influence, on framings that reflect "matters of the heart." These students describe the importance of becoming open to diverse perspectives, earning social respect, developing self-confidence, and experiencing intellectual enrichment and empowerment. Although purely instrumentalist discourse regarding the value of higher education is clearly inadequate to reflect the complex and varied lived experiences of most of these students, such discourse has a firm grasp on our collective and political consciousness. We see all around us just how deeply ingrained are framings that emphasize skills, jobs, and national security, which shape the formation of cultural logics and public discussions of policy and, ultimately, the future of higher education.

AS A NATION, we have grown to accept and perceive as natural the relationship between formal education and success. We accept the idea that a college degree ensures one's place in society and increases the likelihood of not only having a job during economically unstable times but a job that one enjoys and finds challenging—like owning a home, possessing a degree symbolically represents one's having achieved the American dream. U.S. educational systems and their financing mechanisms have over the years grown to accommodate this perceived need for a college degree, a perceived need embraced not only by individuals hoping to attend college or university but by many legislators and employers, who like generations of their predecessors have expressed their belief in the value of higher education. The Morrill Land Grant Acts of the late 1800s and the GI Bill following World War II represented but two moments in our national history that clearly marked movement toward open access and opportunity, all while cultivating a relationship between institutions of higher education and industry.

All the student parents in this study—like Rou, Amber, and Carol—believe that their education will provide them with a better job and their families with a better life. For now, these student parents are surviving and hopeful. They are not among the high number of students who will drop out of the community colleges and state universities that they attend. These student parents accept the ideas and world views that have emerged from our nation's history of higher education, which draw linkages between the economy, a college education, and the American dream. So having been provided with access and a belief in opportunity, how do they select a college, finance their education, and navigate campus? Ultimately, what do their experiences as they attend college reveal about our system of public higher education in the twenty-first century? I now turn to those questions in the following chapter, exploring the various structural and cultural factors that shape the campus experiences of these student parents.

3

"I'm Just Looking for Some Kind of Understanding"

Academic Resources and Campus Culture

Carolyn, a twenty-seven-year-old graphic arts student, hopes to use her skills one day to open a small business of her own. She recently separated from her husband after he returned from serving overseas in Iraq. Receiving very little support from her ex-husband, her in-laws, and her own mother (she hasn't seen her father in years), Carolyn now maintains primary custody of her two young children, ages three and six. When I ask her how she conceptualizes student success, she declares, in exasperation, "College is for kids that don't have kids. That's what it's made for—kids that don't have kids." After a brief moment of silence between us, she continues, "But life takes its toll. You know, I'm not looking for handouts. That's not what I want. I'm just looking for some kind of understanding." Carolyn's words reveal her deep frustration on campus, where she often feels she has to erase her identity as a mother as she endlessly toils to succeed as a student.

Returning to college, particularly after many years of absence, can be a daunting prospect for many of these student parents. They must engage in the practical concerns of accessing previous transcripts, completing application materials, and taking entrance or placement tests. Students with prior college experience must also juggle their transfer credits, figuring out how past accomplishments—or, for some, failures—are going to fit in to their proposed program of study. For those younger student parents who had their children while in their teens or early twenties, weaving together student and parent identities can become exceptionally challenging when peers, professors, and counselors consciously or tacitly stigmatize them. Other parents, like Carolyn may be in the midst of tumultuous relationships or struggling to raise children on their own, all while managing the demands of their professors and campus administrators.

These student parents share concerns about a campus culture that at times feels out of alignment with their complex needs and student parent identities.

In chapter 1, I introduced Swidler's concept of culture as a toolkit and highlighted the importance of examining how specific historical and institutional contexts shape students' meaning and decision making. To that end, in chapter 2, I explored historical policies and cultural trends that reveal just how these student parents came to believe that a college education is available and necessary for success. In this current chapter, I look more closely at institutional policies and resources that ultimately influence both campus culture and student parents' strategies of being. In this way, I follow in the footsteps of many influential educational researchers who have studied the ways that institutional structures and campus culture affect students' college experiences.[1] My intent in this chapter is to reveal the ways that students like Carolyn come to feel supported or alienated as a result of the way social institutions respond to their parenting and educational needs.

Student parents' dispositions, decisions, and interactions are distinctively shaped by a campus culture that consists of classrooms and offices—faculty, admissions, financial aid, academic advising, counseling, athletics—that historically has reflected an organizational logic structured to address the needs of young, childless students. Even the terms that are used in the world of higher education to describe student parents, "nontraditional," or in the case of older students "adult learners," bring to light how they are perceived as distinct from the campus norm. In truth, very few people on campus know which students are parents—they are often an invisible, unacknowledged population. Unless students arrive at a professor's office hours with a child in tow or bring up their familial obligations in conversation, faculty, staff, and administrators are unaware of these students' parenting identities. Such a situation exists in part because parents perceive campus to be a sphere separate from both work and home, and so rarely, if ever, bring their children to campus. Only when in crisis—when a child is ill or child care falls through—do they reveal their identities as mothers or fathers by "outing" themselves, a process that can be fraught with tension or pride. Like the needs of veterans, athletes, first-generational students, and students with psychological, emotional, or learning disabilities, the needs of student parents are often not visible and so can easily be ignored by an institution unless it devotes specific resources to support those students and normalize their presence on campus (Grubb 1999; Morest 2013).

All of the student parents in this study ended up enrolling in regional public colleges or universities due to a complex interplay of individual, cultural, and institutional factors. Once on campus, various interactional and cultural factors determine whether or not the experience of coming out as a parent is one of self-affirmation or stigmatization. A student's age, marital status, race or ethnicity, and gender collectively affect the way professors, staff, and administrators might respond upon learning that a student is a mother or a father. Further, access to key resources, including financial aid and child care, can determine whether or not a student parent is likely to succeed on campus and feel connected to his or her student identity and the larger campus community. These interactions and resources both reflect and shape a campus culture that is felt to be welcoming to student parents or not.

In this chapter, I begin by examining prior literature that explores the cultural logics that shape students' decisions regarding where they choose to pursue their education. This research helps us to understand why these student parents stayed local and how their experiences fit into larger research narratives regarding college in the twenty-first century. I then examine the various ways that these student parents' identities were either challenged or validated as a result of the presence or lack of institutional financial and child care resources made available to them both on and off campus. I also explore their interactions with professors and peers, interactions that either contest or legitimize their student parent identities. In examining these processes, I intend to highlight the ways that institutional policies and organizational culture function in the context of the public colleges and universities that these students attend.

The Decision to Attend a Public College or University

The student parents in this sample, like many students, did not fully consider their options when deciding on a college to attend. Instead, these student parents—of which almost half reported annual incomes of less than $30,000—restricted their educational options, confining themselves to state colleges and universities that are within driving distance of their homes and familial support systems. The thirty-five student parents in this study who were pursuing baccalaureate or master's degrees did not seriously consider attending any of the other at least seventeen private colleges and universities in the small state of Connecticut. They instead chose to attend one of the four regional comprehensive state universities that was nearest their homes and social networks and that was familiar to them.

McDonough (1997) similarly revealed the various ways that families, friends, and schooling organizations establish boundaries regarding the college choices that students perceive as available to them. McDonough relied on case studies of students and counselors in four very different California high schools, highlighting the social dynamics that shaped students' pathways to college. Based on their familial and schooling experiences, she found that students grow to feel "entitled" to a particular kind of college experience and so base their college choices on what feels appropriate for them. Importantly, McDonough highlights the cultural and organizational processes that substantively and differentially shape these feelings of "entitlement," processes that ultimately serve to reproduce social inequalities. Just as many of the low-income students interviewed by McDonough came to believe that community colleges were their best option in regard to postsecondary education, the student parents in this study have come to accept that local state schools best suit their personal and educational needs.

Similar conclusions were drawn by Mullen (2010) in her analysis of interviews with students who attended Yale University and a regional state university in Connecticut, a public university that several of the student parents in this study also attended. Mullen found that the state university students in her sample primarily based their college selection on convenience, affordability, and program offerings. She describes these students' college choices as adhering to a "logic of efficiency," in which cost and expediency are paramount (p. 106). When Mullen interviewed Yale students about their college choices, she found that, like the state university students, most of the Ivy League students limited their choices, only in a very different way—they expected to attend only an elite or highly selective school.

Tellingly, both the state and Ivy League students in her study expressed a desire to attend a campus where they felt *comfortable*. Citing Bourdieu's classic work on cultural and social reproduction, Mullen suggests that "these remarks reflected the students' habitus in their perceptions of the possible and the sense of one's place" (p. 115). In other words, if one's decisions are in concert with one's sense of place, those decisions feel sensible and normal. Both McDonough and Mullen highlight the effects of a complex intersection of social forces that result in these students deciding upon a particular college, a decision that has significant ramifications in regard to their experience on campus and their likelihood of graduating.

The student parents in this study are certainly similar to the state university and working-class high school students interviewed by Mullen and McDonough, respectively. In describing their process of college selection, all of these student parents relied on the very same "logic of efficiency" identified by Mullen. This is not to suggest that these students are making unsound decisions—far from it. As stated earlier, their logic is based on a particular understanding of their position in the larger socioeconomic structure and the system of higher education, even if they do not articulate it precisely in those terms.

For example, these student parents are, on average, correct in their assessment of affordability. A private nonprofit university that is only ten miles away from one of the regional state universities that thirty-one of these student parents attended is similarly rated in terms of its selectivity yet posted tuition in 2013 at just over $30,000 a year, well over three times the cost of the nearby state university the same year. The six-year retention rates for both those universities—that is, the percentage of students who received their college degree within six years—are relatively similar, with the public university reporting 52 percent compared to the private university's 56 percent graduation rate. However, the four-year retention rates of these two universities differ significantly in that only

21 percent of the students at the state university graduate in four years, whereas 46 percent of the students attending the private university graduate in that same time (NCES 2014). One less year in school results in one less year of paying tuition and one more year available to work and potentially reap the financial rewards of having a job for which a college degree was required. When the facts are read in this way, it soon becomes clear that the decisions regarding the costs of a college degree are far from straightforward and are dependent on a variety of complex factors that require careful consideration, a reading that is often belied by these students' "logics of efficiency."[2]

As described earlier, most of these student parents never explored going to college anywhere else. The idea never crossed their minds. First, they are not willing to leave the local area, to move their families—much less move away from their immediate families—or to move away from extended families or friends, who provide important supportive networks. Second, and this is explained by the way culture functions, most of these students did not bother to research alternatives to the community and state colleges that are closest to their homes. They have come to accept the belief that state colleges and universities will provide them with the education that they need to succeed. Those students, and there were none in this sample, who are most likely to possess knowledge of retention rates and to analyze a college degree's "return on investment" are more likely to research their college options and select a campus that provides an educational setting that meets their perceived educational and social needs.[3] Those students are more likely to be from higher socioeconomic backgrounds and have access to more resources that provide them with such information (McDonough 1997; Mullen 2010; Stuber 2011). Such knowledge, or human and cultural capital, to use the language of sociologists who have intensively examined these social processes, ensures that individuals from higher social classes select colleges from which they are likely to graduate.[4] And this is important, particularly when students have a high number of needs due to their socioeconomic status, academic demands, or responsibilities at home.

An institution's average retention rate does not tell the whole story. As already described, some students enter a university with more advantages, many of which result from their families' socioeconomic status. In her examination of working-class and middle- and upper-class students attending two very different colleges, a small liberal arts college and a large flagship state university, Stuber (2011) identifies the various ways that the culture[5] of the campus itself shapes the "experiential core" of students' campus life, influencing their academic and social integration on campus. For the middle- and upper-class students, a particular college's culture had very little effect on their involvement levels on campus—many of these students arrived on their respective campuses with preexisting social networks and predispositions to integrate themselves in ways that will enhance their college experience and improve their likelihood of graduating. Working-class students, on the other hand, are much better off at the slightly more expensive liberal arts college due to a variety of campus-based programs and opportunities, including study abroad programs, clubs, and a vibrant Greek culture, that have been put in place to connect them to the larger campus community.[6] Their chances for long-term educational success are very much influenced by their choice of college.

Armstrong and Hamilton (2013) likewise determine that college choices tend to matter most for low-income women. In their study *Paying for the Party: How College Maintains Inequality*, these two researchers examine women students' experiences at a public research university, revealing how an institutionally sanctioned party culture shapes students' academic success along social class lines. Such a culture, they argue, is produced in part because of the type of students—that is, out-of-state and international students with the means to pay for college but without the drive or academic qualifications to enter a more elite university—that these public universities are pushed to accept during an era of shifting demographics and funding cutbacks. Many of these students come from families that can afford the high tuition and that have provided their daughters with the social connections and cultural capital to survive both at school and upon graduation when entering the workplace. The working-class women, however, are distracted by the "party pathway" that is fostered by their upper-class peers and by institutional practices that support a strong Greek culture. This "party pathway" ultimately renders divergent effects on the educational experiences and futures of these young women, with upper-income women surviving the "party" due to their possession of a network of resources and lower-income women falling behind in school and work. Like the qualitative studies described earlier, Armstrong and Hamilton provide yet more insights regarding the interconnectedness of culture, college experiences, and social inequality.

The pathways that Armstrong and Hamilton (2013) portray play out very clearly in the educational story shared by Drew. Drew, a twenty-three-year-old communications student and father of a two-year-old, transferred from a college over four hours away to a local state regional university when he found out his longtime girlfriend was pregnant. He wanted to be closer to his girlfriend and to the familial networks that would provide them with support as they embarked on the journey that is parenthood. Drew also made it clear that because his father owned a local fast-food franchise, Drew had a ready job as well as a great deal of family support nearby as he worked through his immediate life changes.

However, that was just part of the story. When Drew made the decision to leave a university in a neighboring state, he cites the very different campus cultures at each respective institution as contributing to his decision. He describes his prior school as "expensive" and as having a "party school" atmosphere that did not align with his changing sense of self as he was preparing to become a new father. Certainly he was influenced to return to his home state because a job in his family's business awaited him there as well as a strong network of supportive family and friends. However, he also finds that the regional comprehensive university near his home town is not only more affordable than his prior out-of-state college but also provides a campus culture that he believes will support his educational and long-term career goals. Over 75 percent of the undergraduate students on his current campus are commuter students, and many are similarly working full time (CCSU 2008). These working students have very little time available to pursue the "party" culture that is typically associated with the residential college experience. In sum, Drew found his nearby, public regional university to be a good fit given his changing responsibilities as a new father.

Most private colleges, particularly smaller nonprofits, continue to target what are considered by college administrators as "traditional" students, who most often do not have children, are able to live on campus, and have time to engage in extracurricular activities and programs. Many of the resources described by Stuber (2011) that improved the academic success and retention rates of working-class students would not aid most student parents, who are rarely able to participate in study abroad programs due to their caregiving responsibilities and have neither the time nor the inclination to become involved in a variety of student clubs or Greek life.

So it is very possible that the state colleges and universities that student parents frequently choose to attend are indeed the "best option." Students' "logic of efficiency" may well be working in their favor. Although it may be true that state colleges and universities can provide student parents with the on-campus experience that they desire, it's important to acknowledge that most of these students didn't even explore their options. They have not researched campus resources to determine which colleges might best address their complex educational and familial needs and are not aware of the various campus climates that are cultivated to enhance retention and graduation. Not that there is much information out there regarding campus climates—much of that knowledge comes by way of one's social networks, acquaintances, friends, and family who are familiar with the various campuses or from campus visits, if one has the time and money to travel.

Although student parents' logics of efficiency are steering them toward state colleges and universities, public institutions have experienced severe cutbacks in recent years. Their tuitions are increasing, and students are increasingly expected to pick up the difference. In 2016, state spending in forty-six states remained well below prerecession 2008 spending, and states were spending on average 18 percent less on higher education. In Connecticut, where these student parents are attending college, spending on higher education in 2016 had decreased 12.6 percent since 2008, which translated to approximately $1,951 less spending per student (Mitchell, Leachman, and Masterson 2017). To make up for these cuts, public colleges have both consolidated services and increased tuition. Tuition at

Connecticut's four regional public universities more than doubled over a fifteen-year period from $4,153 in 2001–2002 to $10,079 in 2016–2017. During that same period, tuition at the states community colleges likewise doubled from $1,888 in 2001–2002 to $4,168 in 2016–2017 (Constable 2017). The promise of an affordable college education that students have come to expect is no longer what most will receive—students are paying significantly more than past generations for their college degrees, and with attrition rates so high, the risk of their investment has grown. The students interviewed here are, for now, the survivors. But for far too many students who wish to enter the doors of college, this part of the American dream is increasingly being deferred.

Why Not Enroll in an Online Program?

Interestingly, these student parents have chosen to forgo online degree options that are readily available and aggressively market themselves as convenient alternatives for working adults. Concerns regarding the high attrition rates of such programs and the quality of instruction have permeated public discourse as researchers and legislators question whether or not some of these online programs, particularly online bachelor's programs offered by for-profit colleges and universities, are providing quality instruction and the resources necessary to ensure students are able to succeed (Deming, Goldin, and Katz 2013; Mettler 2014). These concerns are borne in the context of increasing postsecondary enrollments and the diminishing resources for state colleges and universities as outlined earlier (Mettler 2014; Mitchell, Palacios, and Leachman 2014).

When asked about the possibility of enrolling in an online college, over half of these students confessed to trying online courses, but they claimed to prefer a traditional classroom environment, a preference that led them instead to local community colleges or state regional universities. Some students expressed concern regarding the quality of instruction and learning in a purely online classroom format. Lindsey, who is studying to be a high school history teacher, had taken four online classes throughout her college career. As a single mom of an energetic one-year-old, she admits that online classes in general are "a great way to get a course done and not interrupt your daily life too much." However, she states that she would never take an online course again. Of her experience, she laments, "I felt that I was just really on my own. And you know, somebody was just correcting my work and that was it." Lindsey perceives the teaching and learning in the online courses that she took to have been detached and ultimately inferior. At that time, she longed for the accountability and personal response that a traditional classroom provides and now declares, "I'd just rather put a face to the professor and know that this person is going to be angry with me if I don't come to class prepared." Ultimately she determines, "I just find that online courses are not for me."

Lindsey's desire for face-to-face contact was repeated by several other student parents, including Matt and Molly. Matt, a twenty-five-year-old criminology student and single father of a two-year-old, withdrew from the one online course that he attempted because the educational experience lacked a physical immediacy that he prefers. Matt contends that he has "to physically see a teacher, a professor, and I have to connect with him somehow." Molly, a thirty-four-year-old accounting student and married mother of a nine-year-old, echoes these students' comments admitting to preferring on-campus versus online classes because "I like to be here, listen to the professor, take notes, you know, hear the inflection in their voice, get things from them in person, and I think that that's how I learn best."

Jose, a forty-five-year-old father of three, like Lindsey, is studying to be a history teacher after having worked many years in the public school and foster care systems. When asked about his experience with online classes, Jose responds, "I'm more of a visual [learner] and because of all my work experience, I like to be face-to-face and discuss things." Later Jose admits that several of his colleagues and friends suggested that he enroll in a local public college that targets working adults by offering online programs and degrees. Jose rejected that option saying, "I think I'm going to find it boring. I think I'm going to be missing something." What he would miss, he later clarifies is "dialoguing," which is important to him because many of his ideas are developed during the process of interaction and discussion: "I might not know the answer now, but while we're discussing it I'll figure it out." Jose values the process of learning and discovery that can occur within personal interactions, and he has not yet found an online classroom environment that fully replicates that experience.

Other students express appreciation for the convenience that online options provide but question their ability to discipline themselves or focus on their coursework. Ed, a twenty-three-year-old father of two studying computer science, admits, "If I have an online class, I can get easily distracted, and being on your computer right there online, you have the games you can be playing . . . if I'm sitting at home, it's more like, 'I'm at home.'" Elizabeth reiterates Ed's concern when she confesses, "I don't have the self-discipline. I really need to be in the classroom. . . . I can't even check my email without my daughter being on my lap, so it just wouldn't work for me." These parents have come to appreciate the routine and structure that leaving the house and participating in a college classroom provides.

Additionally, time spent in a classroom provides a social respite for many parents. For some of these students, their time on campus was their sole opportunity to interact with other adults without their children around. When asked if she had ever taken an online course, Allie answers, "No. I needed to get out, to be with people, because I've been home for so long with just my children. I needed to be out and socialize." Just under a quarter of the student parents whom

I interviewed referenced their appreciation for the opportunity to engage in adult conversation and interaction in a face-to-face classroom environment.

In 2013, only 17 percent of public colleges and universities offered some courses online as compared to 5 percent of private nonprofit research universities and 2 percent of private liberal arts colleges. In contrast, 34 percent of for-profit institutions provided all of their courses online (McPherson and Bacow 2015). These numbers reveal the underlying objectives and missions of various types of institutions of higher education. For-profit colleges are driven by credentialing and a steadily increasing bottom line, which can be facilitated by offering conveniently accessed and administratively less expensive online instruction. On the other hand, more selective schools address their bottom line by ensuring high-quality college experiences that encourage face-to-face social networking with faculty, staff, and students. Most public colleges and universities fall in the middle of this spectrum, preferring to offer satellite campuses or community colleges to online instruction for those students who are geographically remote from their nearest full-service, public university. However, public colleges are increasingly offering some online options to provide flexibility to address the diverse needs of their student body.

Overall, these students prefer face-to-face instruction, which allows them the opportunity to meet with professors and fellow students and to more clearly separate their home and school lives. Although some of these student parents believe that having online options for some classes is beneficial, they would rather attend classes on a college campus, and none of them are interested in taking all of their courses online.

Where's the Money? Access to a College Education

One important factor shaping a student's sense that they belong on campus is access. All of these students qualified academically for their respective programs at these state colleges and universities, and so access was primarily determined by geographic proximity and affordability. Approximately 85 percent of the student parents in this study rely on some kind of financial aid to pay for their college experience, be it in the form of grants, scholarships, or loans. As described in chapter 2, many aid programs emerged following World War II to address the needs of the evolving economy in the United States and to redress social inequalities. Among the most prevalent forms of aid that these student parents have taken advantage of are the GI Bill, Pell Grants, and Stafford Loans. In the following sections, I briefly describe these various forms of financial aid, in addition to forms of non-education-related financial aid and child care assistance that students sought out but were denied. Collectively this overview provides a window into ways that college affordability has ebbed and flowed for these student parents in recent years.

The GI Bill

The most generous combined federal and state financial aid package is available to veterans. Seven of the forty students in this study benefit from the Post-9/11 GI Bill and Connecticut state tuition waivers, which cover most if not all the costs of tuition, fees, books, and living expenses during the months when students are in school. At the time when I conducted these interviews, Connecticut was one of the few states to offer tuition waivers that veterans can use to attend any of the state colleges or universities as long as they served a minimum of ninety days in active duty, were honorably discharged, and have been officially accepted to the state college or university of their choice. This tuition waiver makes Connecticut a particularly attractive educational destination for veterans, who are expected to pay out-of-state tuition in many other states until they can establish residency status.[7]

These seven students chose to enter the military rather than immediately attend college right out of high school for a variety of reasons—some were pushed to go to college but did not feel ready or were simply not interested in continuing with school, while others felt they could not afford college and so chose to join the military as a means of financing their future education. Whatever their initial reasons for joining the military, these seven student parents are all now enrolled in a public university, and the educational benefits provided to them have made that possible.

It became very clear that these GI educational benefits are a vital financial resource that provides access to low- and even middle-income veterans who might not otherwise consider pursuing a college degree. However, such benefits are more likely to be available to men than they are to women. Because the military remains a male-dominated institution, only 9 percent of all veterans are women, it is no surprise that numerically many more men than women have taken advantage of the comprehensive assistance provided by the GI Bill (U.S. Department of Veterans Affairs 2015).

In the fall of 2015, I met with the director of the Office of Veterans Affairs housed at one of the state universities attended by five of these seven student parent veterans. At that time, the director admitted to being concerned about the lack of women veterans returning to campus to pursue their degrees. He shared with me some of his attempts to reach out to women veterans—for example, offering a complimentary spa day, which he used to promote available educational benefits. Overall, however, he conceded that such events to reach out to women veterans had been unsuccessful. Although the women veterans who participated in these events were generally interested in what he had to say, many of them expressed concern about being able to balance family and work with the demands of going to school. Importantly, veterans are limited as to how long they have available to take advantage of their educational benefits.

The most generous benefits, accorded by the Montgomery GI and Post-9/11 GI Bills, must be used within ten to fifteen years of release from active duty (U.S. Department of Veterans Affairs 2013). If these women don't use their educational benefits within this limited time frame, they lose them.

Pell Grants and Stafford Loans

The Pell Grant and Stafford Loan programs, implemented in the 1970s, continue to enable millions of low-income students of all ages to attend college. According to researchers at the National Center for Educational Statistics, over 36 percent of the students receiving a bachelor's degree in 1999–2000 had at one time or another during their academic career received a Pell Grant. They found that women were much more likely than men to have relied on a Pell Grant, and over 45 percent of those students were aged twenty-five or older (see table 3.1). Pell Grant recipients were also more likely than nonrecipients to identify as racial/ethnic minorities and more likely to be caring for dependents and to identify as single parents (Wei and Horn 2009). These numbers make it clear that the population of Pell Grant recipients who are pursuing a college degree are much more racially diverse and are more likely to be women, older and/or caring for children than are students who do not qualify for such aid.

In my sample of student parents, 63 percent rely on Stafford Loans to cover their educational costs, a figure that is in line with national trends (NCES 2015b). Fourteen students have incomes low enough so that they qualify for and receive Pell Grants, and of those students, 86 percent, that is all but two, are also taking out loans. Although student parents did not share with me exactly how much debt they had accrued up to that point in their college career, researchers have found that the level of debt of Pell Grant recipients on average exceeds that of students whose incomes were too high to qualify for a Pell Grant in the first place (see table 3.1).

The availability of Pell Grants has no doubt improved access to higher education, yet even in 2000, Pell Grant dollar amounts were not enough to equalize the effects of college debt. And over the past two decades, Pell Grant dollars have come to cover increasingly less of the cost of full tuition at public state universities across the nation. Over a ten year period, between 2003–2004 and 2013–2014, tuition and fees at public institutions steadily increased 44 percent from $5,900 to $8,890 (College Board 2014). These increases occurred primarily in response to reduced state funding on higher education, which has been decreasing steadily since 2000 and dropped even more dramatically in the wake of the 2008 financial crisis. Between 2008 and 2013, average state spending on higher education decreased by 28 percent, and 2010 marked the first year that, in public colleges and universities, revenue from tuition was higher than revenue acquired from state and local appropriations (Desrochers and Kirshstein 2012; Oliff et al. 2013).

TABLE 3.1

Comparison of Demographic and Financial Aid Characteristics of College Graduates by Pell Grant Status, 1999–2000 (Percent)

	Pell Grant Recipients	Nonrecipients
Gender		
Women	60	55.9
Men	40	44.2
Age		
Ages 24 and under	54.3	72.6
Ages 25 and older	45.7	27.4
Race		
White	63.3	79.7
Black	11.8	5.8
Hispanic	13.2	5.9
Asian	6.8	5.2
Pacific Islander	1.0	0.5
American Indian	0.9	0.4
Other or more than one race	2.9	2.7
Caregiving Status		
Has dependents	24.3	12.8
No dependents	75.7	87.2
Single Parent	11.4	4.0
Student Loan Status		
Borrowed	86.8	47.1
Did not borrow	13.2	52.9
Average cumulative amount borrowed	$18,500	$17,000

Note: Totals may not equal 100 due to rounding.

Source: Wei and Horn (2009).

In 2013, in-state tuition and fees for one of the state universities attended by approximately two-thirds of these student parents came to almost $9,000, whereas Pell Grants in 2012–2013 were limited to a maximum award of $5,645, with most awards averaging $3,678. In-state tuition and fees at Connecticut's state flagship research university during that same year were over $11,000, well above the average Pell Grant distributed to eligible students. It is clear that the Pell Grant alone is not sufficient to cover the educational costs of these student parents, who have chosen to attend public community colleges or comprehensive regional colleges in part because of their comparative affordability. This helps us to understand why most of these student parents subsequently rely on loans to make up the difference.

Low-Income Parents and Child Care Assistance

Six student parents—Cynthia, Caroline, Drew, Lindsey, Jackie, and Dave—were all told by case managers in local social service agency offices that despite their very low incomes and single-parent status, they were ineligible to receive state supports because they were pursuing a four-year degree rather than engaging in paid work or job training programs. Due to changes in 1996 U.S. welfare laws, many of these student parents, who would have previously qualified for public assistance due to their low-income status, are no longer eligible for cash or child care benefits that would help them to stay in school. According to revisions of welfare policy, which were signed into law in 1996 by then-president Bill Clinton, all welfare program participants are expected to attend workforce training classes or locate paid jobs in order to receive cash and child care assistance. This emphasis on work-first resulted in many states severely limiting their postsecondary education options for parents attending college, resulting in many student parents being counseled by their case managers to put their college goals on hold indefinitely (Pearson 2007, 2010).

At the time when these six students were interviewed, pursuing any degree above an associate's was not considered a legitimate means of fulfilling participants' required "work" hours in the state of Connecticut. Lindsey laments, "I heard from the state that I don't qualify because I'm not in a job training program. That because I'm a student trying to not milk the system, you know, for the rest of my life and trying to make something of myself, that they can't pay for day care." Dave similarly admits, "Obviously the state wants me to get off of them, so I think they try to push me to go to the working programs, but I'm not going to go there and look for a job at Target or anything 'cause I'm getting a four-year university degree!" Both Lindsey and Dave see the requirement of attending job training programs as shortsighted—they do not believe that such programs will help them to attain their long-term career goals, which require a four-year college degree. Dave is studying business and hopes to continue on to graduate school to earn an MBA, and Lindsey is completing her bachelor's degree in secondary education with the intent of teaching high school history. Both are frustrated by the strict welfare requirements that push low-income parents to take resume-writing classes and low-wage jobs in lieu of pursuing four-year degrees and careers.

Dave is the only student parent in this sample who serendipitously found a way around the system because he was assigned a "lenient" case manager with whom he has a good relationship. As long as his girlfriend enrolls in and attends the job placement classes, his case manager is not pushing him to attend them as well. Dave confides, "She just understood how much me being in school helps out. She was real lenient about not making me go to programs and all that kind of stuff but still giving us the assistance." Dave's case manager is breaking with established guidelines and protocol so he can continue to pursue his college education, which both he and his case manager believe to be in his family's long-term, best interests.[8]

Cynthia, Caroline, Drew, Lindsey, and Jackie were not so lucky—their case managers interpreted state and federal regulations more strictly and told these student parents that although they financially qualified for the program, to be eligible for public assistance, they needed to put aside their goal of pursuing a four-year degree.[9] Case managers denied all five of these students' applications for public assistance through Connecticut's Temporary Family Assistance (TFA) and Care 4 Kids programs. Caroline clearly expresses her irritation with the limitations such programs put on students who wish to pursue undergraduate degrees:

CAROLINE: With Care 4 Kids they don't help women who go to school. Why? I don't know. That does not make sense to me, like if a woman's trying to better her education and better herself to get a good paying job, why can't you help pay for day care while she's in school? That does not make sense to me. Like they only go up to associate's. They won't go up to bachelor's. That doesn't make sense to me.

FIONA: A case manager talked to you about that? Did you actually talk with someone about all that?

CAROLINE: Yeah. But they can't! They [say] "I'm sorry but there's nothing I can say. There's nothing I can do. There's nothing I can change. It's documented." Oh my God! That's full of crap! Like here is a, here's a female in front of you that's trying to better herself. . . . When you're on state, they tell you the job's first— it's called Jobs First. And if you're on state you have to abide to these rules for Jobs First, where they help you find a job, they help you put a resume together. And I'm telling them, "I'm in school I have a job, why can't you pay for my school?" "Because you're going for your bachelor's." "But I'm bettering myself!" They just couldn't give me an answer. They didn't know.

Caroline's experience reveals the ways federal and state regulations restricting students' qualifying educational experiences result in uniformly pushing parents toward short-term, not long-term, solutions. These five student parents were financially eligible for public assistance through the TFA and Care 4 Kids programs, but they were unwilling to amend their educational goals to fulfill the programs' requirements.

Connecticut's welfare regulations regarding the Jobs First Employment Services (JFES) program were temporarily relaxed in June 2010, in part a response to record high levels of unemployment in the state. The Connecticut state legislature passed and then-governor Jodi Rell signed into state law a provision altering local welfare policy, allowing students pursuing four-year or graduate degrees to take advantage of child care benefits as long as state unemployment levels remain high. When I called the Connecticut Department of Children and Families at the end of 2011 to inquire as to how many participants in the Temporary Family Assistance (TFA) program were taking advantage of the opportunity to enroll in baccalaureate programs, I was told "not likely many, if any." Legislative changes are notoriously slow to trickle down to case managers and their clients. By 2015, the legislative provision allowing for flexibility in state welfare work requirements had expired and college students enrolled in four-year baccalaureate programs were again no longer eligible for cash assistance and child care benefits.

Forgoing Marriage

Three of the seven student parents who are cohabiting with the fathers or mothers of their children stated that at least one reason why they are not choosing to marry their partner was due to their concerns about how marriage might affect their financial aid status. Marrying their respective partners would increase their annual income, possibly making them ineligible for or reducing the amount of money they might receive from Pell Grants. Jaime, a twenty-six-year-old mother of one, who was pursuing her bachelor's degree in accounting confesses, "That's why [I'm] kind of debating on getting married right now, because if I get married, who knows what happens to my financial aid. Then I won't be able to go to school, which is a problem [laughs]. You know, 'cause, I have like a year left in school, and then after that I'm not even sure if I'm—I might go on to get my master's. So . . . it's all up in the air." Like many of these student parents, Jaime is unclear exactly how changing her marital status will affect her financial aid. She is twenty-six years old and so is not claimed by her parents as a dependent. It is likely that marrying her partner will increase her household income and decrease her needs-based financial aid. But much depends on how much income she and her fiancé make from year to year. He works in construction, and his income varies considerably season by season, year by year, making estimating the financial implications of getting married even more complicated.

Ed, on the other hand, clearly understands the financial implications of such a decision and states that the primary reason he and his partner were choosing not to get married was purely financial. He declares, "Yes, we'd like to get married, but it just doesn't make financial sense right now." Although the GI Bill covers his tuition and books and some living expenses, it does not cover child care. His partner receives child care under Connecticut's Care 4 Kids public assistance program, and because they are not married and Ed is not the biological father of her children, his income and benefits are not considered when she goes to apply for public assistance.[10]

Ed shares that his partner also wants to pursue her bachelor's degree, but given the limitations of the welfare program described above, they together agreed that she will continue to work the relatively low wage jobs that are currently available to her and that allow her to receive the Care 4 Kids child care subsidies. Once he completes his degree and becomes the primary breadwinner and once their child is older and not in need of regular child care, she can then pursue her college degree in education. Ironically, one of the stated goals of welfare reform was to increase the number of marriages among low-income families, yet Ed and his girlfriend are forgoing marriage in order to make the existing complex system of financial assistance work in their favor.

Family Savings

Only six of the student parents in this study are not dependent on federal or state grants or loans to fund their education. Three of those five students—Emma, Leslie, and Joy—are married, have relatively stable incomes and adequate savings, and feel that they can now afford to pursue their college degrees. The fourth student, twenty-three-year-old Drew, is very much supported by his family and is able to use his earnings from a family-owned franchise and his job at a local university to pay for his tuition and school costs. He and his girlfriend live with his parents, who also help out significantly with child care. The fifth student, forty-nine-year-old Snow, recently divorced after many years of marriage and is using her savings so that she may now pursue a degree in counseling with the hopes of attaining a job in a public school. Starting over in midlife, Snow is focused on her career, seeking a job with a reliable income and benefits now that her children are growing older and she is on her own.

The sixth student who is not dependent on federal or state grants or loans is thirty-four-year-old Molly. She had never expected to go to college. Back when she was eighteen, Molly had no intention of continuing with her schooling—never took the SATs—and instead married and gave birth to her daughter soon after graduating from high school. Several years ago, she began caring for her ailing grandfather and grandmother and was designated their conservator, taking on responsibility for their finances and assets. An uncle, who lives across the country and whom she had never met before, wanted to express his appreciation for her caring for her grandparents by sending an assistant to help her. He also wanted to provide her with a gift for taking on the responsibility of caring for his parents and so offered to pay for her college education. Molly says of their first encounter, "My first conversation with him was the day of the probate hearing when I took over my grandfather's conservatorship. And just as the relationship blossomed and he had sent someone out to help me and said to this middle person, 'I want to do something for Molly.' And she said I think that she needs to go to school. It was kind of—I guess she saw something in me that she, she said, 'You know, she needs to go to school.' And just kind of blossomed from there, and so, that's why I'm here!" [laughs]. She started taking classes and was conditionally accepted as long as she did well during her first term, which she did, earning a 4.0 grade point average that confirmed for her that her uncle's investment in her education was worthwhile. Molly is now well on her way to earning her degree in accounting and has gained a newly found appreciation for the learning that can take place in a college classroom.

How Money Matters

The vast majority of the student parents in this sample did not receive much if any financial assistance from extended family members and most relied on state or federally sourced funds, including the GI Bill and a complex system of grants and loans. Any form of financial aid is increasingly necessary as more and more individuals are pursuing postsecondary degrees and as college costs continue to increase. Without such financial aid, many of these student parents are at risk of leaving college altogether.

In response to the failing economy, reduced state and local funding, and increasing college tuition costs, in the fall of 2007 Congress passed and President George W. Bush signed into law the College Cost Reduction and Access Act. This was followed in the winter of 2009 with President Barack Obama signing into law Congress's American Recovery and Reinvestment Act.[11] The acts were hailed as victories for low- and middle-income students because they included provisions that increased the maximum amount available to individuals for Pell Grants, which had remained at the same level since 2003 and increased the amount of income students could receive before they might experience reductions to their financial aid.

Despite these changes, financial aid experts and educational researchers have long noted the decreased purchasing power of the Pell Grant, which in the early 1970s covered nearly 80 percent of the college costs for the average four-year public university but by 2012–2013 covered only 31 percent of those costs (Mettler 2014). Although the U.S. government more than doubled its contributions to the Pell Gant program between the years of 2007 and 2012, almost twice as many students now qualify for the grant, meaning more money has to be disbursed to more students. When evaluated in terms of constant dollars, the maximum individual Pell Grant awards have remained relatively stagnant over the past two decades, while tuition costs have soared (Baum and Ma 2013; College Board 2014).

Further, just because students may have family incomes that are too high for them to be eligible for a Pell Grant does not necessarily mean that they are financially stable or comfortable, as Desiree's and Lucille's respective stories make clear. Desiree gave up a dancing career in New York City at age eighteen when she learned she was pregnant. In order to make ends meet, she now lives in her hometown with her mother, who herself was a single mom. Desiree is receiving no financial support from her daughter's father, although he stays in touch and visits with her two to three times a week when he can. Desiree does not qualify for the Pell Grant because she is, in tax terms, a "dependent." That is, her mother claims both twenty-year-old Desiree and her two-year-old daughter on her income tax forms, and so Desiree reports her mother's relatively high income as a registered nurse on her financial aid forms for college. As a result, she is ineligible for the federal Pell Grant and so pays full tuition at a local community college. One of Desiree's two brothers is also in college attending a public university in another state, and her mother is helping him out as well with his education.

Of her own and her mother's financial situation Desiree confesses, "It's been a struggle," but the entire family is for now able to make ends meet even if the household budget runs tight from month to month. Desiree is taking out loans to cover most of her tuition fees and pays for her remaining tuition, fees, and books with her earnings from a part-time job at a local women's shelter. She is fortunate in that her mother and a close friend watch her daughter three to four times a week—she pays her friend twenty to thirty dollars a week for helping out even though her friend doesn't ask for anything. Without her mother's support in providing housing, food, and occasional child care, Desiree would not be able to afford to go to school.

Of her current situation, Desiree confides, "I mean everything's pretty stable, and you know, I get everything I need. I make enough money to survive at the level that I'm at." But she admits, "I just wish I had more savings because now that I'm a parent, I think about what if this happens, what if that happens, what if I need money to fix my car? What if . . . you know? What if something happens, and I have to move out of my house? There's a million things that can go wrong, and when you have nothing to fall back on, you're that much more worried about what's going to happen 'cause you have another life on your hands." Although she has all the basic resources to survive, Desiree is fully aware of how dependent she is on her family's and friend's generosity in providing shelter, food, and child care, and she is aware of the debt she is incurring as she takes out loans every semester to cover her tuition costs. Desiree's financial situation is secure for now but could change at any moment as she is not able to set aside any savings, and her debt grows with each semester.

Lucille's story differs in the details but is similar in effect. Just over ten years ago, when Lucille was in her early twenties, her parents listed her as a dependent on their tax returns and helped her out with her college tuition. They earned just enough income so that she didn't qualify for needs-based aid but found that they could cover the gap between her own financial contributions from two part-time jobs and the tuition costs for a public state college. However, when her younger sister became pregnant, her parents needed to pull back from assisting Lucille to aid her sister during her time of need. Unwilling to accrue large amounts of debt, Lucille chose to withdraw from college and began working full time in a grocery store bakery, making enough to live on but never enough ever to accrue any savings. She focused instead on getting married, maintaining a household, and starting a family. Now over a decade later with two children, one of whom is autistic, and with her husband recently unemployed, she has decided that the only way for her family to get ahead is for her to go back to school to earn a degree. And the one positive unintended outcome of her husband being laid off is that they currently have a household income low enough so that she qualifies for a Pell Grant. She is augmenting her grant with loans, but unlike before, she has now determined that the long-term debt is worth taking on.

Desiree's and Lucille's stories reveal that many students are struggling on the sidelines, caught in between not or barely making enough to cover their basic household and educational costs, but often making too much to qualify for needs-based grants. And as described earlier, even for those students who do qualify for needs-based aid, Pell Grants are not nearly enough to cover increasing tuition costs at many of our nation's public universities. Further, for those low-income student parents like Caroline, Cynthia, Drew, Lindsey, and Jackie, their choice to pursue bachelor's degrees rather than short-term, certification programs results in their ineligibility for public assistance programs that would provide access to child care and cash assistance.

As public assistance programs retain their restrictions, needs-based financial aid stays flat, and states disinvest in their public colleges and universities, we see tuition costs and borrowing levels increase. Ultimately, students are left to decide what level of risk and debt their education is worth. The answer for many of these students is to turn to loans, which is why we have seen student debt emerge as the second-highest consumer debt category in the United States, following mortgage debt. In 2017, over forty-four million borrowers incurred approximately $1.3 trillion in debt, with the average borrower owing $37,172 (Friedman 2017). And as student debt continues to creep up past the $1.4 trillion mark, the Federal Reserve chairman, Jerome Powell, cautioned U.S. senators in 2018 that such growing debt could soon affect national economic growth (Bauman 2018).

These students' realities reveal an important shift in the funding of higher education in recent decades. That is, we are seeing a steady transfer of risk and responsibility from institutions to individuals. Instead of the government subsidizing public colleges and universities to keep tuition costs low as in years past, financial aid via grants and loans is disbursed to individual students, attending both public and private, both nonprofit and for-profit institutions. And even those students who choose to attend the often more affordable, local public colleges and universities in their communities are now collectively paying more than are states and local governments to fund those institutions (Desrochers and Kirshstein 2012). In sum, we are seeing access to higher education moving out of reach. A college degree is increasingly becoming a private, *not* a public, good.

Campus-Based Child Care

Child care centers are key organizations that shape a culture that is perceived by student parents to be family friendly or not. Not only are on-campus child care centers an integral resource for parents but they provide symbolic acknowledgment and validation of parents' caregiving work. As these students describe the various child care resources on their respective campuses, they cite the importance of convenience, access, quality, and affordability. But they also talk about feeling that they belong and are accepted on campus when they see children and other student parents both in these centers and walking across college grounds and in buildings.

Angie, Heather, Cynthia, and Desiree all attended the same community college and describe the child care center located on that campus. This particular community college–based child care center offers services for students at a discounted rate, three dollars an hour, and is conveniently located on campus. All four of these students used this center, usually to cover hours when family members were not available to watch their children, and found the care to be of high quality and the price affordable. However, that changed when they transferred from the community college to a local four-year university. The child care center at the public university that they now attend is both expensive and limited in terms of the number of students it can accommodate. At the time of these interviews, the center did not provide hourly drop-in care, was inconveniently located off campus, and could accommodate only twenty-six children on a campus with over twelve thousand students.

Desiree expresses her frustration regarding the limited child care resources provided by her current university: "My daughter's been on the waiting list for the day care here since I was pregnant. . . . I went down there about two weeks ago and they told me it's going to be another year and a half." Cynthia ends her comparative description of the community college and state university campus cultures by confessing, "I think there's a day care here [at the university], but I don't really know anything about it." Seven of the thirteen students who compare their community college experiences with their four-year university experiences cite the visible presence of child care or preschool programs on their community college campuses as evidence of a family-friendly culture, a sight not evidenced at the four-year public universities where they are currently enrolled.

Nationally, the Institute for Women's Policy Research (IWPR) found that four-year colleges are more likely than community colleges to have some kind of child care center. However, the IWPR also recently reported that despite increasing numbers of student parents evidenced on college campuses, resources for child care have been steadily dwindling since 2000 (Gault et al. 2014). In

2003–2004, 53 percent of community colleges provided some form of campus-based child care—in 2013, that number dropped to 46 percent. On four-year public college and university campuses, the percentage with on-campus child care fell from a 2002 high of 54 to 51 percent in 2013. Although the decline in child care centers for all postsecondary institutions began in 2004, the most precipitous decrease occurred after the recession of 2008, when public institutions, in particular, began to be hit hard by reduced levels of state support.[12]

Not only is the number of child care centers decreasing but so are the funds that are available to student parents to assist in paying for child care, such as the stagnant funding of the Child Care Access Means Parents in School (CCAMPIS) competitive grant program (Gault et al. 2014). The CCAMPIS program, which was first offered in 1999 under the Clinton administration and provides financial assistance to subsidize student parents' child care costs, has been flat funded since 2003. The number of CCAMPIS grants awarded to college and university campuses has fallen from a high of 341 in 2004 to 86 in 2014 (U.S. Department of Education 2014). Most recently, the current secretary of education, Betsy DeVos, has recommended eliminating the grant program altogether, but legislators in 2018 agreed not only to keep but to increase funding for CCAMPIS (Dzigbede and Bronstein 2017; Kreighbaum 2018). The future of the program remains unclear, but even with increased funding from approximately $15 million to a proposed $35 million, the CCAMPIS program only begins to address the steep child care needs of student parents in college.

Admittedly, nearly a third of the students in my sample would not even need formal child care because they are able to turn to family members or close friends for caregiving assistance. It is because of these networks of support that they were able to return to college in the first place. However, when I ask students to offer recommendations to improve student parents' experiences on campus, nearly all mention the importance of providing on-campus child care. In frustration, Jackie argues, "Even high schools like [City] High have a day care! It's like, they have day care, so why can't the university have a day care?" When child care is visibly present or absent on campus, the symbolic message is clearly communicated to parents.

These students are acutely aware that as parents, they are a distinct minority on four-year college campuses. A visible child care center on campus serves as an affirmative acknowledgment of their parenting identity and provides a place where parents might seek out community resources or meet other parents.[13] Although these students were able to cobble together child care networks that in most cases worked for them, they nonetheless cited the relevance of providing campus-based child care as a means of helping out students who might need such assistance. Doing so would acknowledge the needs of and legitimize the institution's commitment to students like them.

Age, Stigma, and Academic Norms

Most of these student parents attribute their perceptions of acceptance or lack thereof to a campus culture shaped by not only financial aid and child care resources but academic norms and policies. Those student parents who over the course of their college career attended both community colleges and four-year universities additionally describe some of the differences between those two types of campuses. Heather, a forty-year-old mother of four who is now pursuing her bachelor's degree in psychology, specifically addresses the issue of students' age and the norm of bringing one's children to campus and class:

HEATHER: Now, I don't think it's accepted to bring your babies into class like I did when my oldest was little. . . . Maybe that was the school I was in or the area I was in. I don't know, 'cause a lot of girls did. Here I don't see that [*laughs*] you know? I think at [the community college], I had a Saturday class. There was a mom who brought a couple of her kids and then they just sat in the back, but they were fine. The teacher, I think, the professor, they worked it out.

FIONA: But here you feel there's a different culture?

HEATHER: I'm the oldest in my classes [at State U], so nobody has kids. I think there's one girl who has a two-year-old in my class, but I don't think anybody else does.

Heather reveals that not only did she more often see children on her two-year campus but also she perceives professors to have been more open to having children in class than on her current campus. Although most parents in this study did not express a desire to bring their children to class—instead these students described having their child in class as distracting—nearly all of these students describe a time when they brought a child to class or campus because their child care for that day fell though.

These different campus cultures also create a distinct effect on student parents' peer and faculty interactions, and those effects can vary depending on a student's age. Cynthia, a twenty-three-year-old psychology student who previously attended a community college, maintains that "the majority of people" at her local community college "have kids, so it's different there 'cause all the professors know that most of the students in the classes have kids and they're working adults." She contends that the faculty understand "that most [students] really don't have the time to be in school but they try to do it anyway." In contrast she describes the students attending her current university as "younger, they're like eighteen, nineteen, out of high school" and she believes that faculty "don't really know what's going on with the student body—they know most of them work, but they don't know that they have families." Cynthia's perceptions regarding age differences on community college and four-year universities are validated by actual numbers. In 2016, the average age of students enrolled in a community college across the country was twenty-eight (AACC 2016). In contrast, at the four-year state university where thirty-three of the student parents in this study were once enrolled, only 17 percent of the undergraduate student population was over the age of thirty. Nearly 70 percent of the students at that university were age twenty-four or younger (CCSU 2011).

Cynthia confesses to feeling that she is an "outsider," particularly when her professors at the four-year university emphasize the youth and inexperience of their students. She admits to feeling riled when her instructors presume that young college students are irresponsible and know little about the "real" world. Although her young age allows her to assimilate on a four-year campus in a way that older student parents cannot, Cynthia is frustrated when faculty or staff presume that her life emulates that of many of her young peers who devote much more time to managing their social lives than they do their family lives. However, like many of the younger parents whom I interviewed, she also expresses a fear of being perceived and stigmatized as a teen or young parent "statistic," and so she often hesitates to "out" herself in class to professors and peers. Either way many of these younger mothers and fathers feel that they lose, and so they choose instead to remain silent about being a parent.

On the contrary, older students are sometimes reluctant to reveal their identities as parents because they do not wish to present themselves in front of their younger peers and professors as seeking special treatment. Lindsey, a twenty-six-year-old history education major, shares,

> Now that I'm getting into like the professional program, I have a few more parents in the classroom but in just a lot of my lower-level classes or some of my history classes, I'm the only parent in the room. I'm the only person over twenty-two in the room. . . . I'm looked at as the parent in the room, and I think that if I was to ask for an extension because I was sick or anything, if I were to ask for something of the teacher and the teacher gave it to me, the rest of the class would think, "Oh, it's 'cause she's a parent." Or, "It's because she has a kid. She's playing the kid card." Or, you know, like there's some reason that I'm getting this, and the professor would probably give it to anyone in the room, you know, whatever I was asking for, whether it be an extension or to leave early or something like that. "Oh, she must have a day care crisis." I remember last semester, I did get some roll of the eye when a professor who knew I had children, we bonded. We would talk. Like, I'd come to class early, she was in class early. We would talk about our children, and people. Other students would walk in and probably hear this and think, "Oh, she's kind of friends with the teacher. That's not cool." I think people are intimidated of bonds that parents have that maybe nonparents don't have.

Lindsey sees the pros and cons of outing herself as a parent in class—although sharing her parenting identity with her professor provides moments of connection, those moments come at the risk of alienating her from usually younger, nonparent student peers.

Further, even when Lindsey believes most of her professors to be understanding of her parenting needs, she feels guilty for needing to request assistance. She admits, "You know, I never know how a new professor is going to respond, and I don't want them to think that I'm going into some long like soliloquy about, 'Oh, I'm a single parent. I'm on disability.' I don't want them to think that I'm trying to swing their grade or anything like that." Lindsey does not want to be perceived as different or needing special favors. Like Carolyn, who asserts at the beginning of this chapter that she's not looking for "handouts," many students simultaneously want to be treated like every other student but at the same time want professors to understand how their caregiving responsibilities might interfere with their ability to get to class or complete an assignment.

Communicating with professors and classmates that student parents do not expect special favors while nonetheless sometimes needing differential treatment is not at all easy, particularly when regular or emergency child care is unavailable. Elizabeth shares such a moment:

> Last weekend next to me in my logic class there was a girl there who had a baby with her, and I'm like, "Wow! You brought her to school." And she's like, "Well, I had a paper to turn in" and her father had an emergency and he couldn't be there and she's like, "I had no other choice." And I said, "I give you a lot of credit. That's dedication." And she didn't go in the class because they were watching a movie or something, but she made sure she was there to hand it in because she didn't want to disturb the class with her baby, but she was there to hand it in.

Elizabeth chooses to emphasize the lengths to which this student parent went to fulfill her parental and student roles simultaneously. Although not an ideal solution for the mother, child, and professor, the act of coming to school to submit her work was perceived by Elizabeth to be a show of "dedication" worthy of acknowledgment in a difficult situation.

Most of these student parents recognize that their professors are similarly placed in a difficult position when students' familial needs conflict with their educational requirements. Matt describes a time when he was enrolled in an intensive winter session course and his son's day care was closed. Matt knew he could not miss a day of school because one class during the compressed term was the equivalent of a week's worth of classes during a regular fifteen-week term, so he contacted the professor, who allowed Matt to bring his young son with him to class. Matt was grateful to his professor for providing this opportunity, which allowed him to keep up with his class attendance. However, Matt admits that "by like the second hour" his son "was ready to start screaming and go play," and that the entire situation "was kind of rough." He eventually left class early that day and reflects now that neither he nor the professor knew how best to address the situation—locating emergency backup care was really the only feasible solution, but none was available.

Finding a professor who is willing to work with the competing demands of student parents' lives, even if the solutions are not ideal, is far from guaranteed. Matt describes his professors at the four-year state university as being "surprisingly accepting in vast contrast to his prior experience at a private liberal arts college. Of his previous college, Matt contends, "They probably wouldn't know how to react to [parents]. It was just a totally different atmosphere. Whereas here, you have a wide range of different types of people, and there's a large part of the student population that do have children. And the professors are definitely aware and they help out. . . . I appreciate it. It makes my life a lot easier." And most of the student parents find their professors on the four-year state university campus to be supportive as long as students maintain clear and steady contact with them. Lindsey, described earlier, recalls a time when she had to miss class because her daughter was ill. She was concerned because the professor of the class maintained an attendance policy, but when she wrote to her professor explaining her situation, her professor replied that she would not "penalize" Lindsay for the "stresses that are life." Lindsay admits that she "didn't expect that at all, especially coming from a woman with such a strict attendance policy."

But not all professors are supportive when student parents' caregiving responsibilities come into conflict with their classroom responsibilities. Amber, a twenty-five-year-old mother studying English, shares that when her one-year-old daughter was ill, she could not attend class on an important day when a paper was due. She describes bundling up her daughter and trekking over to the university to submit her work, even though she would have to miss the class. The reception she received, however, was unexpected: "I went to school to drop that darn paper off to show that I was a good student, and I didn't want it to be late and ten points off it, etc. etc. And the teacher yelled at me in class in front of the students!" Amber continues, "It took all my composure to leave that classroom, get in the elevator with my daughter, and come home without crying because I wanted to be a good parent and be home for my sick daughter." Amber believes that she was doing the right thing, being a good mother and a good student, but was instead publically humiliated for what her professor perceived as not fulfilling her student obligations.

Jackie describes an instance during finals week, when her exam time conflicted with the time that she usually dropped her daughter off at school. Because she knew that the professor was not issuing an exam and was instead going to use that time to return papers and facilitate a discussion about those papers, she asked if she could pick up her paper at an alternative time so that she could drop her daughter off at school. The professor instead suggested that she bring her daughter to class during the scheduled exam time. Jackie understood that he was trying to be accommodating but felt that he didn't understand that it was more important that her daughter be at her school and not her mother's university. Jackie reflects,

> I told him I couldn't make it, and he said, "What do you mean?" and I'm like, "Um, I have a daughter and she goes to school. You know that." He's like, "What do you mean? I don't understand," and he repeated, "I don't understand." And I took it as an insult. I'm like, what do you mean you don't understand? Like why am I arguing with him? This is ridiculous. Obviously he doesn't understand what it's like. I'm like, "I am a single parent. I don't have anyone else to bring her. What do you want me to do?" "Well then bring her to class." And I felt so pressured by this man that I had to basically shorten my daughter's day [and] bring her to the college campus to the class just so he could sit there for an hour and discuss. I'm like this is ridiculous. My daughter is missing a half day at school because you wanted me to come in here because you couldn't understand that I have a daughter. You know what I mean? I took it as an insult and I felt hurt. I felt like he didn't understand me or anything. It felt so wrong.

Jackie states that she did not feel comfortable pressing the issue any further because the professor held positions of power at the University. She admits, "You don't know how people are. You don't know if they are going to take you personally and hold something against you."

As she relates this story, she mentions several times that this professor made it clear that he did not have children, and she attributes his lack of understanding of her situation to his unfamiliarity with the responsibilities of parenting. She ultimately arrives at the conclusion, "That's probably why he doesn't understand. . . . He doesn't have children. . . . I guess he was honest like he really didn't understand." Her beliefs were confirmed when she brought her daughter to class that day. She states that her classmates welcomed her daughter, exclaiming how "cute" and "well-behaved" she was. When I ask whether or not her professor interacted with her daughter during their two-hour discussion, she responds "Not at all."

Students also perceive that faculty who themselves divulge that they have children are perceived to be more open and understanding of their caregiving obligations. Nicole maintains, "If the faculty member doesn't have children, it tends to make a big difference." When I asked Snow to share an example of a time when she felt her parenting needs were acknowledged and supported on campus, she provides not one but two anecdotes. The first is of a professor who was likewise in a child care bind during a day when the local schools were closed due a teacher's professional day. Snow recalls, "When I asked her ahead of time, can I bring my son, she said, 'Absolutely. You know, my daughter's coming in, too. We can put them in the back, and we'll give them something to do.' So she really made an effort to make me feel comfortable in doing that, and even had a little something planned for the kids." Snow felt comfortable talking to this professor about her child care needs because she knew in advance that this instructor fully understood her obligations as a parent. Snow goes on to describe an encounter with a different professor when she missed class in order to trick-or-treat with her son on Halloween. She was hesitant to ask her professor, whose parenting status was unknown to her at that time, but was surprised when her instructor validated Snow's desire to be with her son—according to Snow, her instructor claimed that she respected Snow's decision to "put family first."

When I ask Allie if she finds the campus to be supportive of her educational goals and family needs, she answers by differentiating the organizational structure of the campus from the human dynamics of students and professors. She maintains,

> I think it's more the teachers than the campus itself because I think the campus is more concrete than the teachers. The teachers have feeling, understanding, warmth as people; whereas the campus is an organization with just the written policies and things. So I really do think it's, it's the teachers that count. I had a sociology teacher who had children . . . she had a younger child, so she didn't experience any of this. She had child care and all that lined up. This [other] teacher, he had two or three children and he commuted from Massachusetts or something. But he understood. Things come up, kids get sick, you're commuting, whatever, and he said that in class. So there was one day I had to call him and tell him—this may have been one of the days it was a snow day—and I said I'm going to be late for class or I can't make it to class because it's a snow day. And he understood. And I was very grateful for that—that he understood.

Allie highlights a key point here—although she unwittingly denies the influence of "policies and things" to shape campus culture, the campus itself is not structured to accommodate the needs of parents. That is, the campus, like most workplaces, is structured to address the needs of the organization, sometimes at the expense of the individual people moving within that organization. Instead, Allie attributes the creation of a family-friendly campus culture to individual professors. And for most campuses, the institution's stance on the presence of children is left to the discretion of professors, thereby freeing the institution from having to take a principled position.

One of the community colleges that six of these students attended had created clear policies regarding the presence of children on campus—those policies require that children be supervised at all times and require students to receive permission of the instructor before bringing a child to class. The four-year state universities that thirty-five of these students attended did not have any formal policies in place, reaffirming these student parents' perspectives that the presence of children in class is not a paramount concern on these campuses. It is by default that, at the four-year university, discretion is left up to the professor or staff member who is faced with addressing the needs of a student parent who has a child in tow on campus.

When the needs of student parents are not acknowledged, much less legitimized, on a college campus, even the academic opportunities available to mothers and fathers can be limited. Nowhere is this more clear than in Lucille's experience that resulted in her leaving her original program of study due to scheduling conflicts. Because Lucille has to put her nine-year-old son on the school bus every weekday morning between 7:45 and 8:00 A.M., she has not been able to register for a core class in her social work curriculum. Each semester, the class is only offered at 8:00 A.M.. She met with the chair of the department, who stated that if she planned to remain a social work major, she would have to rearrange her family schedule so that she can take this 8:00 A.M. class. Because her husband works the early shift, she does not have anyone else whom she could depend on to put her son on the bus each morning. So Lucille decided to switch majors. She knew that regularly attending an 8:00 A.M. class would not work for her at this time in her life.

Ultimately these students feel trapped in an institutional setting that functions most efficiently when their parenting identities are not acknowledged. As a result, these student parents are reliant on individual-level supports during times of crisis. Although most did not expect administrators and professors to treat them differently, the fact is that at times they needed those individuals and the institution to treat them differently. Believing that the campus culture is not likely to change anytime soon, they are left to their own devices to seek support from potentially sympathetic individuals. In some cases they find it, and in other cases they don't.

What Institutional Support Can Look Like

Colleges and universities are ever concerned about retaining students, which is why entire administrative divisions devoted to student life have emerged over the years to address students' nonacademic needs (Barr and Dessler 2000). First-Year Experience programs, learning communities, and extensive student and faculty mentoring programs are increasingly present on college campuses as a means of recognizing and responding to students' academic and social needs. Veteran's programs, disability services, and equal opportunity programs target the distinctive needs of specific student populations, helping those students to identify and navigate available resources. In recent decades, educational researchers have closely examined how these programs and offices, as well as social organizations, including Greek life and student clubs, collectively shape a campus culture where students feel connected, or not.[14]

None of the campuses attended by these forty student parents had an organization, office, or club devoted specifically to addressing the needs of student parents. However, some of these parents found institutional support in unexpected places. Next I describe the experiences of Dave, Heide, and Nicole, who shared with me the contexts in which they found validation of their parenting identities and responsibilities on campus. These examples demonstrate how supportive networks or services might take shape so that student parents can succeed on campus.

In Dave's case, institutional commitment came by way of a program designed to serve the needs of another student minority—athletes. Due to their intense training schedules, athletes are provided with priority registration benefits and scheduled study halls that are facilitated by academic coaches. Dave entered the state university as a scholarship athlete but had to leave the track team at the end of his first year of college, when his son was born. At that point, Dave found that he was not able to maintain his strict academic training schedule while simultaneously caring for his newborn son. However, the coach allowed him to continue with the team so that he could continue running part time and maintain some of the academic benefits accorded to team members. Dave was therefore able to use his priority registration benefits to arrange his classes around his son's day care and his partner's work schedules. In addition, he continued to attend athlete study halls as he found that they helped him to keep up with his schoolwork. He admitted that receiving these perks helped to keep him in school.

Dave's former coach not only allowed him to continue to receive special services and benefits reserved for athletes but also helped him to land a summer job at as a camp counselor working for a local town. As Dave put it, his coach "had a lot of pull" and chose to use his influence to help out Dave in his time of need. His coach also actively worked with residence life in an attempt to provide campus housing for Dave, his partner, and their child. At the time of our interview, Dave had little hope that such a benefit would be provided, but he expressed sincere appreciation for his coach going to such lengths to provide support for his family and demonstrating such respect for his responsibilities as a father as he pursued his degree. Dave admits that without this assistance and mentoring, he likely would not have made it through his second year of college.

Dave's experience was unusual in that most student parents did not identify specific individuals or programs that assisted them in multiple ways as they wove together their student and parenting identities. As I highlighted earlier, most students describe a specific moment when they experienced support or ran into obstacles. Dave's experience reveals how institutionalized assistance by way of priority registration, study halls, and an encouraging mentor can provide the support necessary to manage one's student and parenting labor. Comprehensive programs like those provided to athletes are similarly provided on many campuses to veterans, students with disabilities, or those who are first generation. Colleges and universities have come to recognize that if they are to graduate students and maintain high retention levels, they must acknowledge the unique needs of these particular populations of students and so provide then with the resources necessary to succeed (Hamrick, Evans, and Schuh 2002; Long 2012).

Additionally, several students identified particular departments on campus that they perceived to be family friendly, or at least child friendly. Heide entered her fall semester when she was just over six months pregnant and ended up delivering her baby earlier than expected at the end of October in the midst of the term. She shared that all of her professors were very understanding of her situation and allowed her to make up missed assignments and complete her coursework. She attributed the willingness of many of the faculty to work with her during her time of need to their being psychology professors who themselves study infants and children. Heide explains, "I think that taking psychology really helped . . . they were really nice . . . Dr. [X] she studies infants' cries. And the other class I was taking, she was my Child Psychology teacher, so they allowed me to bring the baby into class and show the class and stuff because we were learning about birth, and I got to bring in the pictures and stuff, so she kind of liked me being there because then I was her example!" [laughs]. Three other students likewise stated that they in part selected psychology as a major because they believed that the professors and students in those classes, in other words the department as a whole, would be more supportive of their parenting identities and needs. Within the context of this educational environment, which was shaped by both the subject matter of the discipline and the attitudes of the professors and peers, these student parents believed that their attempts to be good mothers and fathers were not only validated but respected.

Finally, Nicole described a weekend retreat hosted by the university's Women's Center as rejuvenating and empowering as she transitioned to campus life. Nicole is twenty-nine years old and so is older and more experienced in life than many of her student peers in her four-year program. By the end of her first term, she was feeling disconnected on campus, but after participating in the retreat, she admits to experiencing "more of a sense of community that I didn't feel last semester." During that weekend, she connected with both the director of the Women's Center and a group of women students with whom she remains in contact. The director and several of the women students who regularly associate with the center have long been working to create a family-friendly campus that addresses the full range of needs of student parents. In addition to providing household financial advising and stress reduction workshops, they are an integral force in ensuring the construction and maintenance of lactation rooms and have continuously advocated for increasing child care resources on campus. When I ask the director of the Women's Center how student parents on campus use the center's resources, she shares her view that "such spaces on campus are crucial to supporting the needs of student parents." She continues, "Very often when such spaces are provided to student parents, they provide student parents networking opportunities, academic support, emotional support and the ability to engage socially with those balancing similar life experiences ... [allowing] for relationship building, which leads to additional child care support, academic and parenting tips, ability to schedule classes to support one another's child care needs." It is, therefore, unsurprising that Nicole would find support and legitimization of her mothering and parenting identity within this campus-based space and group.

Importantly, Heide's and Nicole's experiences reveal not only how student parents can benefit from having access to a supportive department or center but also how the academic environment for all students can actually be enhanced by the presence of student parents. Nicole found that many of the nonparent students working in the Women's Center were very much interested in learning more about her parental experiences and needs as they sought to address large-scale gender inequalities on campus and in the world of work. Heide found that her classmates and professors in her psychology classes were very much interested in learning more about her experience as a new mother, for reasons both personal and academic. Students who were not yet parents learned from these mothers and fathers, demonstrating quite clearly how a diverse student body can increase opportunities for the creative exchange of ideas and information.

A CAMPUS'S ORGANIZATIONAL culture influentially intersects with each student's individual needs and dispositions. Student parents are more likely to succeed when a college's or university's culture legitimizes those students' identities as parents and acknowledges and addresses their unique needs. When needs-based grants do not go as far as they used to in covering the costs of state college and university tuition, when students are prohibited from applying for public assistance, when child care is not provided on campus, when face-to-face interactions with professors and campus staff result in stigmatization or even punishment, student parents do not feel welcome. When federal and state-based aid covers all tuition and even provides a living stipend as do recent GI Bill programs, when students are provided with affordable and convenient child care, and when professors and staff recognize, acknowledge, and understand the challenges facing student parents, then mothers and fathers on campus are more likely to feel that they belong. Ultimately, when students feel that they are expected to be there and to succeed, they are much more likely to persist and fulfill their educational dreams.

The examples at the end of this chapter detail the ways that institutions can both recruit and retain student parents by working to create an organizational culture that validates their needs and provides concrete supports. These examples are limited to student parents' experiences on a team, within a department, or in a center, yet they reveal how a culture can be created that facilitates student parents' attaining their college goals. These student parents and the people on campus who helped them or learned from them have created a culture where "understanding," as Carolyn calls for the beginning of this chapter, can be cultivated. And understanding is necessary for substantive, sustained cultural and structural change to occur.

4

What Students Want and Why

What do we expect from a college education? To answer this question, the Pew Research Center in 2011 surveyed a random sample of U.S. residents to find out what they believed to be the purpose of college. The researchers found that 47 percent of respondents say that providing work-related skills and knowledge was most important to a college's mission, whereas 39 percent said that helping a student to grow personally and intellectually was most important (Taylor et al. 2011). When I asked student parents in this study what they believe to be the purpose of higher education, nearly all of them at some point framed their answers by emphasizing the relationship between education and acquiring job skills and career preparation. All of these student parents have been exposed to such instrumentalist discourse at home, at school, in their communities, and in the media. Like most of us, they have come to accept the idea that, for most people, it is just common sense that attending college is necessary to succeed financially.

That said, students in this study varied significantly in how much and how deeply they relied on instrumentalist discourse to articulate their understanding of the purpose and value of their own college education. Like the 39 percent of respondents surveyed by the Pew Research Center who said that colleges should prioritize personal and intellectual growth, 35 percent of these student parents described the value of their college experience in ways that moved beyond the mere acquisition of job-related knowledge and skills. In analyzing these student parents' responses to my questions, I found that students tended to fall into one of three groups in regard to how they described their student identities: job seekers, practical explorers, and self-reflective learners.

In the sections that follow, I describe how each of these three groups reflects a distinct disposition toward higher education that in turn shapes the way that members of each group discuss their understanding of the college experience.

To that end, I explore students' strategies of being—that is, how they make sense of their perceived needs and sense of self by embracing, modifying, or rejecting complementary or competing cultural logics, all in the context of their access to social resources. Such an analysis allows us to understand more fully how institutions and culture play out in student parents' lives, shaping their processes of meaning making and their dispositions to action.

Although the three categories that I describe are distinct, I must emphasize that individuals' cultured capacities and strategies of being emanate from a complex interplay between specific situations and cultural and institutional forces that are at any moment open to change. As Ann Swidler (2001) reminds us, "People may also develop new cultural capacities by modifying ones they already possess, or by prolonged contact with models whose styles and habits they can imitate" (p. 209). As I describe later, some students describe their former, often much younger, student selves in ways that reveal they would likely have been categorized differently years earlier. That is, students might be more or less likely to embrace particular cultural logics during different stages of their life course. However, this snapshot provides an opportunity to examine the various ways students have come to understand and reflect upon their educational motivations and expectations and then place those expressions of meaning making in the context of educational and economic opportunity.

Job Seekers

Just over a third of the student parents I interviewed discuss their educational dispositions largely in terms relating to their anticipated job. They are "job seekers," who are focused on skill building or credentialing and completing their degree as quickly as possible with the intention of obtaining economically rewarding jobs. Job seekers may fleetingly reference the importance of taking classes to become, in their words, "well rounded," but they do not talk with any depth about what that means or how such educational experiences might shape their sense of self beyond making them more attractive to potential employers. They rely overwhelmingly on cultural logics grounded in instrumentalist discourse to make sense of their educational motivations and expectations.

Jackie and Dave: Economic Security

Although not all job seekers are from low-income or lower-middle-class backgrounds, nine of the fourteen students who qualify for and receive Pell Grants fall into this group. It is not at all surprising that individuals experiencing economic precariousness would be more likely than those coming from more economically stable households to turn to talk of jobs and the logic of economic security. When I meet with Jackie, a thirty-one-year-old secondary education student who is living with her parents so they can help her to care for her daughter, she never once mentions an educational motivational factor that is not focused on a job. Jackie is wholly convinced that "you have to have money or some kinds of means of support," and that "the only way you can have more finances is with education nowadays." Jackie tells her seven-year-old daughter, "College is not an option. You have to do it; it's mandatory." Because she is in effect a single mother—her daughter's father pays child support but is not involved in their day-to-day activities—she feels particularly pressed to obtain a job that will provide security and a stable income. She is interested in becoming a high school English teacher, but her 2.7 grade point average is too low for admittance to her college's teacher education program. Neither of her parents, who emigrated from Puerto Rico when Jackie was young, possesses a college degree. Nevertheless, they fully support her educational ambitions, viewing them as a means of attaining a steady job that will allow her to become financially independent and economically secure.

Dave, as described in the previous chapter, is a twenty-year-old father whose girlfriend became unexpectedly pregnant during his first year of college. After his girlfriend gave birth to their son, Dave found that he couldn't balance his parenting, educational, and athletic responsibilities. In his own words, "it was kind of too much all at once." He had been accepted to the university on a track scholarship, but after learning he was going to be a father, he found his attention was diverted. He performed poorly in his classes, was placed on academic probation, and so lost his track scholarship in the middle of the season during his sophomore year.

When I ask Dave to describe the purpose of an education, he immediately addresses the pressure he feels to provide for his family, adding, "We're living like, we're in a bad area. A lot of drugs, gangs—all that kind of stuff. And I see this and that happening here. And I really see the influence of it. . . . I just want to get out of here." Later in our interview, when I ask Dave about obstacles to his education, he immediately describes his family's financial hardships:

> The bills sometimes are overwhelming and—I'm still paying the gas bill off of last winter. And the energy assistance, like the state really doesn't help out much. Like the energy assistance, we're still on a waiting list for that. They say they help out. They help out the people they haven't turned off already, so we have to wait until January for that, and it's probably not going to come through. And the Section 8 helps you pay for your rent, by your income, so you pay like a percentage, pay like 15 percent of the rent, but we've been on a waiting list since my freshman year, so it's like three years. We're not waiting for that, because there's no limit on that—once you got it you got it. So it's hard to get openings, and you have to get an opening in your city. If it's in [another city], I'd have to move there, and then I can't go to school if I'm living there. So like financially it's hard.

Dave has come to understand the grim reality of relying on strained and bureaucratic public assistance agencies and feels the weight of living paycheck to paycheck. As described previously, Dave was one of six students to financially qualify for cash and child care public assistance, and was the only one of the six to actually receive that support because his case manager was willing to overlook his attendance in a four-year baccalaureate program in lieu of short-term job preparedness programs. In Dave's mind, a college degree means primarily two things: an opportunity to forgo dependence on unreliable and bureaucratically complicated public assistance programs and to move his family out of poverty.

Dave feels pressure from both sides of his family to fulfill the position of breadwinner, which helps to explain why he so strongly relies on a cultural logic that conceives of the value of his education in terms of alleviating financial hardship. Upon the recommendation of his college-educated father, Dave began pursuing a degree in management, with the hope that he will later be able to go on for his MBA. Earning a business degree makes sense to Dave, a seemingly practical goal that he hopes will lead to steady employment so he can move his family out of their "bad area," pay his bills, and become economically secure.

Victoria and Ed: Human Capital and Skills

Victoria learned that she was pregnant over the summer between high school and college. During those summer months she was enrolled in a college access program that provides high school graduates who otherwise do not meet a local state university's acceptance requirements with the opportunity to take college preparatory courses that will allow them to gain admittance in the fall. She finished out the summer program and successfully completed the fall semester of her first year before giving birth to her son. After her son was born, Victoria felt particularly motivated to return to school the following fall and complete her degree because she never wants her son to have to feel financially responsible for her well-being:

> Looking at my family's past and their education and also looking at jobs today, it's important to have a higher education. And I want to lay a foundation—not just for him—but for myself as well. That may sound a little selfish, but I know that as I get older, regardless of our smaller age gap, there may be a situation where I get sick or something like that, and I want to know that I can take care of myself rather than putting it on him and having him stop his life in order to support me.

Like Dave and Jackie, described in the prior section, economic security is paramount to Victoria, who believes that obtaining her degree will provide her with the "foundation" or human capital necessary to get what she wants, "a good paying job."

Victoria was nineteen years old when I interviewed her, and she was studying both psychology and criminology. She perceives her general educational courses as being "unnecessary" and confesses, "I skipped past them to tell you the truth. I took a lot of the basic classes in high school. . . . I got that all out of the way." More important to Victoria are the work experiences and connections that college will provide. She believes, "I think you should know what you're getting into before you get into it. As well as, have experience in it, and I think that college allows us to do that with internships with the professors. I have professors who are prosecutors, judges, and bail bondsmen and everything, so you, you experience it before you get in there." When I ask Victoria about the purpose of an education at various points during our interview, she exclusively refers to job training and employment. Even when I ask about her son's father and his education, she focuses solely on how his education will lead to a specific job. Her son's father is enrolled in a local community college but is considering enrolling in a local for-profit college that offers degrees that will train him to become an auto mechanic. In Victoria's mind, a college education ought to first and foremost develop human capital, training future workers and providing the knowledge, skills, and experiences that are necessary for landing and keeping jobs. That's what keeps her going to school.

Ed, a twenty-three-year-old veteran who is using his GI benefits to pursue a computer science degree maintains, "You still have the other, like, general [education] classes to fill in gaps and learn some more stuff," but he appreciates that his current track is more "focused on whatever your major is." Ed didn't go to college straight out of high school—instead he chose to enter the army. Of that decision, Ed claims that when he graduated high school, he wasn't interested in his courses, was just coasting through, and thought going into the army would be "cool." Once he was actually in the army, he found that the experience wasn't quite what he had expected. He didn't like the strict structure and the job he was doing, so he left after his first four-year assignment and decided to take advantage of the educational benefits offered to veterans.

Ed, who is helping to raise his girlfriend's two children, became a serious student, evidenced in part by his accomplishment of graduating from his bachelor's program with a 4.0 grade point average. He contends that his experience in the military provided him with a sense of motivation and discipline that he didn't possess when he first graduated high school and entered the army. Although he works hard in all of his general education classes, he focuses most of his attention on the skills that he is acquiring in his computer classes. Whenever I ask him about education and his classroom experiences, he talks exclusively about how they might relate to a future job in computer science. As he sees it, the purpose of a college education is to "set you up and get you going in the right direction and have the skills required to actually start up and start a job."

Cynthia and Nicole: Credentialing Hoops

Although most of the job seekers emphasize the skills that they expect to acquire while pursuing their college degree, two student parents flatly reject the logic of human capital theories that stress the connection between education and job skills. Cynthia and Nicole express their skepticism regarding the true value of the education that they are pursuing, which they perceive as disconnected from the work they hope to engage in after graduation. In discussing her educational goals, Nicole, a twenty-nine-year-old mother studying business management, exasperatedly declares, "I don't think [education] really matters, but I guess a little piece of paper does." Cynthia, a twenty-three-year-old psychology student likewise responds with frustration when I ask her to explain what she believes to be the purpose of education:

> I don't know. I just think it's just really . . .'cause I live in the real world, so I kind of see it as pointless. It's real hard because I know you need it to get your foot in the door. Certain employers will hire you 'cause [you have] a four-year degree, and even though it doesn't say specifically what major you get it in, they just want someone who has a four-year degree. But once you get into the job, you really don't use it. For most entry level jobs, you really don't use it. So I kind of see it as pointless for students that really want to seek it. Unless they're going to something specific like what you're doing or like being a doctor, things like that. But for everyday skills, I don't think it's really necessary.

Both Cynthia and Nicole are aggravated by what they perceive to be the credentialing hoop propped up by colleges and universities and reinforced by employers who can then use it to narrow a pool of applicants to those individuals who have acquired, if not specific job-related skills, at the very least a degree. They acknowledge the credentialing function of education, a role highlighted by researchers in the 1960s and 1970s who were critical of the ways that an ever-expanding system of higher education was legitimizing not only its social function but growth (Berg 1971; Collins 1979; see also Bills and Brown 2011).

Nonetheless, Cynthia and Nicole, like all the job seekers, persist in pursuing their education to get a job. Their strategies of being reveal how individuals can turn to competing or alternative logics, yet nonetheless end up reflecting the same overall disposition as the other job seekers. It is clear from Cynthia's earlier comment that she is not at all convinced by the logic of human capital and skills. However, she adheres to the logic of economic security, believing that having the degree is necessary to "get your foot in the door" and obtain a job that will allow for upward mobility. When I asked Cynthia why employers might require a degree, she allows, "Well I guess they can sort of see that you're dedicated to something. You can actually push through and do four years of school and you're literary—you can read and write. Maybe they see you as more competent than someone who doesn't have an education." Cynthia believes that the degree that she is pursuing will not necessarily provide her with specific knowledge or skills that she will use in the workplace, but the degree will communicate to potential employers that she is among the educated—she is capable of acquiring the status of college graduate. She fully understands the credentialing function of degrees in the current job market. In this "contest mobility" system of education (Collins 1979), she will have moved up to the next level, and her degree will reflect that accomplishment.

Practical Explorers

Twenty of the students in my sample are more expansive in how they describe the value of their education than are the job seekers just described. These practical explorers appeal to a variety of logics that very often are rooted in a desire for economic mobility but also explicitly emphasize social mobility and status. Practical explorers don't want to have to worry about money and hope that their college degrees will help them to land financially lucrative jobs, but they are also interested in acquiring the respect and confidence that accompanies a rise in social status when one enters the college "club." These students further differ from job seekers in regard to their strategies of being in that they value intellectual curiosity and express a genuine interest in learning more about themselves and the world. Rather than primarily focusing on the end result, practical explorers are for the most part enjoying the ride, relying on cultural logics that allow them to view their education as an experience and not just a hoop, an opportunity and not merely a bureaucratic requirement.

Amber, Jose, and Charlie: Opportunities and Fulfilling Work

Amber is a twenty-five-year-old student studying English with the expectation that she will go on to obtain her master's degree in education so that she can teach high school. As described at the beginning of chapter 2, she and her husband divorced fourteen months ago, and her son, for whom she has primary custody, just celebrated his first birthday. When I ask Amber about the purpose of a college education, she first highlights the career opportunities that higher education can provide that allow for a "better life," opportunities that have been denied to her parents who did not pursue an education beyond high school. Amber reflects, "Neither of my parents went to college, and I see them and they have decent jobs. They pay the bills. They're just not happy. I mean they go to work 'cause they have to. It's not because it's something that they want to do." Of becoming a teacher, Amber proclaims, "This is something that I want to do. I want to have a job that I wake up and look forward to going to every day. And to me being a teacher would be that job. So I have to do that."

Although Amber talks about the career benefits of earning a college degree, she is also very clear that the college years should be a time to explore subjects and learn more about the world. She contends that college students ought to express a "willingness to learn and openness," and laments the fact that so many younger students feel pressured to link their college experience to specific jobs or careers. In mulling over her educational journey, Amber reflects, "You're in high school; you have to decide what you want to do when you grow up. That's a big decision. And half the time it doesn't even turn out that way. You'll go start doing that and you go to law school and realize, Hey I want to be a painter [laughs]. Just doesn't work out right."

Like most of the older student parents whom I interviewed, Amber's educational history is rife with stops and starts. In chapter 2, I describe how she temporarily left school during the second semester of her sophomore year to finance and plan her wedding and then how she was essentially pushed out halfway through her junior year when she discovered that she was pregnant. She did not believe that continuing with her degree was possible as she prepared for the birth of her child and navigated a failing relationship with her new husband—they ended up divorcing in her eighth month of pregnancy. No one on campus followed up with her when she disappeared, and her family encouraged her to focus her immediate attention on her son. Fortunately, Amber has a strong familial network who encouraged her to resume pursuing her educational aspirations and help her out with child care, and although she has primary custody of their son, she describes her ex-husband as being an "involved dad." Looking back over her educational career, Amber believes that having had the time and opportunity to take a variety of classes has both made her more "open" and helped her to develop and understand her love of English. She expresses a passion for reading and learning and is confident that she has selected a degree that will allow her to move into a teaching career that will allow her to continually stretch her intellect.

Most of these practical explorers spoke about the perceived purpose of education in similarly multifaceted ways. For one, like Amber, they rarely clung to one logic when describing their educational motivations and expectations. Instead they moved between narrative threads that focused on varying dimensions of their educational, job, and general life experiences. These practical explorers not only articulate their concern with securing a job that will provide economic stability, they also express a desire to obtain jobs that are intellectually or emotionally fulfilling. They are not solely moved by "practical," job-related concerns; they additionally describe their appreciation of learning that promotes self-growth and enhances their comprehension of the world and their place in it. They are internally motivated to broaden their knowledge base and to demonstrate to their children the value of learning and continuing their education in life. These practical explorers overtly share their concern with obtaining a job that will furnish at the very least a middle-class standard of living, but they perceive of their college and career experiences as part of a larger journey to be appreciated and not just as means to ends that must be endured.

Jose, a forty-five-year-old father of three who is majoring in history, believes that his college education will allow him to engage in work that aligns with his sense of self. When asked to describe a successful student, Jose recounts some advice that he provided to his college-aged son who was at the time struggling in his first year of college. He advised his son that students need "to know that [being a student] is really what they want to be and what they want to do." Jose stresses that he does not care what kind of job his son obtains upon graduation; he states that if his children want to "to pick cans" for a living, that is up to them to decide. What is important to Jose, however, is that his children feel fulfilled by their educational experiences and eventually obtain college credentials.

Jose himself lives by this maxim. He left a steady job as a social worker, making $50,000 a year with only a high school diploma, but claims he did not like the work. As he describes it, "in his heart" he wanted to become a teacher, and so he left his job in social services to return to college and work part time as a paraprofessional in an elementary school classroom. Jose to some degree wishes that he had pursued this educational and career path sooner, but he also values his life experiences, which allow him to engage in class discussions armed with information that he did not possess over twenty years ago when he was a young college student. Although Jose is certainly job-focused in his current educational quest, he is also intensely concerned about his quality of living, which is not defined by income alone. He describes teaching as a "calling" and perceives himself to be a "teacher." He has even obtained classroom experience as a long-term substitute in a fifth grade classroom but lacks the education and formal credentials that will allow him to follow that career pathway. There is no doubt that Jose is concerned with the exchange value of his college education in regard to obtaining a job, but he is also driven by the belief that the degree he will receive will allow him to obtain work that will fulfill his sense of self.

These older student parents have been working for a number of years and many, like Jose, desire a change and so seek an education that will provide them with a job that will foster their intellectual curiosity and provide continued learning and growth. Charlie, a thirty-four-year-old veteran and father of two is excited to be enrolled in a local community college's computer information systems program. When I ask why he is choosing to pursue his associate's degree, Charlie opens his explanation by deriding some of his younger college classmates, whom he claims are only there to "get a good job," an objective that he claims to understand even though he finds his classmates' perspective somewhat limited in scope. He dismisses their single-minded focus on money and emphasizes that his own motivation to return to college runs deeper. After years of performing what he refers to as "mediocre jobs for minimal pay," he would like to earn a decent salary, but more importantly he hopes to create a future in which he will "be able to get up in the morning, to go to work, and to be happy to do it. To not really look at it as a job, but look at it as an experience . . . to learn." He sees his younger classmates as motivated purely by the potential income that might come with a degree in computer technology and not excited by the learning that is taking place in the classroom. In addition to sharing his appreciation of his classroom learning, Charlie expresses his need for work that is intellectually challenging and that will allow him to continue to learn.

Leslie and Drew: Social Status and Self-Confidence

Another dimension of the value of higher education described by many practical explorers resulted from their developing sense of confidence and satisfaction now that they are resuming and potentially completing a degree that they started many years prior. Leslie attended a regional state college over fourteen years ago following the birth of her son but then withdrew because balancing school and an infant was just too much to handle at that time in her life. She recently returned to a local community college to pursue again the music degree that she had begun so many years earlier. When I ask her about the purpose of an education, Leslie launches easily into a lengthy description of her family's educational history and goals, admitting, "At my age [what is important] is confidence. It just gives you a sense of I've done something, I've finished. I finally completed something and earned it." She confides that having a degree contributes to "feeling good" about herself, and she is eager to fulfill her educational goals.

Such self-confidence, however, is not wholly internally derived; Leslie also acknowledges the value of a college degree within the context of social interactions. In short, Leslie desires the societal status that a degree can confer, a fact made clear when she shares, "I've worked in factories. I've worked for lawyers. I've worked for private corporations, oil companies, the Danbury hospital, boutiques, retail stores, and I think the more education you have, the more respected you are. And more people treat you differently." Not only does Leslie believe that pursuing her education will boost her self-confidence but it will likewise boost other people's confidence in her as well and will provide her with increased social status. Leslie unequivocally adopts the language of human capital theory as she explains how all of her classes will serve her long-term career goals, discussing the job-specific skills that she will acquire in her general education courses. However, she also refers to what many sociologists refer to as cultural capital, when she states that her courses will provide her with "interesting things to talk about" and that "being well spoken is going to help you in any line of work, whether you're teaching or in business or a public speaker or a professor." It is not just job-specific skills that colleges and universities are expected impart, but also knowledge of culture that is deemed valuable in the context of conversations and social interaction with others who share that knowledge.[1] And such knowledge will not only help her in her chosen career but will also garner social respect in her community.

Drew, a twenty-three-year-old father studying communication, additionally describes the value of acquiring social capital, a concept that refers to the social relationships that an individual forms that can enhance one's social and economic opportunities.[2] When asked about the purpose of education, Drew maintains, "You really want to learn as much as you can about yourself, about the world, about where you belong in the world and what you want to do. I would say probably that and you really just, you want to meet other people and network yourself. I mean, that's kind of a business thing, but you know, network yourself and enjoy your time of being away and having an environment that's open." Over half of the practical explorers acknowledge the value of acquiring cultural and social capital in college and highlight the respectability that possession of both types of capital can confer. When Leslie states that a college degree "helps you in life as far as being respected," she echoes Randall Collins's (1979) observation that, a "college education, once an incidental accompaniment of high status" had become by the latter part of the twentieth century a "prerequisite of mere respectability" (p. 129). These practical explorers are seeking entrée into the college "club," and they fully believe that a college education and degree will procure that access.

Practical explorers are very clear that they are in school so that they might pursue jobs that are otherwise off-limits to them because they lack a college degree. However, these students are in most cases highly engaged in their studies and interconnect their classroom learning and what they hope to do as a career with various dimensions of their sense of self. They may question some individual curriculum requirements—for example, Diane, a thirty-four-year-old mother of three, is not convinced that she needs to take calculus if she plans to become an elementary school teacher. Another practical explorer, forty-two-year-old Sam, questions the value of taking a history course as he works toward earning a degree in physical therapy, even though he frequently mentions how another general education course, Introduction to Psychology, has fundamentally transformed the way he perceives learning and approaches parenting.

Overall, these students find value in most of the classes that they take and link what they are learning with experiences in other classes and in their lives. Practical explorers are concerned with acquiring skills and knowledge that will benefit them in the job market, but they more broadly define that which might benefit them to encompass cultural and social capital. They expect that from their college experience they will secure knowledge that will enhance their self-confidence and their attractiveness on the job market, all while gaining the respect of potential employers, friends, and family.

Self-Reflective Learners

Six student parents rarely if at all mentioned jobs when discussing the value of education. These self-reflective learners instead emphasized abstract skills, such as the importance of creative and critical thinking, introspective inquiry, and exploring diverse perspectives. They expect that good jobs will come their way in the long term, but at this moment in their academic career, they most value the opportunity to exercise their minds and to grow intellectually.

Joy, Molly, and Sara: Personal Enrichment and Growth

When asked about the purpose of education, Joy stops for a moment before working her way toward the following answer: "Wow, that's an interesting question. Well, you know, first, honestly what comes to mind for me is not self-improvement so much—although I think it does lend itself to that—but just enriching. It's so enriching. I love being in school. I really do. I could, I could be a student forever. I just love to learn. Learn, learn, learn, learn, learn, learn about all sorts of things." Joy already possesses a master's degree in early childhood education that led her to a job in a preschool that she eventually left because it did not make financial sense for their family for her to continue working full time while paying for child care. After many years working as a massage therapist, she is now interested in returning to college to pursue a degree in counseling. However, she mentions this career goal only once during the course of our interview; instead she spends much of our time together describing in very abstract language what she expects from her educational experience—she values her time in school, describing it as "enriching" and appreciates the sense of "fulfillment" that her experience as a student provides. Like so many of the practical explorers, a job for Joy serves a practical function in her life, but unlike them, she does not articulate self-fulfillment primarily in the context of the job she expects to attain.

Molly and Sara similarly describe their educational experiences as personally enriching, and highlight moments when their awareness of the world and their place in it grew. When asked about the purpose of education, Molly replies:

> I think [the purpose of education is] to get out of your comfort zone and your egocentric little world, because I think that the one thing that I've learned is that there's a whole big world out there. I probably could have stayed very contentedly in my little house with my little job and my little family and really not have had my eyes open to anything. But being here I think has just given me a sense of how small the world really is and that the possibilities are endless and that you need to think more about community and other people besides yourself. I come from a family of people who really haven't gone that far, geographically or in any other way. So I think that it was kind of eye opening to get into a college atmosphere

and university atmosphere and just kind of the diversity on campus and things like that.

Molly then shares an anecdote from an anthropology class that challenged her to "think in ways that I never did before." Her professor had the students read and discuss a book about whiteness, and she confessed, "I'd never thought about things like that and never pictured myself to be prejudiced . . . and then you kind of realize that inherently we kind of all are, whether we want to be or not. . . . And he just put things into perspective really." Along the same lines, Sara reasons, "If you just get stuck in this closed up mind where, 'Oh, well, I know what I know, and that's all I need to know,' then you don't really learn anything. You don't grow. There's just so much to learn and so little time" [laughs]. Sara admits that "if it were up to me and I had all the money in the world, I would never leave school."

Rose and Lucille: Emotional Empowerment

Two self-reflective learners speak poignantly and very specifically about their education being emotionally empowering. Rose, a twenty-five-year-old psychology student, talks at length about her Islamic identity and her current difficult familial situation. She began our interview by sharing her family story, which spilled from her steadily as she shared her frustrations and self-analyzed the complexities underlying her emotions and well-being. Rose moved to the United States when she was fourteen years old and is now trapped in an arranged marriage with a man who she believes will never grow to love her and who is dealing with a debilitating gambling addiction. She knew from the beginning of her marriage that there were problems—although she didn't yet fully understand the depth of his compulsions. Her parents convinced her that she could change her potential husband, tame his wild streak and make him a good family man. Her family tried to support her, providing shelter and resources in times of need, but she felt her life was crumbling around her—she was financially and emotionally dependent on an addict, who seemed to have little respect or love for her. She had hoped that having a child together might change their relationship for the better, but instead she is finding that her husband is withdrawing even deeper into his addiction.

When Rose talks about the purpose and value of higher education, it soon becomes clear that being in school contributes to her feeling more hopeful and liberated. Rose credits her classes with teaching her how to open up and express herself:

ROSE: This year I took this psychology class, but it changed my life. You know, I'm more open now, more expressive, can express my, my feelings, my ideas. You know I'm more . . . I'm working on it. You know I'm not like perfect right now but, yeah I think I have a feeling that I'm going there. It helped me with my relationship with other people as well, outside school.

FIONA: How so? Can you remember a time?

ROSE: Anything. As I said, I'm more expressive now. Before if people said stuff to me, I would just like keep it in me and have that sad face—just keep it in you. But now I can say, "Oh, that kind of bothers me," you know, like, "Hope that you don't do it or say it anymore." I'm more open, more talkative, more communicating with people.

Her interest in communication, culture, and behavior ultimately led her to major in psychology, and she is now considering a career as a high school counselor.

Rose's parents are first-generation immigrants from Turkey who did not attend college and adhere to a system of traditional religious beliefs, but she feels that they very much support her educational and professional goals, in part, she confides, because they feel guilty that they pushed her to marry her husband. Her husband's family is also supportive of Rose and her educational goals, but they are rarely in the United States. They recently visited for six months to prepare for and celebrate her brother-in-law's wedding—her brother-in-law and his new wife now live with Rose and her husband.

With her sister-in-law now living in the same household, Rose feels responsible for her well-being and is pushing her to become more self-reliant and economically independent. Even though Rose believes that her sister-in-law is not as educationally motivated as is she, Rose admits, "She's learning. She's a teenager, you know. I can't expect more from her. . . . She realizes I'm supporting her. She even tells that—she even tells to her mom. She'll be like, "Oh Rose is really like telling me to go to school, really encouraging me to go to school." That is nice that she realizes that." Rose feels "stronger" as a result of her education—learning how to reconcile varying strands of her identity as a woman, as a Muslim, and as a wife—and she hopes to pass on these ideas to her young sister-in-law and daughter. She expresses some regret for not waiting a few more years before giving birth to her daughter and pursuing her college education sooner—she finds it difficult now to balance her classes and duties at home. This belief is in part what is driving her to help her sister-in-law not to fall into the same predicament and to encourage her own daughter in her schooling.

Going to college has been a particularly liberating experience for Rose—as her words below reveal, she has gained strength from the communication and analytic skills that she has developed over the years:

Education makes you a better person I believe. So you're not ignorant, you know? I believe with that I'm stronger. I can defend myself. . . . Because I'm Muslim, I cover up. People think, "Ah whatever," you know? They don't think that I could accomplish something. . . . Because everybody thinks Muslim people stay home, cook, clean and that's it. . . . Some people think that I don't even speak English, you know? People speak slow or whatever.

I mean covering up—it doesn't make me old fashioned. But being modern, what is it? Being modern is wearing short clothes or showing your body, showing your hair? Is it being modern? I think people tend to think that way. I think being modern is in your mind. What is in your mind? How are you? Are you ignorant, or are you more accepting, more acknowledging about other cultures, you know? More understanding. This person may do something. Why that person did that, you know? There's always a reason behind, maybe cultural, maybe religion, maybe personal. Try to understand about the person, just like not judge it right away. . . . That's what I have become, you know, more acknowledging. If I see something, I just draw a conclusion or I stop and think, "Why, why does this happen?"

In addition to being afforded opportunities to refine and gain confidence in applying her analytic skills, she was able to access and make use of counseling resources on campus, and that alone changed her life tremendously. All of these experiences resulted in her feeling more empowered in both her personal and her public life.

In another section of our interview, Rose describes a moment in one of her psychology classes, when she learned about a study regarding gamblers and addiction, which helped her to understand more comprehensively the nature of her husband's ailments. Throughout our interview, Rose interweaves discussion of her home life with that of her classroom and campus experiences, exposing the deeply ingrained interrelations between her conceptualizations of self, family, and education. She mentions her career goals once when I explicitly ask her to share them—she would like to become a high school counselor, a goal that she determined only recently, toward the end of her junior year. She is propelled to seek financial independence, so she can potentially leave her husband, but she primarily conceives of the value of her education in very abstract terms, focusing most of her discussion on the importance of expanding one's understanding of oneself and the world.

The six self-reflective learners all similarly emphasize their desire to learn and the empowerment that can come from gaining knowledge. Lucille, who is introduced in chapter 3, is a thirty-three-year-old mother of two young boys. She shares, "Education for me is learning the skills that I need to make change." Lucille is a student who is politically motivated to enact social change and is more concerned about the knowledge that she acquires in her classes than she is about the grade she receives. She admits, "I have to care to a certain extent 'cause . . . that's the way I get my financial aid. But when I walk into a class, I don't care if I get an A or if I get a C. I just want to know that I learned something." She describes learning as "building up your artillery" and argues that "you've got to have all your tools and everything in line." Like Rose, Lucille attests to the many ways that she has grown due to her experience in the classroom—she feels more knowledgeable about herself and the world, and the information that she has been exposed to encourages her to believe that she can improve her life and the lives of those around her.

As described previously, Lucille's educational journey has been fraught with diversions and obstructions. Lucille returned to school after a ten year absence, optimistic and eager to finish up what she had started. However, the transition was not so easy and when I met with her, Lucille was experiencing some tough times. For one, she was negotiating the educational needs of her autistic son who was enrolled in a public school that was not providing the resources that he needed to succeed. In addition, she was working two jobs because her husband had been laid off unexpectedly. Despite these everyday hardships, Lucille found the time and energy to become heavily involved in campus life, eventually serving as Senior President during her final year as an undergraduate student. She delivered a powerful speech regarding social justice and education at commencement in front of an audience of thousands. For Lucille, education confers a "state of mind" and an "artillery" of "tools" that she can then use to improve her own life and the lives of others.

These self-reflective learners embody the values espoused by public commentators defending the core of a liberal arts education (Roth 2014; Zakaria 2015). These students are motivated internally to expand their understanding of themselves and their world. They believe that their education is enriching their relationships and making their lives better, not just in terms of increased opportunity but in terms of their intellectual and emotional engagement. Easily drawing connections between their classroom lessons and their lives, these students are invested personally and deeply in their education.

Why Understanding Cultural Logics and Strategies of Being Matters

Attending college requires a significant investment of time, money, and emotion, and so the reasons why students attend college are predictably complex. Although all students are familiar with and generally accept the argument that possessing a college degree will increase their chances of achieving financial success, their educational expectations differ due to variations in how they come to understand the value of their education. As I describe earlier in this chapter, some students are primarily concerned with acquiring skills that they expect will secure future jobs. Others additionally express interest in acquiring cultural or social capital and value a college degree because of the social mobility it promises, not only in economic terms but also in regard to the level of respect or status that a degree garners in the context of social interactions. And yet others are very much internally driven to take advantage of the learning opportunities that a college education can provide, opportunities that contain the potential to lead to self-fulfillment and a greater knowledge and appreciation of their local and global communities. This latter group may indeed consider the career and social status benefits of acquiring a college degree, but they alternatively artic-ulate their motivations in terms that reflect a deep concern with self-growth, a desire to impact positively the lives of others, and emotional empowerment.

Because cultural logics are embedded in individual and sociohistorical con-texts, both micro- and macrolevel social factors shape whether or not students will embrace, reject, or modify particular logics, emphasizing aspects of their individual identities that reflect the dispositions of a job seeker, practical explorer, or self-reflective learner. In my sample, the stability of a student's household structure and access to financial resources are frequently connected to a student's strategy of being—as is one's age (see table 4.1). The ranges of stu-dents' ages are similar for each of these three typologies; however, as a group, the job seekers are younger and less likely than the other groups to be in a stable relationship with a partner, which has the potential to negatively affect their financial stability.

Several of the practical explorers and self-reflective learners, particularly the older student parents, describe their former student selves—which for most of them existed in a place and time before they became parents—in ways that reflect the dispositions of job seekers. That is, they may have started out their student lives as job seekers but *became* practical explorers or self-reflective

TABLE 4.1

Student Parents' Educational Dispositions by Household Family Structure, Age,[+] and Income Status*

| Job Seekers | | | Practical Explorers | | | Self-Reflective Learners | | |
Single	Divorced	Partnered	Single	Divorced	Partnered	Single	Divorced	Partnered
21*	26*	19*	25	26	20	22*	29	25
23*	27	20*	34*	23	27		29	
26*	49	23		27	31*		29	
28		26*		34	34			33*
31*		29*		35	38			34
		29		40	41			52
				42	44			
				45*	54			

[+] Numbers refer to age in years.
* Students who are receiving Pell Grants.

Source: Author.

learners over time. Heather, who began her college career at a selective non-profit private school over twenty years ago as a premed student, admits, "You have to want to be there, like back when I first started, I didn't." She dropped out after a semester and then jumped around from community college to community college until she had her first child and then turned her attention to family. As Heather describes her prior student self, her reflections reveal that she possessed the disposition of a job seeker—she chose premed primarily because she desired a stable income and was only in school because she felt that was what was expected in order to succeed financially. Heather now reflects the disposition of a practical explorer and is studying psychology as she weighs options for graduate school. She describes the opportunities that an education can provide and expresses the belief that college "has to be something you're passionate about. What you're studying, you have to really want it."

Of the three typologies of student parents described in this chapter, those students who are most likely to be disenchanted with their college experiences and classroom learning are the job seekers. The job seekers in this study value the degree they intend to acquire but often question the value of their college learning experiences, particularly those experiences that they do not see as being directly related to their anticipated jobs. As a result, they are less connected to their student identities than are both the practical explorers and self-reflective learners. The hope that job seekers will graduate is no doubt diminished by the fact that they are less intellectually engaged in many of their classes than are their peers.[3] Further, given the relatively large number of job seekers in this study who are single parents and whose low incomes result in their being eligible for and receiving Pell Grants, we ought to be highly concerned about their educational futures as a result of their more precarious social and economic contexts. Low-income students have the most to lose in regard to socioeconomic status if they should either not complete their education or see their educational credentials go unrewarded in an economy in which middle-class jobs are steadily dwindling (McMillan Cottom 2017; Mettler 2014).

Some of these job seekers will indeed graduate and locate positions that provide a viable income and economic mobility, in part due to the familial and social resources that are helping them to navigate college life. Even though Ed, a job seeker, primarily views his college education as consisting of a series of requirements to "get through," he understands that he needs to do well in all his classes. He is a good student whose college-educated family members support his educational goals, especially his father, who teaches adjunct classes at the university that Ed is attending and can therefore help him to search out and make use of campus supports and offices when necessary. Ed also credits his military experience as providing him with the discipline to forge through classes that he might not enjoy but that he feels are necessary to complete to achieve his long-term goals. Further, the military provides him with tuition waivers and a living stipend, so he feels he can afford his education at this particular time in his life. With all of these resources available to him, Ed can focus on his educational goals and hopes that the skills that he acquires in his computer information technology classes will aid him in landing a job in the burgeoning field of network security.

However, as I also describe in this chapter, another job seeker, Jackie, is struggling in many of her classes, and her goal of being accepted into her university's education program and eventually becoming a teacher is not looking likely. Jackie's parents do not possess college degrees, and although they express support for their children's educational goals, they have few experiences of their own to draw upon when providing guidance to them in regard to their college education (Rondini 2016). Jackie's younger brother was the first in her immediate family to graduate from college and now teaches at a local high school, while also pursuing his master's degree. According to Jackie, "He's basically the American dream," and she hopes to follow in his footsteps. However, she is at this moment struggling academically. If she were to leave school, she is not convinced that the cosmetology certification that she received from her vocational high school, a much more narrowly focused and lower-level credential than a baccalaureate degree, is going to lead her to achieving financial independence, much less the American dream.

Ed's and Jackie's stories reveal the complex interplay between structural forces, such as financial resources and familial dynamics, and their educational dispositions as job seekers on their potential for success in college (Wells and Lynch 2012). Although Jackie's parents provide her with a place to live and reliable child care, they cannot help her to navigate campus life in the way that Ed's father can. Additionally, Ed's partner is the primary caregiver of their two children, whereas Jackie is her daughter's primary caregiver, and she receives only intermittent financial help from her daughter's father. Ed is also granted significantly more federal and state financial support than is Jackie due to his GI benefits. Although both these job seekers are primarily interested in the job opportunities that their degrees may provide, for Ed, that may be enough to maintain his educational engagement and get him through his degree program. For Jackie, it's not so clear—because job seekers are less connected to their learning experiences and student identities than are practical explorers and self-reflective learners, their access to supportive resources that will help them to stay in school is particularly important. Ed's and Jackie's stories demonstrate that students' strategies of being do not function deterministically. How the effects of a particular disposition play out in a student's life is highly dependent on the social supports and resources available to that student.

HOW STUDENTS MAKE SENSE of the value of their college experiences varies widely and reveals their reliance on cultural logics that reflect key dimensions of long-held instrumentalist and liberal arts framings. The distinct dispositions that subsequently emerge are themselves embedded in an intricate web of social relations influencing action and potential success. For job seekers, education is a stepping-stone to paid work and, hopefully, a financially secure existence. These job seekers express motivations inspired by utilitarian framings that are only tenuously connected to their student identities. Practical explorers likewise seek economic security but also desire the prestige and social respect that possessing a degree can confer—a degree provides access not only to an advantageous income but to a desirable status and career that they expect will be intellectually and personally satisfying. Self-reflective learners identify first and foremost as students, who through their learning will gain insight about themselves and their world and hence control over their futures. Less concerned with the specific job skills that they might attain, self-reflective learners believe that education emotionally empowers people and in following their passion, they will become successful in all dimensions of life.

These educational dispositions, however, tell only part of each student's story. Educational access and opportunity are tempered by a variety of institutional, economic, and cultural forces that are shaping their everyday actions and college pathways. As a result of the obstacles described in chapter 3, some of these students, particularly those job seekers with the fewest supportive resources, are at risk of not making it through and graduating with degrees—the obstacles they face are many and high. Other student parents are nearly assured of succeeding due to the value that they place on their student identity or their strong support networks and resources. Most, however, loom somewhere in between.

If student parents are to have the opportunity to realize their goals, they need sufficient financial, familial, and academic resources, but they also need policymakers and administrators to acknowledge the diverse cultural logics shaping their educational dispositions and expectations. Public colleges and universities were established to address the varied needs of communities, and we are now in the position of deciding whether or not those institutions are obliged to service those needs in all their complexity. A more full and nuanced understanding of students' dispositions reveals that most students are not only concerned with their place in their local economies but also with the well-being of their minds, families, and communities.

In the following two chapters, I adjust the focus of this analysis to explore how more ideologically common, or broadly accepted, cultural logics function in students parents' lives shaping their family and work experiences in the context of their educational journeys. An exploration of these moments reveals how students forge new meanings, particularly when a firmly entrenched cultural logic fails them. I now turn to these students parents' home lives, to see how their educational experiences and dispositions shape their strategies of being outside of school.

5

Weaving Existing and New Identities at Home

Angie grew up in Puerto Rico, where she was the first in her family to graduate from high school and enter college. When I ask about her educational history, she seamlessly strings together details about her family, culture, and schooling experiences:

> I just wanted to go to college because that was like my dream. You know like in Puerto Rico not too many, I don't know, adolescents think about going to college. . . . When I grew up, like all of my cousins, and even my sisters, they were younger than me, all of them like drop [out of] school, high school, you know? So I said, I don't know. . . . My father is working and he's always like, his kids are going to college. So I always love my father so much. I grew up with my grandmother, so I just wanted to make the difference. But I also, I wanted to do it for them, but for me too because I liked to study always, I always liked to study. . . . Everybody in my family was happy and proud. I went to college, and that was my goal because I wanted to have a better future for me and to be a professional and have a better job.

Early in our interview, it becomes clear that Angie has identified strongly as a student since she was young. She is a practical explorer who talks quite explicitly about the professional and economic mobility that a degree can provide. She also perceives herself as someone who enjoys studying and values the pride that her family members have taken in her educational accomplishments over the years.

Angie is now twenty-seven years old and close to finishing her bachelor's degree, all while maintaining a 3.1 cumulative grade point average and raising two young children. When I ask Angie if her husband, who has not attended college, has been supportive of her educational goals, Angie responds, "He say he understand, but I know in the bottom of the heart he doesn't understand yet how much work [it] is to go to school and to work and take care of the kids." Her husband has his own flooring company and so has some control over his daily schedule. He helps around the house minimally with cooking and child care during the year, but Angie handles most of the domestic chores and caregiving work. Although they are traditional in regard to their gender roles both in their relationship and in their domestic contributions, Angie sees herself as feisty and similar to revolutionary feminists of the past. She confides, "Sometimes I just . . . maybe that's why I just don't, I don't pay too much attention [to] what he says, and sometimes I should. Like you know like sometime the decision he makes, I don't agree, and I don't change my mind. And he doesn't change his, and I don't change mine, and I'm going to still do it! [laughs]. And you know, I think sometimes I'm more like that style, like '70s style."

Two months ago, Angie broke down and told her husband that she needs more help getting the kids ready in the morning. He has since started to help more, but his job often takes him out of the house before the children wake up, and so she is still discouraged by his lack of assistance with domestic duties. Angie admits, "I cannot say he doesn't help, because he helps, but then I feel I'm doing too much [laughs]. Yeah I think mothers . . . I don't know—nothing like a mother!" Angie understands what is expected of a "mother" and so understands why a gendered division of labor has evolved in their household, but she also believes strongly that their current household dynamics are not working for them. In her eyes, if she is to fulfill her personal goals of attaining a degree and a professional career, what it means to be a mother and what it means to be a father need to change.

Angie is also discouraged because she feels that her husband has begun only recently to grasp just how difficult her life as a student can be:

> He used to say I was the hope for our family, you know, like economically when I finish my school. . . . But he didn't realize I did study. He say, "Oh what are you doing? She's just studying." And I said, "But what!" You know like I used to get upset, "What the hell you mean I don't do anything? Come on and read those chapters and do my homework and do my paper!" . . . I would pay somebody to do my homework [laughs] because I'm so tired! And he didn't realize it.

Angie's work as a student is important to her and she is frustrated that her husband narrowly values her student role in abstract economic terms for their family's future and does not value nor even recognize the educational labor that goes into maintaining her student identity.

When Angie was hospitalized for a back injury a year ago, she talked at length with a nurse about their respective schooling experiences. Angie's husband overheard their conversation and only then, she feels, began to understand how difficult her life had been these past few years:

I used to cry a lot, because I was so frustrated. . . . I want a break and I couldn't have a break, because even those free weeks that sometimes we had, you have to still work on the papers. You know? It's not a break. So he didn't realize that. But—and if that [nurse] didn't say something about school, you know, or how difficult it is—he didn't realize it. And that happened like, a year ago. And I've been studying all these six years and he realizes a year ago. He, he didn't understand me. That's why we have too many problems [laughs]. It's not easy.

As Angie's experiences reveal, an individual's relationships with spouses, partners, children, parents, siblings, and friends are in no small measure affected and often changed when returning to college. And those changes can cause significant strain. A mother who used to have dinner on the table every day at 6:00 P.M. or a father who has regularly worked overtime to cover the household bills may not be able to take on these familial roles once fall classes begin. What it means to fulfill parenting roles and be a good mother or father is contested, negotiated, and, sometimes, reconceptualized.

In many instances, perceived success is elusive as Heide, a twenty-two-year-old white mother, makes clear when she confides, "It's hard because . . . whatever is making you more of a successful parent is probably making you less of a student" [laughs]. However, in other ways, many of these students find harmony between their student and parent identities and believe that being a good student can help them to be a better parent. Heather, a forty-year-old white mother, describes taking her seven- and nine-year-old daughters with her to study at the library. She sees her parenting and student identities as connected and believes that she is teaching her daughters to value education "because they see me study, they see me, you know, forty years old, how long I've been doing this and how important it is to me."

Angie, Heide, and Heather, like all the student parents in this study, are negotiating evolving gendered selves. Angie values both her student and mother identities and strongly believes that her experiences as a student enrich her understanding of herself as a parent. In answer to a question about her success as a student, she describes how she came to declare her major in psychology. She then seamlessly steers the discussion to the subject of her children and how she hopes that she can use her own educational experiences to guide them toward a path of success. Although she perceives these two identities as complementary, she does not believe that her husband fully understands nor appreciates the caregiving, household, and educational labor that is required to construct and maintain these aspects of her identity. According to Angie, one of her biggest challenges at home is helping him not only to understand the value of her educational labor but also to engage in household chores and caregiving responsibilities. Doing so, however, will require him to reconceptualize what it means to be a good father and what it means for Angie to be a good mother.

In the sections that follow, I examine how student parents are engaging in strategies of being, negotiating the value of domestic, caregiving, and educational labor so that their understanding of that labor aligns with their parent and student identities. To this end, I focus much of the following analysis on one particular cultural logic, that of gendered separate spheres, which hierarchically differentiates labor in the private sphere (primarily in the home) from labor in the public sphere (primarily in politics and the economy). The student parents in this study often turn to the logic of separate spheres when seeking to describe their experiences and legitimize their actions and beliefs, such as when a father discusses going to school as a means of increasing his ability to be an able breadwinner for his family. In this latter instance, traditional gendered logics regarding masculinity that emphasize men's roles as breadwinners are maintained by such meaning making. In other instances, separate spheres cultural logic may fail student parents, such as when the same father has to explain how his leaving a current job in order to go back to school makes him a good father—here, separate spheres logic and the logic of masculinity are rejected or modified as the father forgoes the role of breadwinner and engages in unpaid educational labor and, often, increased responsibilities at home.

All of these student parents are reevaluating their familial relationships and either turn to, reject, or modify cultural logics in ways that allow them to enact strategies of being that bolster their sense of essential well-being and worth. Further, how these students come to define good parenting and what resources they have available to them influence how they come to weave an evolving sense of self, not just as mothers and fathers but as men and women.[1] As these student parents seek to affirm their gendered parenting and student identities— whether or not they are job seekers, practical explorers, or self-reflective learners—they challenge those around them to likewise value their caregiving, household, and educational labor. These overviews provide a glimpse into the strategies of being that students experience at home, negotiations that some days weigh them down but other days free them from social constraints and stretch their imaginations.

Separate Spheres: In Transition

When individuals turn to cultural logics to make sense of their actions, values, and beliefs, they are guided by what cognitively makes sense and also by what *feels* right. Attending to the moral and emotional dimensions of the meaning-making process helps us to understand why social actors might rely on, reject, or modify particular cultural logics, thereby creating opportunities for transformative change.[2] Gender and labor researchers have long examined how household and caregiving labor became devalued and feminized over the past two centuries as a result of various economic and social changes.[3] Alongside the rise of capitalism in the nineteenth century arose a culture of domesticity that divided the masculinized public world of politics and economy from the feminized private world of the home (Williams 2000). Within this socioeconomic and cultural context, the masculine norms that came to define contemporary notions of the ideal worker emerged as gender and labor became intertwined. Although these separate spheres were very much defined by not only gender but also race and social class, they nonetheless produced cultural ideal types of femininity and masculinity—the angel in the house and the breadwinner—that men and women of all races and classes are frequently compared against and judged (Douglas and Michaels 2004; Hays 2003).

Both the mothers and the fathers in this study were highly cognizant of various gendered social idealizations of parenthood and the ways in which household and caregiving labor have come to be feminized and generally devalued in a world dominated by the logics of the marketplace and separate spheres. Although these student parents acknowledge the effects of gendered separate spheres in their lives, they describe themselves, their strategies of being, and the value of their own household, caregiving, and educational labor with more nuance and complexity. In reality, these spheres are far from wholly separate for most parents. In this chapter, I describe how students accept, reject, or modify this logic, exploring how they make sense of caregiving and household work, potentially altering the value of such work and its connection to gendered identities. I then explore how the general flexibility of academic schedules allows parents to reconceive of and redistribute household and caregiving labor. Finally, I examine how such change shapes parents' conceptualizations of effective parenting and what it means to be a good mother or father. When parents return to college, they create opportunities for new experiences, reflection, and debate as they negotiate the meaning of gendered separate spheres and the value of caregiving, household, and educational labor in the context of their families.

"Punching the Time Clock": Domestic and Caregiving Labor Is Work

All these student parents are engaged in varying levels of household and caregiving labor that they see as contributing to their identities as mothers and fathers. How they come to value that work and connect it to their sense of self varies immensely and is shaped by a number of factors, including their familial support systems, their racial/ethnic or religious background, their socioeconomic status, and their gender. However, all of these students recognize that household and caregiving labor is deemed invisible in much dominant discourse about work—a "working mom" is someone who participates in the paid labor economy, not necessarily someone who cooks dinner. Molly, a thirty-four-year-old white married mother, articulates her understanding of cultural contradictions resulting from the invisibility of household and caregiving labor when she admits, "I kind of feel funny when I say I don't work because, you know, it gives a misconception about what else I do with my time. But, technically I don't work" [*laughs*].

Allie, a thirty-eight-year-old white married mother, demonstrates her desire to validate her household and caregiving labor when she rejects cultural logics that narrowly define work and lists "homemaker" alongside two other paid jobs in the "Work History" section of a brief survey that I asked her to complete in advance of our interview. As we discuss some of the obstacles that she has faced while pursuing her college degree over the years, Allie describes how she and her husband have come to manage household and caregiving labor:

> So I had to teach him kind of—not deliberately teach him, but guide him like, "Okay, this is what you need to do." I wasn't about to be the one that did everything and you come home and you put your feet up and fall asleep and watch TV, and I'm going to make you dinner. Nuh-uh. 'Cause I work seven days a week, 24 hours a day. "You only work nine to five or whatever the time is Monday through Friday or whatever time you work. Then you come home and you don't have to do anything that you consider work." So I had to tell him, "When you come home, you have children that need you." So he had to learn that. Oh, this is what being a father is all about.

Allie not only redefines work for herself and her husband as including household and caregiving labor but also equates being a good father with taking on the labor of the second shift at home.[4] She claims that her husband was likely responsive to her "guidance" because they have extended family members for whom the breadwinning and primary caregiving roles are gender reversed, with the wife working full time and the husband staying home to care for the household and children. These couples in her immediate family life model alternative approaches to structuring gendered family dynamics even if their arrangement doesn't necessarily challenge traditional definitions of work. However, she further believes that because her husband was raised in a single-parent household, her husband became open to participating in caregiving and housework because, while growing up, he was required to assist around the house. As a result, she is convinced that he may have been receptive to Allie's requests for help in caregiving and domestic chores in part because they were already familiar to and valued by him.

Allie is now adamant about teaching her two children to expansively understand work as including domestic labor and to value such work around the home—she is particularly intent on transgressing gender boundaries and showing her children that particular kinds of domestic labor are not inherently suited to men or women: "In my house, everybody does something. It's not my daughter does the dusting. My son does the garbage. . . . My daughter does the garbage now, and my son does the dishes. I'm teaching both of them to cook. I'm teaching both of them to clean the house. Both of them are responsible for finding their own things for school. So it's, for me, I'm trying to raise my children that, 'You're no different than anybody else. You're a girl, you're a boy. It doesn't matter.'" Allie maintains that because her children cross traditional gender boundaries in regard to household labor, they are learning "what they can expect when they have relationships later." It's nonetheless clear from my review of Allie's detailed daily description of her household dynamics that she shoulders most of the responsibility of managing domestic duties and caregiving. However, in talking about these gendered household dynamics, she emphasizes that she perceives her family to be in transition. To facilitate that transition, she rejects the separate spheres logic that prioritizes and more highly values paid work. She is conscious of the need to break through gendered boundaries as she guides her family members to value household and caregiving labor and to see such labor as *work* in which both men and women engage.

Jim, a thirty-seven-year-old white married father, is no stranger to the idea that household and caregiving labor is difficult work. He invokes the language of the public sphere to describe his family's home life when he admits, "We always joke about punching the time clock, you know? 'Okay now, your shift, my shift.'" Although Jim's wife spends much more time with their son due to Jim's full-time job and part-time school schedule, Jim nonetheless perceives himself to be an involved dad who acknowledges and engages quite actively in caregiving labor—he manages his son's morning routine each week day and solely cares for his son every other weekend when his wife, who has a job in retail, is required to leave home for her job. When his son was experiencing cognitive and behavioral issues during his toddler years that made finding able child care providers nearly impossible, Jim considered leaving his job so that he could stay home and tend to his son's needs full time. Eventually he and his wife were able to locate counseling resources and suitable child care for their son, but Jim claims that those were difficult years that resulted in his better understanding the obstacles facing parents whose children have extraordinary physical or cognitive needs. Although Jim is less conscious than Allie of the gendered implications of separate spheres logic and is less intentional in challenging the gendered dimensions of that logic, he nonetheless conceives of labor more broadly and values the caregiving labor required of his son.

Like most of the married and cohabiting student parents whom I interviewed, Allie and Jim see their mothering and fathering identities as not wholly in line with separate spheres logic but as in transition. Although eighteen of the partnered students described their relationships as relatively traditional, with the mother taking on significantly more of the caregiving and household labor than the father, two of the separated or divorced fathers had primary custody of their children and nine of the partnered parents in this sample believed that they were challenging the logic of separate spheres and traditional gendered norms in the context of their relationships. Six of the student parents described their relationships with their partners as egalitarian in regard to their engagement in domestic labor. Detailed portrayals of a "typical day" revealed that they shared both caregiving and household roles and duties with their partners. Five of the student parents described home dynamics in which fathers took on the vast majority of caregiving and household labor. Within those five families, two of the mothers had partners who were stay-at-home fathers, and three of the student fathers were either stay-at-home dads or possessed primary custody of their children.

It is not clear whether or not the three gendered household structures—female-dominated, male-dominated, and egalitarian—existed before student parents' entry into college. However, it is clear that a return to school required many of these parents to renegotiate their household and caregiving labor in ways that often challenged both existing gendered household structures and parents' conceptualizations of motherhood, fatherhood, and separate spheres logic.

Opportunities Provided by Flexible Academic Schedules

Many sociological researchers have documented the differing and various benefits that both mothers and fathers experience when they are provided with more flexible work schedules (Lyness et al. 2012; Nomaguchi and Johnson 2016; Williams and Boushey 2010). As I describe in more detail below, these student parents' home dynamics and their reliance on the logics of separate spheres and gender are similarly altered, sometimes monumentally, when academic schedules shape their daily routines.

All but one of the fathers interviewed were attending college full time and, as Rou and Raul describe a typical day, they make it clear that their flexible academic schedules allow them to engage in high levels of caregiving. Rou, a fifty-four-year-old, white married father, admits that even after he finishes his degree and reenters the paid labor economy, he hopes to match his work schedule with his daughter's school schedule, as he is doing now, so he can remain actively involved in her caregiving. Raul, a forty-two-year-old Hispanic father whose youngest child just turned one, decided to leave his job so he could focus on managing the household, while taking evening classes to complete his degree. His girlfriend works in a hospital during the day and for the last nine months has been the breadwinner, providing the sole income for their family. These fathers specifically cite the flexibility of their academic schedules as providing them with increased opportunities to engage with their children and to devoting more time to housekeeping and preparing meals.

Jose, a forty-five-year-old Puerto Rican married father, declares that leaving his job and going back to school full time "helped our family dynamic." Of these recent changes, he notes, "It's a lot better. We're a lot more closer. Now, myself with the kid, myself my wife, she sees a lot more of me. And, yes the financial part is the tricky part, but if you look at the other part, the social part, I mean all that has improved a lot better than what it was." Jose spoke at length about how his role as a father differs from his father's generation. He is choosing to leave behind a career in social work to become a teacher in part because the teaching schedule is more amenable to his family's needs and his fathering identity. He recently left his job and is going back to school full time and has found that his academic schedule allows him to be present at his three children's schooling and social events and tend to their day-to-day needs in a way that he could not when he was both working and going to school. It helps that his wife's employer has been flexible and allows her to work from home four days a week. Jose feels that their life is "in balance," and it is due in great part to such flexibility.

All of the mothers, on the other hand, discuss the effects of their academic schedules on their mothering identities very differently. They instead focus on how going back to school has required them to seek out caregiving assistance from partners, older children, parents, other relatives, or friends. Mothers also talk more than fathers about the effects of their academic schedules on their ability to complete household labor. Several mothers, and none of the fathers, describe how they have cut back on their household labor in order to attend classes. Amber, who recently divorced and has primary custody of her son, admits, "I've definitely learned to let things go, like the cleanliness of my house and that kind of thing."

Most of the married or cohabiting mothers describe how they sought out more household assistance from their partners. When I ask Diane whether or not her husband supports her going back to school, she responds,

> He's frustrated that he has to do everything, but I'm like, I did it! When I was home with the kids, it wasn't frustrating for you that I had to do it all the time! [laughs]. It's funny how that works. . . . It is a little sore subject in our household. He gets a little peeved, like, "You don't appreciate all the things I do!" And I say, "You don't appreciate all the things I do!" [It] can definitely dissolve into a fight, so, sometimes it gets avoided but, yes, it is an interesting dynamic. He realizes now that the laundry is unending [laughs], unending! As soon as you clean up a mess in this room, you turn around and there's a mess in the next room! [laughs]. I think it's driven home to him—the point has been driven home to him.

Diane believes that her husband has come to recognize household labor as relentless, unending *work*. For many student mothers, academic schedules provide a relief from household labor, either because it is not done or because partners and older children, if they are present, step in and assist. Although it's not clear how relieving themselves of such labor affects these women's understanding of themselves as good mothers, it is clear that in some cases, like Diane's, fellow family members come to gain an appreciation for the labor involved in caregiving and domestic work when that work is not done or they have to take it on.

Further, although some married and cohabiting mothers and fathers describe their household and caregiving labor as equally shared or at least in transition, student parents' descriptions of their daily routines reveal that mothers devote more time both to performing and to delegating household and caregiving labor. Such findings are in line with conclusions drawn in prior studies and nationally representative time-use diary reports, which reveal that mothers spend more hours engaged in household and caregiving labor than do fathers (Bianchi et al. 2000, 2006; England and Srivastava 2013). Additionally, mothers are still much more likely than fathers to retain primary custody in divorce cases or to identify as single parents, a fact realized in this sample and in national statistics (Grall 2009). However, surveys also reveal that the percentage of people who believe that both parents should be equally involved in caregiving has steadily increased over the course of the twentieth century—82 percent of those surveyed who were born after 1965 believed in such parental equality (Bianchi et al. 2006: 128). What equal caregiving looks like in the context of a particular family structure may not be universally agreed upon, but these students' experiences reveal that when men and women go back to school, the shifts in daily schedules often result in men and older children engaging in caregiving and household labor more frequently and subsequently understanding and valuing that labor more highly.

Challenging Gendered Moralities

Although many of these parents perceive themselves to be in transition in regard to their sharing household and caregiving labor, the logic of separate spheres continues to loom ominously over their efforts. The influence of the logic of separate spheres persists in part because it is so firmly entrenched in core beliefs regarding women's and men's gendered identities. Kathleen Gerson (1985, 1993, 2010), who has devoted much of her career to exploring how men and women negotiate their household and caregiving responsibilities, notes that "since the rise of industrialism the social organization of moral responsibility has expected women to seek personal development by caring for others and men to care for others by sharing the rewards of independent achievement" (Gerson 2002: 8). Women who are unable or choose not to engage in caregiving labor may find that others question their very womanhood. Men who are unemployed may come to feel emasculated. In this way, "a framework of gendered moralities" shapes the likelihood that men and women will act in accordance with gendered norms and thus "justify inequalities and stigmatize those who do not conform" (Gerson 2002: 11). We see here how the labor of mothering and father-ing has come to constitute cultural logics that are wrought with gendered moral implications (Blair-Loy 2003; Christopher 2012; Doucet 2006; Duncan and Edwards 1999; Duquaine-Watson 2017; Gerson 1985, 1993, 2002, 2010; Hays 1996, 2003; Ruddick 1989; Williams 2000).

Rou, introduced above, describes the pressure he feels from his wife's parents to cut back on the hours he spends caring for his four-year-old daughter and taking classes at a local community college. He claims that "they still feel that I should be out there looking for a full-time job and getting the support kind of thing that a male should be doing." However Rou believes that his in-laws are out of touch with the reality of contemporary family life. He contends, "Society's changing. It's gotten to the point to where both [parents] need a full-time job. But then again, too, if the wife has the dominant career or pulls in the money, why is it the man has to too? I mean that's the old school." Rou claims that his in-laws are coming around to the fact that he is a successful "Mr. Mom," and he strongly believes that they are slowly beginning to value his labor in the household.

On the other hand, Diane, a thirty-four-year-old married mother who iden-tifies as white and Hispanic, is finding it difficult to give up the role of primary caregiver in her household. Several years prior, Diane's husband lost his job, and she took on the role of breadwinner while he transitioned into a new career. Although she was able to bring in a high salary as a mortgage broker, she found the hours untenable and decided to return to school to work on a degree in elementary education, a degree that she hoped would lead to a career with hours that would allow her to weave her worker and mother identities into a more self-fulfilling life pattern. These past few terms, however, had been particu-larly difficult, and although she appreciates the opportunities that her absence in the home provides for her husband, she feels that she is sacrificing her per-ception of herself as a good mother. Diane confesses, "This semester has sort of propelled my husband into top caregiver spot which has killed me, killed me! Absolutely killed me! But in some respects, I can see when I look back that it has been good for their relationship, that he's been sort of the primary guy. He's had to cook dinner four nights a week. He's had to take people to dance and do all the things that I would normally pick up the slack for. So it's been tough, but I think in some ways it was a good, a good thing." When I ask Diane to clarify how it "killed" her, she shares an anecdote from two weeks prior when her son, who was feeling emotionally distraught, called out in the middle of the night for her husband rather than for her. Although gratified that her son felt that he could turn to her husband when in emotional need, she simultaneously felt concern that her son did not first turn to her for consolation.

Diane's recounting of this experience reveals that movement toward a more egalitarian relationship often involves a loss of power and control over either public or private spheres and types of labor that fundamentally shape an individual's sense of self. Just as many men have been reluctant to give up their roles as primary breadwinners, many women have been reluctant to give up their roles as primary caregivers, and there are morally infused motivations underpinning such resistance.[5] Diane and her husband are engaged in a new level of emotion work as they renegotiate their roles and parenting and gender identities.[6] When the tensions from such emotion work were particularly high, Diane fondly recalls that her husband reminded her that the work that they are both engaged in is "a marathon, not a sprint." Together they are attempting to direct their attention to the long-term benefits of what in the short term may sometimes cause moral strain or discomfort as they weave together new parenting and gender identities.

For several of these student parents, the logic of separate spheres retains a strong hold on their imaginations, even if their actions belie adherence to such logic. Raul's return to school, described earlier in this chapter, resulted in his becoming a stay-at-home dad and taking on primary household and caregiving labor while his wife became the primary breadwinner. However, Raul expects that when he completes his master's degree in computer science and obtains a job, his girlfriend will cut her hours and again take over the primary caregiving responsibilities in their household. When I ask Raul what it means to be a successful parent, Raul declares,

RAUL: I believe that . . . the person that is in the best position [to stay home with the children] is probably the woman.

FIONA: That's interesting because you're in the reverse position.

RAUL: And I'm in that situation, but I'm hoping that won't be that forever. That is my purpose.

FIONA: Right. So you feel it's something temporary.

RAUL: Yes, temporary.

However, Raul is not so traditional as to turn over the caregiving responsibilities for his young son to his parents, in particular his mother. When I ask him whether or not his parents are supportive of his caregiving roles and provide him with assistance, he explains,

They are unfortunately—you know, my father works, my father still works. My mother she, she likes to go to bingo, she likes to go to the store, so I try not to ask them too much because . . . not because she's not going to be careful enough, but I don't want to put the burden. . . . My son is my responsibility . . . and I see that he puts a lot of stress in my life, and that he's my son. So even though my mother's his grandmother, I can imagine the stress that he will put on her. And you know they help me out, for a little bit. Like today I told them I'm going to stay in for a couple hours and she's graceful enough to say, yes. But just telling them to watch him the whole day, I think is unfair.

Raul feels responsible for the care of his son, and he is enjoying this opportunity to be intimately involved in his son's early life. He could pass on the care of his son to his mother, but he instead chose to leave his job as a bus dispatcher to focus on his college education and his caregiving and domestic responsibilities. Importantly as described previously, his flexible academic schedule allows him to be a more active caregiver.

Raul has two older children from a previous marriage and admits to having been not as involved in the day-to-day activities of their upbringing. He confesses, "With my two older children I didn't get to spend as much time as I spend with this one. . . . I missed a lot of events in their life." With his youngest son, things are different: "Being there when he cries and needs something. Being there to change his diaper, to feed him. You know just being there for him. . . . Now with this one I'm really involved, not willing to miss anything when he's growing up. And yes, it has been a whole different experience." Although Raul expects, like several of the fathers in this study, to revert to the role of breadwinner once he graduates and obtains a job, his experience managing the caregiving and domestic responsibilities in the home have made him aware of the expenditure of emotional and physical energy that is involved in performing such care work. When weekends arrive, Raul admits to needing a break and telling his wife, "I know you're tired. I'm tired too." He affirms to having increased his understanding of the intensity and amount of labor that is required in the home and having refined in his mind what it means to be a successful partner and father.

Raul's experiences reveal the difficulties of challenging firmly entrenched gendered logics and of the complex relationship between these morally infused logics and one's sense of a gendered self. His views, however, are also very much influenced by his belief that in the United States, Latino and African American fathers are not shown the same respect as white fathers. He laments, "When it comes down to fatherhood, you know, it's more valuable if you're white, not if you're a minority." Raul believes that African American and Latino fatherhood is not valued in the larger culture because of stereotypes that minority low-income fathers are overly reliant on social services and welfare. It is likely that Raul cannot give up the belief that women are more suited to caregiving, even though he has been serving as the primary caregiver in his own household, in part because he desires to combat those stereotypes regarding low-income Latino fathers. He is currently content to serve in this feminized role temporarily but resists viewing it as permanent. Such a perspective is not surprising in a culture where the logic of masculinity is intertwined with that of the breadwinner as a result of not only gendered but also racialized hierarchies. As a Latino father, Raul feels particularly pressured to negate stereotypes of deadbeat dads and show that he is a capable provider. Because economic and social power comes with the role of being the primary provider, it can be difficult to give up that position in both the family and the larger culture.

Rose, a twenty-five-year-old married Turkish American mother, talks at length about her difficulty in getting her husband to help around the house. Rose identifies strongly as a Muslim and respects her Turkish culture but does not necessarily believe that the strict gendered separate spheres that shape gender relations within her extended family and Turkish American community ought to be the ideal. Rose confesses to envying some U.S. American couples when she shares, "U.S. culture I really value and adore. They're willing to do things. If a mother is working, father will pick up the child in school, you know? They're more willing to share roles in the house. They'll cook, they clean, they help with the house chores if a mother is working a lot, if she's not able to do it. I like that, I really like that. I value that. It's not happening with my relationship, not in Turkish culture." As is described in more detail in the prior chapter, Rose is a self-reflective learner who is pursuing her degree with the hope that she will be able to obtain a job that will allow her to leave her gambling-addicted husband. She is also committed to helping her younger eighteen-year-old sister-in-law to pursue her education, so that she too can feel empowered to challenge some of the gendered norms that circumscribe their familial, religious, and community relationships. Education for Rose provides a means of understanding and reconciling contradictions that she is experiencing in her relationships and in the gendered logics of contemporary U.S. culture and her Turkish and religious cultures. She is in the process of redefining what it means to be a good mother, a good Muslim, and a good woman, and she believes that her education, and in particular the learning that is taking place in the context of her psychology courses, is providing her with the opportunity to explore the contradictions shaping her complex life experiences.

Overall, these student mothers and fathers are challenging and, in many cases, dramatically reconceptualizing how their engagement in household and caregiving labor contributes to their sense of self as mothers and fathers, as well as women and men. Their multiple responsibilities at home, work, and school result in their having to restructure their daily lives in ways that fundamentally challenge the ways in which they have come to define themselves as gendered beings. They find that the logic of separate spheres often fails them as they negotiate alternative gendered strategies of being, and so these student parents are creating space for new logics and innovative ways of understanding both gender and parenting.

Social Class, Gender, and Educational Labor

In addition to reframing the value of their household and caregiving labor, student parents are acutely aware of the social value or lack of social value often ascribed to their educational labor. Like household and caregiving labor, studying and other educational labor cannot be easily commodified, and student parents often find it difficult to negotiate the value of that labor, particularly within the domestic sphere. Family members are not always willing to accept that having to read a book or write a paper is legitimate work, particularly when such work doesn't yield direct tangible rewards, such as providing money to pay the bills or meals to feed the family.

All of these student parents value educational labor in part because they hope that their efforts will improve their economic standing. However, as described in the prior chapter, many practical explorers and self-reflective learners are additionally interested in learning and acquiring cultural and social capital that will increase their self-knowledge and sense of self-worth. The sections that follow explore in more detail the experience of negotiating the value of educational labor and some of the strategies they have employed to legitimize the value of their educational labor and student identities.

Navigating Gender and Educational Status

Those students whose own parents and family members are college educated find that their efforts in school are usually highly respected, which is evidenced in not only general expressions of encouragement but also tangible support, which can include financial, emotional, or caregiving assistance. These dynamics are also very much shaped by gender and the expectations that partners and other family members have of mothers and fathers in the context of separate spheres logic and their fulfillment of breadwinning or caregiving roles.

Philoso, a twenty-nine-year-old Sudanese Dominican father, is currently separated from his partner and attempting to gain primary custody of his two-year-old daughter. He served as her primary caregiver until just three months before our interview, when he returned to school to pursue his master's degree in psychology. Philoso, whose mother possesses two bachelor's degrees, one in fashion and one in nursing, and whose father completed his MBA, describes the various ways that his immediate family "keeps pushing" him because in his family "education is big."

However, he believes that his in-laws, neither of whom has completed a bachelor's degree, do not respect his current educational efforts—he describes his mother-in-law as saying that she supports the idea of his going to college, but when he asks her to watch his daughter when he needs to go to campus, he confides that she "snickers" and derides his reading books in lieu of earning a paycheck. Philoso's intersections of social class and gender function very differently in these competing familial settings, which vary in how they value educational labor in the context of separate spheres logic. According to his parents, being a student will allow him to be a good father and provide for his daughter in the long term, but according to his in-laws, being a student is compromising his immediate ability to fulfill the role of breadwinner and hence be a good father.

David, Ed, and Rou describe similar situations—Ed's and David's parents are college educated and support their academic goals and provide encouragement and assistance when times are tough. However, Ed's, David's, and Rou's in-laws are not college educated and neither are the mothers of their children. They describe some of the tensions that can result in their relationships when they are pressed to complete school readings or assignments and their partners do not understand or are frustrated by how much time and energy is required to perform such labor. Rou shares some of the discontent that his wife expresses when he has schoolwork to attend to:

> She felt that . . . it would take away from things that I needed to do in terms of getting a job and stuff like that. I said, "Look, the only way that I'm going to do this effectively is to do it full-time." It's the shortest period of time, and it's really the only way that the government will pay for it. And it took a while for her to understand that. So now she's beginning to understand what I've been trying to tell her from the very beginning. So you know and especially my in-laws, they're one of the . . . they're from the old school and the man provides, you know.

Ed and David similarly describe their partners' frustrations but are propelled forward to pursue their educational goals by their own college-educated parents, who both value and understand educational labor and the potential long-term rewards of such labor.

None of the mothers in this study describe experiencing the conflict that many fathers express in regard to encountering pressure from non-college-educated family members to forgo school and take on a paid job. Mothers instead describe how immediate and extended family members issue abstract support for mother's academic goals; however, those family members, and particularly non-college-educated family members, often do not understand the nature of that work and how it might alter student mothers' ability to engage in household or caregiving labor. As a divorced mother with primary custody of her one-year-old son, Amber would not be able to attend school without a network of supportive caregivers. Of that support, she reflects, "My family is supportive as far as me actually going to school and the whole idea of me going and getting a degree and all that kind of stuff. I don't think they actually understand how much it actually takes with the going to class and the writing papers and doing projects and that kind of thing. . . . They don't really realize how much effort goes into it." When family members do not actually understand the time and energy commitment required of educational labor, they may be unwilling or hesitant to assist with household work or caregiving. Amber continues to explain that her own parents are "a little touch and go as far as the support, with helping me with [my son]." However, her ex-husband and in-laws provide a great deal of caregiving assistance, and so she is able to successfully navigate her otherwise complex and demanding work and schooling schedule.

Negotiating the value of educational labor can be particularly difficult when partners or family members are non-college-educated and may be envious of student parents' achievements or resentful that student parents are pursuing goals that are not immediately relevant to the well-being of their relationship or family. Allie admits that she believes her husband may be envious of her student obligations and identity. When I ask about her husband's support of her educational goals, she explains that her husband sends her "mixed messages: 'Sure, go to school, but . . . I don't think I can help you out in terms of making it easy for you to go to school.'" She ruminates, "I don't know if he's jealous that I'm in school and I'm doing well and that I might do better than him when I go to work." Allie senses that her husband may be expressing his discomfort with both the changes in their household dynamics that require him to engage in more domestic and caregiving labor and the potential shift in status and power that may occur as her student and their mothering and fathering identities evolve.

Molly expresses a similar concern, not about her husband, whom she describes as being her "biggest cheerleader," but about her parents and siblings. None of her immediate family members are college educated, and she describes her dad as being "relieved" that none of his children sought a college degree because he believed he could not afford it. Molly muses, "I think that they almost . . . I don't really know how to word it. I think that they're almost afraid that I'll outgrow them. Does that make sense? If like . . . nobody else has gone to college. Nobody else has aspired to do much." Just over a third of these student parents describe their partners or immediate family members as being uncomfortable with their student identities and not understanding of the time-intensive educational labor required of them as they pursue their degrees.

The examples just described reveal that these negotiations are often complicated by the realization, consciously or subconsciously, that educational labor can be implicated in the processes of upward status mobility and shifting gendered power dynamics. Potential changes in status can be particularly disconcerting for family members who adhere to separate spheres logic, particularly in regard to men's breadwinning role in the family. Additionally, the very cultural and social capital that practical explorers and self-reflective learners, as described in the prior chapter, hope to attain can increase students' social status while simultaneously alienating students' family members who do not possess those resources and status. In sum, less formally educated family members may express pride in a student parent's educational successes in the abstract, but often do not understand the nature of educational labor and may resent the challenges to traditional gender roles and the social status changes that can result from a parent going back to school.

Legitimizing Student Identities

As these student parents talk about their educational labor, they share their strategies of being for conceptualizing the value of that labor and legitimizing their student identities at home. Job seekers, who see going to school primarily as a means of attaining a degree to gain status in the marketplace, possess the weakest connection to their student identities. It is not surprising then, that they speak least about the value and benefits of their educational labor as it is only tenuously connected to their sense of self. Practical explorers and self-reflective learners, on the other hand, weave their student identities into their sense of self. They are more likely than job seekers to discuss strategies of being that allow them to merge their student and parent identities and to refer to cultural logics that encourage validation for their educational labor from family members on the home front. In the following sections I briefly describe three cultural logics that these students use to legitimize their student identities in the context of family and home.

STUDENTS MAKE SAVVY PARENTS. Sara, a self-reflective learner introduced in the previous chapter, explains what she perceives to be the value of education and in doing so weaves together dimensions of her student and parent identities:

> I even see it within my own family, my mother and my father. My husband and I try to tell them something that we're excited about, right? And they sit there and they're like, "Well, that's not true." And we're like, "Well, here's all the research. What makes you think it's not true?" . . . And they sit there, "Well, I have experience or this and this and that." And we're like, "Well, that's your experience. Have other people experienced this? You don't know. You have no idea." And they're kind of like stuck, "Well, this is the way. That's your opinion. This is my opinion." And my husband's like, "It's not my opinion. It's research!" [laughs]. And so it's—I think that I don't want my children to be so closed-minded about things like that. Because I do find a lot of people that are very closed-minded and don't want to consider anything else possible. And I want the kids to experience a different world than what most people tried to teach us. I want them to not say, "Well that's blue 'cause it's blue." Let's see why it's blue. Why do we see it as blue? Things like that. I want them to think outside the box.

Sara and her husband are trying to teach their children to think critically and to value those researching and analytic skills that she and her husband have developed as students. She reveals how deeply integrated are her parenting and student identities—she believes that her educational labor is valuable because it is helping her to expand her children's experience of the world, thereby empowering them to be deep thinkers and making her a better parent.

Several students also refer to specific knowledge that they have gained from their classes and how that knowledge has improved their ability to parent successfully. Philoso, also a self-reflective learner, is convinced that college-educated parents are "more savvy" because they are skilled in asking questions and seeking "resources and stuff." He believes that the information that he has gleaned from his psychology classes, particularly those classes that focus on developmental psychology, have shaped his parenting strategies and made him a better father.

Drew, a communications major and practical explorer, describes how he limits his son's media consumption because of the knowledge he has gained from his communications classes and from various readings. He also discusses how knowledge gained from a current sociology class is shaping his views regarding feminism and men's and women's roles in society at large. The class has helped him to make sense of his parents' relationship and of his current relationship, which he believes "should be equal." Drew, like many of these parents, believes that all this knowledge acquired in school has shaped his fathering identity in ways that make him a better parent.

STUDENTS MAKE GOOD ROLE MODELS. Many of the practical explorers and self-reflective learners also describe the value of modeling student labor, particularly with older children. Emma, a thirty-five-year-old practical explorer, who is working toward her bachelor's degree in management and organization, describes the pride that she feels when her children see her studying: "They think it's nice that I'm going to go to school. And Dad's in school next semester as well. . . . Everyone goes to school and we all get to do homework. Yeah. They're 'I have to go do my homework now.' They think it's cool. 'Mum, do you have homework? You're a grownup!' And I, yes I do have homework. They like that." Emma believes that she is modeling positive student habits and that in doing so she is being a good parent.

In addition, many of these student parents expect that in earning their college degree, they are engaged in the hard work of paving a path that will ensure that college is part of their own children's educational future. At barely two years old, Drew's son is too young to fully understand the value of his dad's educational labor, but Drew is motivated to continue because he believes that possessing a college diploma will symbolically function in his life by setting an educational bar that he hopes his son will likewise reach: "Obviously some people don't have the best circumstance, so you try the best you can. I've been fortunate to have decent circumstances, so I've been able to come to school and hopefully get my degree and move on past there. That's why I'm hoping to do the same so I could do one better for my son. Send him away just like I did and go and experience the good college life and get a degree and get out there and you know make something of yourself. That's what I'm hoping." Thirty-five percent of the student parents in this study described similar educational role-modeling moments or aspirational outlooks. They expect their children to learn from their example as they read, study, and complete projects, highlighting for their children the difficult work that constitutes educational labor.[7] In this way, these student parents legitimize the value of educational labor for their children, their families, and themselves.

STUDENTS NEED WORK SPACES. In legitimizing the value of their student identities and education-related labor, these student parents also develop means of consciously understanding and evaluating the worth of such work and engage strategies that validate their labor, such as consciously carving out specific physical locations to study and read. Elizabeth, a practical explorer, explains how she escapes to a local coffee shop or the public library, leaving her husband at home to manage their five children. When she can't get out of the house, she admits to sometimes locking herself in her bedroom and having her husband tell her youngest daughter that she had to leave to run errands, so that her daughter doesn't seek her out.

Some parents identify specific spaces in their homes, such as spare bedrooms or basement corners, that serve as home offices where they can engage in educational labor. Rou, a practical explorer, explains that it has taken him several months, but that he has finally convinced his wife that he needs a space at home that he can retreat to in order to study. Rou told his wife, "If you want me to be home, then I have to have my time to study. I need a place." They arranged a space in their home that now serves as his office and affirms his student identity. When the door is closed, both his wife and daughter understand that he is working.

Because she lives with her extended family, Rose, a self-reflective learner, has given up finding a place around the house where she can regularly study, but she has successfully arranged for child care so that she can spend extra time on campus. She claims that campus is the best place for her to read and complete projects. Because she has access to reliable family members who can help in watching her daughter, she is able to take advantage of the campus library, computer labs, and various lounge areas to affirm her student identity and complete her class work. Many students express a preference for coming to campus to complete work, because there they are free from family distractions and can focus on their coursework. Most, like Rose, currently rely on a patchwork of family members or friends to watch their children to enable them to come to campus, where they can engage in educational labor and so legitimize their student identity.

MANY OF THESE STUDENT PARENTS are weaving new identities by rejecting or modifying the gendered separate spheres logic and attempting to legitimize their household, caregiving, and educational labor in the context of their homes and off-campus communities. These student parents make visible the gendered household and caregiving labor that they are everyday negotiating as they construct their identities as good mothers and fathers. This is not to say that the distribution of this labor is equal in all cases. The process of reconceptualizing both gender and the value of domestic, caregiving, and educational labor is collectively shaped by students' strategies of being and access to structural resources.[8]

My findings reveal that as students negotiate household and caregiving labor at home, several of the most salient individual-level factors shaping these negotiations are their gender, partnership status, and racial or ethnic background. When it comes to single-parent caregiving, four of the five single student parents in this sample are women, a gendered ratio in line with national figures (Grall 2009). Among married and cohabiting student parents, household labor is disproportionately borne by mothers. That said, many mothers and fathers describe a model of co-caregiving as the ideal to which they aspire.[9] Those parents who are least likely to describe their parenting ideals in this way, like Raul and Drew, nonetheless are fathers who are currently engaged in high levels of caregiving. Raul and Drew continue to rely extensively on the separate spheres logic as they envision their familial roles and fathering identities in the future, but their present strategies of being and actions reflect a more nuanced portrait of fatherhood that is in reality more transitional than traditional.

In legitimizing household and caregiving labor, these students are destabilizing the logic of gendered separate spheres and creating opportunities for new logics of parenting and doing gender. Although going back to school functions differently for mothers and fathers, the effects of engaging in educational pursuits often result in these parents altering their household and caregiving labor routines and reconstructing household dynamics in ways that move toward more egalitarian gender models. Their family members' education levels and their own educational dispositions as job seekers, practical explorers, or self-reflective learners affects the connections they make, or do not make, between their student and parenting identities. Finally, structural factors, such as flexible academic schedules and access to available study spaces, also very much influence the outcomes of these negotiations. They share their belief that their education provides them with knowledge and opportunities that inform their parenting and instills in their children a valuing of education, particularly a college education.

In the words of gender theorist Joan Williams (2000), these student mothers and fathers are engaged in the "hard work" that comes with "flights of the imagination" (p. 219). They are by example showing their children what it means to weave together their gendered parent and student identities and, in many cases, opening up the possibility for more fluid conceptualizations of gender and greater gender equality. These kinds of unintended benefits of being a student have never been included in traditional metrics for assessing the value of higher education. To explore further how we might more expansively assess the value of going back to school, I now turn our gaze from the home front so that we may analyze and assess how student parents' experiences challenge yet another ideologically common logic; one that focuses on the relationship between education and work.

6

False Promises?

Go to College, Get a Job

The true way to nurse patriotism . . . is to inspire our people with confidence, by giving them proper training, that they are equal to their mission and that failure is impossible.

> –Hon. Justin S. Morrill, *Speech to the House of Representatives,*
> Washington D.C., June 6, 1862

In order for our citizens to be able to seize the opportunities of a new era, they're going to have to have skills that can be only learned through a post-secondary education. . . . We're living in a global economy. And we've got to stay competitive as we head into the 21st century, and the best way to stay competitive is to make sure people have access to good education.

> –President George W. Bush, *Signing of HR 2669–College Cost Reduction
> and Access Act,* September 27, 2007

We've got to make sure that more Americans of all ages are getting the skills that they need to access the jobs that are out there right now. But more than ever, a college degree is the surest path to a stable, middle-class life.

> –President Barack Obama, *College Opportunity Summit,*
> Washington, D.C., January 16, 2014

In the nineteenth century, U.S. political discourse that linked higher education with the economy found fertile soil in a young country eager to grow and spread its influence. Colleges in the United States initially emerged to address the classical and moral educational needs of young clergy and sons of the elite, but the purpose of a college education and certainly the discourse that has influenced our understanding of higher education in the nineteenth and twentieth centuries became with each decade more tightly connected with the economy. As described in chapter 2, the historically interconnected relationship between colleges and the economy, industry, and science has indelibly shaped the instrumentalist discourse and cultural logics that many people in the United States draw upon to conceptualize and discuss the purpose of college.

Sociologists studying education have long identified the correlation between social status and educational systems, noting the role that educational systems relentlessly play in perpetuating rather than alleviating social inequalities.[1] In recent years, several researchers have specifically focused on the college experience, exploring the various means by which colleges and universities, both within and between elite and state institutions, often exacerbate existing social inequalities (see for example Armstrong and Hamilton 2013; Goldrick-Rab 2016; Mullen 2010; Stuber 2011). Much of this research similarly finds that students' social class significantly shapes their higher educational expectations, opportunities, and experiences. Students coming from families with a history of collegiate success or socioeconomic privilege, which are most often linked, are generally less pressured to imagine the outcome of their education in terms of specific jobs or potential incomes. Instead, these students rely on their families' social networks or the prestige of the universities from which they receive their degrees to facilitate connections upon graduation that will increase their likelihood of obtaining desirable, high-income jobs. On the other hand, students coming from families in which they are the first to attend college or who do not possess extensive socioeconomic resources are understandably much more concerned with how their education will improve their opportunities for obtaining a job and experiencing upward social mobility.

Given these findings, it is not surprising that most of the student parents in this study not only talk about their education in relation to the jobs they hope to obtain but also select majors in applied programs—such as social work, education, or criminology—that will lead to very specific jobs that are perceived as better than the jobs they currently hold. Unlike many liberal arts programs, which offer a curriculum that provides a broad-based education in the humanities and social sciences, applied programs are more practicum-based and tend to address the defined needs of a specific sector of the economy. Applied programs are widely offered at most state colleges and universities, where all of these student parents were enrolled. Even those student parents in this study who are practical explorers or self-reflective learners and are majoring in traditional liberal arts programs—English, history, and psychology—are for the most part planning to enter into job-specific secondary teaching or counseling programs subsequent to receiving their baccalaureate degrees.

Whether or not our current system of higher education is successful is under question as academics, politicians, and students themselves evaluate the current state of higher education in the United States. As described in chapter 2, the success of a postsecondary institution is frequently measured in terms of retention rates and job placement. Although these factors are certainly important in evaluating the effectiveness of a college or university, my findings in chapters 4 and 5 reveal additional expectations for and unintended effects of going to college for these student parents. The practical explorers and self-reflective learners are further interested in acquiring social and cultural capital, serving as an educational role model to their children, growing intellectually, and feeling respected and emotionally empowered. And some of these mothers and fathers unexpectedly find that as their labor in the domestic and caregiving spheres shifts—in part a result of academic demands and schedules—so does their and their families' conceptualizations of motherhood and fatherhood, which creates the potential for developing more egalitarian understandings of doing gender and parenting.

These student parents' stories reveal that traditional metrics for evaluating educational success are narrow at best. The kinds of perceived benefits cited by practical explorers and self-reflective learners are rarely if ever documented by public colleges or universities or national accrediting agencies.[2] And both Republican and Democratic politicians focus nearly exclusively on cultural logics that emphasize the relationship between higher education and the economy. That said, the job outcome expectations of job seekers and all of these student parents should be scrutinized, particularly given the rising costs of tuition and students' increasing reliance on loans to pay for their degrees. As will be revealed in this chapter, accurately measuring the success of our system of higher education involves looking at more than the traditional measures of institutional retention rates and job placement.

In the pages that follow, I describe the job and educational histories of three older students, a job seeker, a practical explorer, and a self-reflective learner. These student parents' educational and work trajectories, particularly those of older student parents, reveal a complex interplay of additional factors that influence retention rates, job placement, and economic upward mobility. Although these students' dispositions regarding the purpose of higher education vary, these three students are similar in that they have moved in and out of higher education over the years with varying levels of economic success. An examination of their educational and job histories reveals some of the limitations of current measures of institutional success that focus on employment and demonstrates that a correlation between education and economic opportunity is far from neat or direct.

Allie: Job Seeker

Allie, a thirty-eight-year-old mother of two, expresses a refrain that was oft repeated by the job seekers in this study: "If you want to escape low-wage labor, you must earn a college degree." Allie bluntly proclaims, "As I tell my children, if you go to school and get a degree, you can make more money, and you can do and get the things that you want. If you don't go to school, you're going to work at a $7.00 an hour job, and then you won't get or do what you want to do or be where you want to be." Even in an era marked by high levels of college graduate unemployment, job seekers in particular strongly believe that having a college degree continues to be their best defense against the low-wage labor trap. Importantly, just over 60 percent of these job seekers already have associate's degrees or certifications for professions such as cosmetology and dental assisting. Allie clearly believes that a college education is necessary to not only survive in the twenty-first-century economy but also have the freedom to "do what you want to do or be where you want to be." Allie possesses a two-year degree and is now back in school because she has found that her prior education has not provided her with access to jobs that will provide long-term career success.

Allie began her college journey over fifteen years earlier at a satellite campus of the state's flagship university. She had aspirations of becoming a college professor teaching English but soon realized that she was not ready nor willing to continue with her education at that time. Allie confesses, "I went because I thought I had to. I didn't want to. I was burnt out from going to school for thirteen years. It was boring." Subsequently, she dropped out of the flagship university and took on various office jobs before returning to a local community college to pursue her degree in early childhood education.

Four years later, she eventually earned her associate's degree and then worked in a day care center until her first child was born. Upon taking the time to examine their household budget, she left the center because she and her husband determined that they would be better off if she quit her job rather than pay for someone else to care for their newborn son so that she could work. As she reflects back on that time, she shares,

> I had some long-term personal goals of wanting to be a good mother and getting a background for that. And then I thought I would have my own business of child care and I thought that would make good money at that time. And then I actually went into just being a caregiver in a day care center, and it doesn't make any money. And it doesn't cover child care bills. . . . It didn't make sense to put my baby in child care for forty or forty-five hours a week for me to bring home eighty dollars. So, I decided that's not what I want to do. . . . I took time off to be a parent because it was cheaper.

Financially, it made more sense for Allie to stay at home—the extra eighty dollars a month, after deducting child care from her paychecks, simply wasn't worth it.

The one educational regret that Allie now holds is that she in the past pursued a job-specific degree that will never produce the income needed to sustain a decent standard of living. Although plenty of jobs exist in early child care education, and her degree provided her with a step up in regard to her employability in that field, Allie found that she earned little more than minimum wage, which left her with an income that barely covered her own child care costs. When I ask her what she would change about her educational past if she had the chance, she states that she wishes that she had explored more degree options and careers before selecting a major:

ALLIE: I wouldn't have done early childhood education. I probably would have researched jobs more thoroughly or careers more thoroughly. And it would have been nice to know that you could go into college on a general—I don't know what it's called . . .

FIONA: General education? Or liberal arts education?

ALLIE: Right. Like for the first year or two. And then when you find out what's out there, then focus in and concentrate on that. 'Cause then I wasted four years in college. Not really, but, in terms of work, there's no money in it.

Upon completing her associate's degree, Allie applied to a local regional public university to continue with her degree but withdrew before the beginning of the semester when she found out that she was pregnant. Ten years later, she returned to that same university and is now majoring in criminal justice, a degree that she finds interesting in content yet practical in regard to the kinds of jobs that she might be able to attain upon graduation. Although she is primarily concerned about the job prospects of her chosen major, Allie is similar to many of the older students in that she is also motivated by a desire to "finish" what she started almost two decades ago.

When I later ask her to describe what makes a student successful, she describes some of her younger peers in ways that are reminiscent of her former student self:

Young people today don't take it seriously. . . . Students need to understand that when you go to school, it's for your future. And I don't think they look that far ahead. That they're just there for today to do the work, to get out as soon as they can for the day, to be with their friends, party, you know. . . . If they had to pay for their classes themselves, I think they would take it more seriously and understand. I'm paying for this. It's benefiting me to do this because I'm going to take it with me when I graduate so that I can do something good in the workforce. . . . I just want them to have a respect for school, really. I think they go just to get it done. And I just don't think that way. . . . It's a privilege, really, to me.

Later in our conversation, she identifies some of the characteristics that she believes makes her different from these younger students and from her younger student self. She continues, "I know that if I don't do well, in the future . . . I won't be able to prove myself at work. Because if I just float through school, how am I going to apply that in the workforce? So I better get it right now, so I don't have to mess up later. So, I'm just a go-getter. I'm ambitious and I want to do the best I can." Allie is excited by her studies in criminology and the prospect of going on to graduate school and working in forensics. After fifteen years of stops and starts, she again has concrete job goals and sees the relevance of her present coursework in regard to her future occupation.

Sam: Practical Explorer

Another student, Sam, a forty-two-year-old father studying to be a physical therapist, is back in school because he is ready for yet another career change. Before the birth of his four children, who at the time of our interview ranged in age from seven to eleven, Sam received certification from a heating, ventilation, air conditioning, and refrigeration (HVACR) program at a local for-profit institute. The twelve-month program at the for-profit institute was equal in cost to four years at the local state university for an in-state resident. Despite its expense, Sam chose the short-term applied program, hoping that the skills acquired would provide him with access to a job that would provide a stable income. He ended up not using much of the knowledge procured from his year-long program when he began working as a machine operator in a metal fabricating factory. Later, when the factory where he worked turned its attention to the production of circuit boards, Sam enrolled in an electrical technician program offered by his employer to develop skills in this new area of interest and demand. But then the company went bankrupt and folded.

Sam is now working as a custodian at a school, a job that provides a middle-class income and lifestyle but that, like his former factory jobs, is physically demanding. It is possible that his relatively expensive HVACR certification helped him to land his current position in facilities, but he is now ready to leave this job. At the time of our interview, Sam was studying at a local community college to become a physical therapist, a job that will continue to guarantee his middle-class income but will be less taxing physically. He has suffered from several health issues recently—three knee surgeries and a pinched nerve—so he knows he needs a job that requires less physical labor. Because of these injuries, he has regularly visited physical therapists in recent years and finds their jobs to be interesting, a fact that was validated when he took a job inventory test at the middle school where he works and "physical therapist" emerged as one of the listed career choices that matched his personality assessment.

I ask Sam what he believes to be the purpose of college, and he launches into a somewhat rambling discussion that ultimately reveals his contradictory feelings about the topic. He takes seriously accounts shared over the years by several of his colleagues who have college diplomas but describe them as "useless" and not at all necessary for their jobs. When I ask him to clarify, he maintains, "One thing I don't like about the program is there's a lot of classes that I have to take that I'm like, Well where does this—where is this relevant? Where does it actually fit in?" Although Sam is critical of college curriculums that require classes that are "just not necessary," he also believes that his being in school is both testing his endurance and stretching his intellectual capabilities. He reflects, "What I learned in psychology is our brains definitely change, keep learning, keep absorbing education, and if we don't, we, we bottom out. We just forget everything we ever learned, and I just didn't want to wind up fifty years old going, 'Uh-huh?' [laughs]. So I'm always interested in education. I push my kids to do the best that they can as far as their education. I sit down and do their homework with them. And I throw my homework at them and see if they can do it" [laughs]. He continues by sharing that he has friends and family members who have never gone to college and he notes that their "mentality is slowly declining" and that "they only know their environment."

Additionally, Sam is committed to completing his physical therapy program because he aspires to the status that such an accomplishment represents in the larger social sphere. Sam summarizes his current perspective when he confesses, "Coming from where I came from, growing up in the projects, it was almost guaranteed that you weren't going to have an interest in education. You weren't going to go to college. You weren't going to get established in anything. And I'm just one of those statistics that have been proven wrong." Sam is rightfully proud of his accomplishments. He has a comfortable job that provides a stable middle-class income but is now seeking a position that is more intellectually and less physically challenging and a college degree that will communicate to others that he is not a "statistic." He sees himself as living evidence that college graduates can emerge from the "projects" and achieve the American Dream.

Joy: Self-Reflective Learner

Like Allie, Joy worked in early childhood education, but, unlike Allie, she has earned not only a bachelor's degree in human development but also a master's degree in early childhood education. She earned the master's degree after she had started working in a child care center and before she had children. Joy is additionally certified as a massage therapist and occasionally teaches classes at a local massage therapy school to supplement her family's income.

Joy values her past educational experiences but has found that those degrees and certifications have not guaranteed her access to jobs with high incomes. Joy laments,

I mean I read on these graphs, you know, a high school education will get you this amount through your lifetime. Add a master's to that, and it goes to here [she raises her hand in the air]. Well, I've got a master's already, and it's in early childhood education, and that field did not net very much money at all. I was doing incredibly important work and the janitor in the building made more money than me! Because of the gender inequality with the—that NOW position statement, women make what? Seventy-five cents to the dollar! There you go. I've been in traditionally female occupations and so the financial compensation is not there.

Joy highlights structural inequities reflected in the pay differentials between feminized and masculinized occupations. Not only that, she perceptively notes that the higher pay of many masculinized occupations persists despite the higher educational qualifications necessary to attain leadership jobs in early childhood education, an occupation dominated by women.

Like Sam, Joy can afford to attend school because her household income is stable as a result of her husband's job as a lawyer. However, because her husband is self-employed and health care costs have increased significantly over the years, she is seeking a job in the public sector that will provide additional household stability in regard to their health care. These factors shaped her decision to pursue a master's degree in counseling with the hope that she can obtain a job in a school that offers the health care and retirement benefits that will improve her family's fiscal situation.

Importantly, Joy now feels that she has the "time and energy" available to pursue her degree in educational counseling and work full time: "As a mother, that meant by the time I had three kids, I wanted to just put my energy into them. And so I focused on them, and when my time and energy opened up a little bit, I took it into working at the massage therapy school and now, when my youngest is in high school and he'll be gone all day until four every day, and my other two will be away at college, then my sort of scope opens and I can focus on a full-time job." Joy was able to return to school previously to earn her certification in massage therapy because family members were able to step up and assist with child care. Her husband's aunt watched Joy's infant son when she began taking classes, and then her mother-in-law watched the children when she began working part time as a massage therapist. Now that her youngest child is thirteen years old, child care is less of an issue, and she feels comfortable and ready to return to college to pursue her master's degree in counseling.

As described in chapter 4, Joy is a student who loves learning and being a student. In clarifying just what makes a student successful, she explains,

The students who really reflect on what they're learning, recognize its value for them in their life, really take a personal interest in their learning, get the most out of it, it seems to me. Very clear. . . . People who really take the learning and want to make it their own are so much deeper and so much richer than people who just regurgitate the material they need to in order to pass. So I think personal interest is what makes it successful for a student. Because those people, I think, are the most content with what they're learning and feeling the most fulfilled by what they're learning.

Throughout the course of her interview, Joy reiterates the value of learning and focuses on the value of being a positive student role model to her children and encouraging them to appreciate the "enriching" opportunities that all education can provide.

Unlike Allie, however, who blames herself for making poor educational choices, Joy finds value in all of her past educational experiences and instead points blame at an economic system that undervalues the work of feminized occupations. Joy has acquired a sophisticated means of analyzing and articulating her educational and career history that links her individual experiences with larger social inequalities. Joy fully recognizes that her personal experiences are shaped by gendered career tracks and institutions that contribute to the creation of gendered social inequalities. She has earned not one but two degrees that facilitated her entry into fields that are socially valuable and where jobs are ample but financial remuneration, particularly the health and retirement benefits, is insufficient.

Gender, Credentials, and Social Mobility

All of these student parents' experiences reveal distinct trajectories that reflect the value of higher education in larger social and economic spheres. Allie's and Joy's experiences bring to light the ways degree programs that focus on specific skills do not always promise economic success and social mobility, particularly in highly feminized degree programs like early childhood education. Although Allie found plenty of employment opportunities upon graduating, she acquired only limited skills and knowledge in her two-year program. The skills that she acquired prepared her for caregiving work, which, although abundant in opportunity, provides very little in terms of compensation.

Joy is particularly frustrated that her postgraduate degree provides her with a sense of educational accomplishment, yet is not providing her with access to an adequate income despite the social importance of the work. For Allie and Joy, there exists a disjuncture between educational attainment, income, and social mobility. In a feminized occupation such as early childhood education, even a graduate degree rarely provides access to high-income jobs. On the other hand, Sam has been able to succeed economically, attaining a middle-class income with his factory and custodial jobs. Although he has rarely used the knowledge gained from his experience in a relatively expensive certification program at a local for-profit college, he has succeeded in finding and obtaining jobs that provide a middle-class income in two different masculinized fields.

Researchers have long noted the disparate economic returns for students graduating from distinctively feminized or masculinized programs and entering into male- or female-dominated occupations (Charles and Grusky 2004; England 1982, 2010; England and Li 2006; Jacobs 1996). Although women have outnumbered men receiving college degrees since the mid-1980s, women's average incomes remain significantly lower than men's in part because traditionally female-dominated occupations, such as nursing, child care, and teaching, are on average compensated less than traditionally male-dominated occupations, such as construction, computer information technology, and engineering. England (2010) notes that although women have been steadily moving into many traditionally male-dominated programs and professions—including business, medicine, and law—men have not countered by moving into traditionally female-dominated professions. Further, such movement is very much class defined, with middle- and upper-class women more likely to move into male-dominated fields than are working class women. England in part explains this class difference among women as being a result of opportunity—that is, middle- and upper-class women have no other means of social mobility and so feel pressed to move into male-dominated fields in order to advance economically, whereas working-class women can move into higher-status women-dominated occupations, such as nursing or teaching. Collectively this research reveals how gender and culture are firmly entrenched in perpetuating income inequalities.

For all three of these students, the actual relationship between education, skills, degrees, jobs, and income is far from straightforward, a fact belied by cultural logics and political rhetoric that reductively promotes education as a solution to poverty and unemployment. And as was highlighted in chapter 4, an alternative logic regarding the relationship between education and social status emerges—Sam, in particular, is highly cognizant of the cultural value of earning a degree and, like most practical explorers, is motivated by a desire not only to gain skills but also to gain status and respect in his family and community. He admits, "I push my kids to do the best that they can as far as their education," and he accomplishes this in part by role modeling as a student parent, demonstrating that he is adamant about not being a "statistic."

To deepen our understanding of the differences reflected in these students' education and job trajectories, I turn to the work of sociologists and educational researchers who have long been critical of unidimensional framings and cultural logics connecting education, job skills, and the economy. Their arguments and theories help us to understand the diverse social functions of contemporary colleges and universities, functions that are rarely if ever mentioned in public debates regarding the future of higher education. Nonetheless, evidence of these rarely articulated functions permeates these students' stories, emerging as common threads weaving together elements of these narratives. Only then can we understand why these student parents and *we* continue to believe in the power of education to alter their future opportunities.

It's the Economy: The Credentialing Function

In the latter part of the twentieth century, Ivar Berg (1971) and Randall Collins (1979) were but two scholars offering critical perspectives in response to the emergence of an expansive system of public colleges and universities. Specifically, Berg and Collins sought to expose colleges' legitimizing functions in the economy as those institutions became increasingly influential.[3] As described in chapter 2, these scholars rejected economists' "human capital" theories that primarily conceive of education as an investment in one's future occupation, focusing on "output" and higher earnings.[4] Berg (1971), in *Education and Jobs*, and Collins (1979), in *The Credential Society*, instead contend that the human capitalists' central claim that colleges and universities are providing students with technical knowledge and skills for jobs is for the most part a social fiction. That is, the skills and knowledge one needs for most jobs in the contemporary economy could, and often are, much more efficiently taught in the workplace itself.

Collins and Berg argue that in lieu of providing job skills and training, colleges and universities serve a credentialing function, signaling to the larger community, including potential employers, degree-holders' positions within the educational and, hence, social hierarchy. The degree itself and the general cultural competence that various degrees are presumed to reflect is of much more relevance than any supposed job skills acquired while in school. In the end, this credentialing function feeds a system fundamentally based on status hierarchies, creating competition and social inequality between the credentialed and the lesser credentialed or noncredentialed.

Within this "contest mobility" system (Collins 1979), students primarily strive to attain the next degree level, at the highest-prestige institution, with fewer and fewer students moving up the degree ladder at each level. Collins further contends that from an institutional perspective, because the degree level is more important than the actual program content, the educational curriculum in all higher-education institutions and programs is likely to become similar in general content over time. Unlike in a country such as Germany, where students remain on a single educational track beginning at age thirteen or fourteen, directing them to either vocational or academic studies, students in the United States can ostensibly move between institutions and tracks, changing their college or program based on the openings and opportunities available (Brint 2017).[5] As a result, even professional and technical colleges in the United States offer a core general education curriculum that promises to provide students with the knowledge necessary to access the next level of degree available.

In sum, within a system of higher education like that which has developed in the United States, the particular program in which one enrolls or the specific curriculum of an institution is often less important than the prestige of the institution and the level of degree an individual attains. Certainly, some educational programs are more skills or knowledge based, and specific training may be required for entry and success, particularly as an individual moves up the degree ladder. Medical students will have to acquire basic knowledge in anatomy, senior-level engineering students will have to survive physics, and elementary school student teachers will have to learn classroom management skills so that they can become credentialed. However, the U.S. system of higher education is structured in such a way that movement between programs is eminently possible—a student possessing a bachelor's degree in English may certainly apply to medical school, and a student with a bachelor's degree in philosophy can gain entry into a master's in a social work program.[6] Although admissions committees may express preferences for certain degrees from particular institutions and some fundamental courses may be required for entry into more technical programs, ultimately the universal basic criterion is that students are credentialed at the lower level before they are allowed to move a level higher.

Ostensibly, the flexibility reflected in the U.S. credentialing system of higher education allows for students' growth, change, and upward social mobility in an economy that is ever evolving as a result of technological advances. But is the educational system as open and flexible as it appears and is it providing for socioeconomic opportunity?

Most of the student parents participating in this study tend to articulate their perspectives regarding the purpose of education using the rhetoric of human capital theories and credentialing. They discuss the specific skills that they hoped to acquire and generally accept the idea that a college degree is necessary for their career and attaining advantageous jobs. As I argued earlier in the chapter, discourse that equates education with job preparation is readily available for appropriation. Therefore, it is unsurprising that students like Allie and Sam attempt to articulate their motivations for pursuing their degrees by turning to talk of job skills and human capital. Even when some of Sam's colleagues talk about the "uselessness" of the knowledge acquired from attending college and their degrees, Sam is convinced that the degree that he is pursuing is worthwhile. Sam is committed to his education and values the prospect of earning a credential that will allow him to work as a physical therapist. Further, like many fellow practical explorers, he is eager to achieve the social status of being a college graduate and joining the college "club."

However, this credentialing system when understood in the context of human capital theories that focus on individuals and their choices masks some troublesome facts about higher education in the contemporary economy. One, because the number and proportion of high-status positions in any economy is finite, it is simply not possible for every credentialed individual to attain a politically or economically elite position. In 1979, Collins contended that as the system of higher education expanded, both access increased and the number of credentialed individuals grew. Suddenly jobs that historically had not required a college degree could now limit the pool of applicants to those possessing at least a few years of postsecondary education. Such was the case when Collins was writing in the depressed economy of the late 1970s, and with income inequality growing over the past four decades, such is the case today (see for example Armstrong and Hamilton 2013; Mullen 2010; Stuber 2011). Contemporary economists have determined that due to the growing bifurcation of the job market into high-paying and low-paying positions, those graduates who do not land high-status positions are increasingly likely to end up needing a degree to obtain low-paying, service-sector jobs as middle-paying, white-collar jobs slowly disappear (Autor and Dorn 2013).

We see these effects playing out in Allie's and Joy's cases described earlier—their jobs in child care that in prior years required only a high school degree now require additional credentials in many states. In Connecticut, legislation passed in 2011 mandates that by 2020 all lead teachers working in early childhood education classrooms in centers that receive any form of state funding must possess a bachelor's degree. The intent of these changes is to ensure an educated workforce is teaching our youngest children, thereby providing a high-quality early education experience. As a means of steadily working toward that 100 percent goal, by 2017, half of all lead teachers were expected to possess a bachelor's degree (Connecticut Office of Early Childhood 2017). Although most centers reached this goal, corresponding wage increases were not required nor evident in this feminized field that is already marked by low pay (Institute of Medicine and National Research Council 2015). In other words, educational expectations have increased but wages have remained relatively stagnant for many jobs at the lowest end of the pay scale.

Another consequence of such a credentialing system, along with popular discourse and cultural logics that emphasize human capital, is that they together mask failures of the economy and job market by directing attention to individual choices and achievements. Failures of the economy are instead perceived as failures of individuals who lack educational preparation. As alluded to earlier in this chapter and outlined in chapter 2, U.S. and global economies have changed dramatically over the course of the past century. Contemporary economists have noted that job growth is occurring in the highest- and lowest-paid fields, whereas jobs in the middle, both in the blue- and white-collar sectors, are being replaced by computerization and outsourcing (Autor and Dorn 2013; Autor, Katz, and Kearney 2006).[7] Many jobs that previously provided middle-class wages that were defined by "routine tasks," such as organizing or manipulating objects or information, have been replaced by technology. Factory workers and bookkeepers are but two examples of the types of jobs that have decreased in number in the United States due to a combination of sourcing out their labor to other countries or replacing or dramatically changing their labor with technology (Autor and Dorn 2013). In sum, many middle-income jobs are disappearing. Although the net returns in regard to job opportunities and income cannot be guaranteed, employers, politicians, and higher-education institutions themselves nonetheless promote education as the primary means by which an individual can stem the tide of underemployment or unemployment. It is simply easier to assign responsibility or blame to individuals and their educational choices than to censure and alter the course of an entire economic system.

We need only look back at the case of Sam to see how these trends and forces can play out in a person's life. Sam's experiences clearly reveal the mismatch between the skills he acquired from his expensive twelve-month program and the jobs he eventually took on throughout his career. It's not clear that Sam's certification is paying off in quite the way that many human capital theorists might predict or that he expected. The skills that he needed to succeed as a machine operator and school custodian were primarily acquired on the job and not in the classroom of the costly, for-profit technical institute that he attended. This is not to say that the certification he received was of no value; he likely obtained transferable skills—for example, general problem-solving, basic writing, technical, or management skills—that will benefit him in any career that he pursues. And most importantly he has that paper, that degree. If we are to accept Collins's claim regarding the credentialing function of education, we would also conclude that Sam's certification is primarily valuable not because of the skills he acquired but because of the status that certification imparts when Sam competes for access to jobs. Compared to individuals lacking any sort of degree or certification, his HVACR certification may confer an advantage.

Although Sam is fortunate to have been able to sustain a solidly middle-class lifestyle—he describes his two-car garage and pool as personal accomplishments symbolizing his economic success—his career trajectory reveals the difficulty of maintaining that success, particularly at a historical moment when factories in the United States are more likely to close their doors than open them and many middle-class white- and blue-collar jobs are disappearing due to advances in technology. The degree that he is now pursuing will provide him with access to a white-collar job that requires interpersonal rather than routinized manual skills, a job that he hopes will provide not only a middle-class income but also increased job stability. Physical therapists can't be outsourced overseas in quite the same way as factory workers.

In becoming a physical therapist, however, Sam will forgo the stability that his current union provides in regard to health and retirement benefits. Bivens et al. (2014) argue that men's declining wages since the late 1970s are in part a result of the declining real value of the federal minimum wage and diminished bargaining power of unions across the United States. Even though the U.S. economy has steadily grown, inequality has increased between the nation's highest and lowest earners, and men's wages have declined significantly. Between 1979 and 2013, productivity grew by 64.9 percent yet median wages grew by only 0.2 percent annually for the same time period, with much of that growth going to the top 5 percent of workers and the bottom 70 percent experiencing either flat or falling wages (Bivens et al. 2014). Sam hopes that should he end up working in a hospital, his income and benefits will remain competitive with his current collectively bargained salary and benefits. He is entering into a steadily growing field—the U.S. Department of Labor's Bureau of Labor Statistics (2018b) predicts 28 percent growth in the need for physical therapists between 2016 and 2026. With this associate's degree, Sam will certainly be able to obtain a job that is less physically demanding than his current position as a public school maintenance worker, but it is far from clear whether or not his salary and benefits package will improve as he will not likely be unionized.

Sam, unlike Allie and Joy, has undoubtedly benefited from the higher pay that defines many masculinized occupations (Charles and Grusky 2004; Padavic and Reskin 2002). The number of pink-collar jobs in child care, for example, has steadily increased over the years (U.S. Department of Labor, Bureau of Labor Statistics 2018b), but as Allie's and Joy's experiences reveal, college degrees in this field of study do not neatly translate into economic success. For Allie and Joy, there is no mismatch between the skills acquired in school and the skills that they needed in their jobs—in their case, human capital theorists' arguments provide only limited understanding of the complex gendered institutional dynamics that shape economic opportunity. The skills that they acquired in school are necessary, but the feminized jobs that they were prepared for in college do not provide an income and benefits necessary to acquire middle-class status. In 2017, the median annual income for child care workers in the United States was $22,290, well below the poverty threshold for a family of four (U.S. Census Bureau 2018; U.S. Department of Labor, Bureau of Labor Statistics 2018b). In 2017, the median annual income for child care workers in Connecticut was $26,000, and many of those workers, like child care workers across the nation, are not unionized and often make so little as to qualify for public support programs that provide cash or food assistance (U.S. Department of Labor, Bureau of Labor Statistics 2018a; Whitebook, Phillips, and Howes 2014). The jobs that they have been prepared for in school simply do not provide the income necessary for economic stability much less social mobility.

In all these cases—Sam's, Allie's, and Joy's—these parents' job opportunities and experiences were shaped by many more factors than merely their educational achievements. When their jobs failed to provide an adequate income or simply disappeared, education alone could not ameliorate their job situations. All three of these student parents believe that continuing to further their education will alleviate some of the difficulties that they have experienced in the job market thus far. The statistics seem to bear this out, and that is the message promoted all around them that they have come to accept as true, even though their past experiences reveal the relationship between education, skills, and jobs to be far from simple or direct.

Implications of Starting Over

Another key takeaway from a close examination of these three students' life stories is how frequently students move in and out of institutions of higher education. They share stories of needing a break from school or of having children, expectedly or sometimes unexpectedly, and deciding to forgo higher education to focus instead on family and paid work. Some chose the military or pursued certifications in vocations such as cosmetology or business travel. Others went straight to four-year colleges and ended up dropping out for one reason or another. And others went on to community colleges and sought associate's degrees in disciplines including early childhood education, liberal studies, or computer information systems. Most of them completed degrees or certifications at each step along the way, but some left without any terminal degree and often with some debt.

The model of education envisioned by Truman's President's Commission on Higher Education, which allows for free community college with the opportunity to transfer to a four-year regional university, would actually work for many of these student parents. We see that with Sam and Allie, who have decided to build on their prior education to address their new occupational goals. We also see that the credentialing system is working for Joy, in that she too is building on prior credentials to attain her occupational goal of working as a middle school counselor. Having that undergraduate degree under her belt is helping Joy to move forward more quickly than if she had never received that credential.

However, Allie and Sam both spent time and money taking classes that are not necessary given their current career goals. As stated earlier, Sam could have paid for a four-year college degree at a public university for the money he spent on his HVACR certification at a local for-profit postsecondary institution. And when Allie transferred to a four-year public university, many of the credits earned at the flagship university she attended fifteen years ago and for her associate's degree in early childhood education did not transfer. The transfer and articulation relationships between these three public systems—the flagship university, the public regional universities, and the community colleges—were not streamlined at the time Allie chose to return for her most recent degree. As a result, she took and paid for many classes over the course of the past fifteen years that she believes were "not necessary" for her current criminology degree. Now, some of those classes may indeed be unnecessary and part of an outdated curriculum.

But some of those "not necessary" classes may have nonetheless imparted soft skills, like communication or collaboration, or knowledge that may not be directly related to her criminology degree but that provides her with a deeper understanding about history, human behavior, or world cultures. All of that said, Allie has not been prohibited from changing her career direction and is able to apply some of those past classes to her new program of study. Although, she believes that the process of transferring classes could be improved, Allie is ultimately benefiting from the flexibility afforded by a system of higher education that allows for program change over an extended period of time.

Advertisements for credentialing programs in higher education, particularly for-profit institutions, often target older adults, encouraging them to take control of their future and return to school to improve their skills and marketability. Because many of those programs are expensive and often result in students' incurring relatively high levels of debt, as compared to their public counterparts, and because some of those programs are unaccredited, researchers and legislators have argued quite forcefully for increased federal monitoring of predatory, for-profit institutions.[8]

In response to such calls, the U.S. Department of Education (2015b) under the Obama administration implemented regulations requiring for-profit and certificate-granting postsecondary institutions to publicly report retention, student loan debt, and job placement information. As noted in the analysis earlier in this chapter, retention and job placement statistics are certainly imperfect measures to assess the U.S. educational system's success as a whole, but this information at least provides some transparency regarding students' potential debt to income ratios for individual institutions. Additionally, in 2016 the Obama administration finalized regulations that broadened the legal rights of students who had acquired school loan debt from for-profit colleges that had intentionally misled or defrauded them (U.S. Department of Education 2016).

In 2017, the Department of Education (2017b) under Betsy DeVos began to walk back these two sets of regulatory changes, delaying the requirement for for-profit institutions to report retention and gainful employment statistics and "pausing" the implementation of the borrower defense regulations designed to protect students from predatory for-profit institutions. In 2018, DeVos announced that the Department of Education will begin the process of eliminating the requirement that only for-profit institutions report retention and gainful employment data and that they be punished by losing federal funding if their student debt to income ratios are deemed too high. DeVos argues in part that such reporting resulted in the stigmatizing of for-profit career and vocational postsecondary institutions (Green 2018). Legislators and researchers will be watching carefully to see how such "pauses" and rollbacks will play out in future months and years.

With student debt reaching new highs, the concerns about predatory, for-profit colleges and institutions are warranted, and policymakers and legislators should certainly heed those social forces that have influenced the growth of the for-profit sector in recent decades. According to a U.S. Senate 2012 report from the Health, Education, Labor and Pensions Committee, the recent surge in growth of for-profits is a result of two factors: (1) "an era of drastic cutbacks in State funding for higher education" and (2) "an enormous growth in non-traditional students—those who either delayed college, attend part-time or work full-time while enrolled, are independent of their parents, or have dependents other than a spouse" (p. 1). This second point is no doubt heavily influenced by a conflu-ence of social and economic trends that explain why Allie, Sam, and Joy are back in school: gendered jobs, gender inequalities, outsourcing, the demise of labor, and technological advances. As cited previously in chapter 2, community col-leges were conceived to address the diverse needs of local communities, but in the wake of growing economic inequality and disinvestment in public educa-tion, community colleges have been hurt hard by state cuts to their funding. As a result, community colleges have not been provided with the resources neces-sary to keep up with their for-profit counterparts, which recruit aggressively and charge significantly higher tuition, charging on average four times the tuition of comparable programs at community colleges (U.S. Senate 2012).

In order to increase financially sound choices for all students, researchers and progressive legislators in recent years have called for reinvestment in our nation's public colleges and universities (Mettler 2014; Zornick 2017). They argue that community colleges should be provided with the resources they need so that they can work intensively both with local employers to provide the skill training that is needed in particular employment sectors and with local four-year colleges and universities to provide opportunities for further educational advancement for those students who choose a more traditional academic path (Mettler 2014). Programs like those implemented by Tennessee governor Bill Haslam, which inspired President Obama's America's College Promise initiatives in 2015, begin to address rising student debt by rewarding community college students with good grades by covering their tuition. In recent years, several cit-ies and states, from San Francisco to Rhode Island, have passed legislation promising free community college for their residents, and some states have implemented or are exploring offering tuition-free four-year degrees as well.[9]

In creating tuition-free programs, however, we must acknowledge the diverse life trajectories, particularly of older students and student parents. We must acknowledge that not every college student enters right out of high school and not every student moves seamlessly through an associate or baccalaureate program in two or four years, respectively. Many of the free community college programs that are cropping up across the country place limitations on qualify-ing applicants, restricting the opportunity to only low-income students, recent high school graduates, or first-time college applicants (Kobosco 2017; O'Brien 2017). Imposing such restrictions may make short-term financial sense for administrators, since many of those younger students are less likely to have familial obligations that might interrupt their progression through a program of study. But it also ensures that older students, who are more likely to be parents and caregivers, cannot access financial resources that will aid them as they work to complete previously unfinished degrees. Students like Allie and Sam, who are among those who possess the lowest levels of credentials in my study, would not qualify. And student parents, as these stories clearly show, are often highly invested in the future of their families. With the costs of tuition steadily increasing, potentially denying them these opportunities would be a mistake.

POPULAR DISCOURSE and cultural logics that highlight the role of higher education in the twenty-first century all too frequently devolve into narrow discussion that focuses on jobs, skills, and the economy. The stories of these three students, however, make clear that the relationships between education, skills, jobs, and economic success are often tenuous and varied. The stories shared here reveal how the relationship between higher education and jobs is more complicated than is often relayed in aggregate statistics correlating degree levels and income. Numerous social factors—including but certainly not limited to economic and manufacturing trends, gendered industries, gender inequalities, the demise of labor unions, outsourcing, and changes in technology—have collectively shaped Allie's, Joy's, and Sam's job opportunities.

As described earlier in this chapter, the prevailing instrumentalist discourse that pushes individuals to pursue higher levels of education too often displaces critical discourse of the contemporary economy.[10] It is simply easier to blame individuals' lack of education for their failures in the job market than to target complex economic shifts or deeply rooted gendered inequalities that may shape an individual's job trajectory. In this way, the inequities of our current economic system are hidden in plain sight under a blanket call for more education. And then when postsecondary institutions fail to provide immediate access to jobs, individuals and schools are often blamed for not meeting the needs of an ever-changing, overwhelmingly service-oriented economy.

It is important to note that, with the exception of the job seekers, most of these student parents turn to cultural logics that reveal that they expect more from their education than merely jobs and skills. Some of them yearn for the credential and status of being college graduates and the respect that is accorded that status in their families and communities. Some are interested in acquiring social and cultural capital that allows them to participate more fully in their social world, sharing their understanding of history, literature, economics, or politics. Others are merely curious and eager to be intellectually challenged, while advancing their and their family's opportunity for upward social mobility. As described in chapters 4 and 5, the meaning and value of a college education vary significantly for these forty student parents, and so public colleges and universities are tasked with addressing these students' diverse needs and expectations.

However, one thing is clear. Higher education by itself cannot solve the troubles inherent in our current economy. No amount of early childhood education will change the economic prospects for graduates in that field. As multiple prior researchers have determined, the system of higher education is fraught with inequalities (Armstrong and Hamilton 2013; McMillan Cottom 2017; Mullen 2010; Stuber 2011). Earning a degree may not fully redress the problem of growing inequality, but these student parents want that degree anyway. When these student parents are able to go to school without incurring high levels of debt, they believe their lives to be better. The practical explorers and self-reflective learners engage in learning that they believe expands their understanding of themselves and the world and positively influences their parenting. Ultimately, these student parents value the opportunity to start over, to finish, or to continue on an educational path of their choosing.

Historically, state colleges and universities provided an affordable option for students to pursue their goals. However, in recent decades we have seen steady disinvestment in our public institutions, so their costs keep rising and students are forced to dig deep into their pockets, often relying on loans to gain entry into the collegiate club. A student used to be able to choose to attend college for a variety of personal and professional reasons, but we are increasingly living in an era where a degree cannot promise social mobility and is becoming prohibitively costly. We have to ask ourselves as a nation, are we willing to continue moving in this direction?

7

"It's a Marathon, Not a Sprint"

Final Thoughts

> The mission of liberal learning in higher education should be to teach students to liberate, animate, cooperate, and instigate. Through doubt, imagination and hard work, students come to understand that they really can reshape themselves and their societies.
>
> –Michael S. Roth, *Beyond the University* (2014: 195)

In 1946, Truman's President's Commission on Higher Education was asked to determine "the functions of higher education in our democracy and of the means by which they can best be performed." Now, over seventy years later, it is again worth our tackling this task. College campuses are very different places than they were in the immediate wake of World War II. The substantial investment in public colleges and universities and advances in technology have made it possible to find a college classroom within miles of one's home or even within the confines of one's living room on a computer with internet access. We are caught in a moment of history when higher education is not only accessible but seemingly expected of nearly anyone seeking at least middle-class status. A college degree denotes both success and achievement of the American Dream, as young and older returning parents are enrolling in postsecondary programs with the hopes of improving their future opportunities. Even as tuition costs spiral upward, the student parents who are the focus of this study have decided to seek out those educational opportunities that are available to them.

However, as many researchers in recent decades have made clear and as this study affirms, not all students are benefiting from increased access. Not all students who enter college end up graduating, and too many students accrue high levels of debt with no credential to attest to their educational experience. The student parents whom I interviewed have decided to attend community colleges and state universities that are geographically close to their homes. Unfortunately, the retention rates at these public colleges and universities are often lower than those at private nonprofit colleges, which as a group are not only the most difficult colleges to get into but also some of the most expensive colleges to attend. That said, the retention rates at public colleges and universities are higher than their usually more expensive, private for-profit college counterparts (U.S. Department of Education 2016). As a result, public colleges serve as a reliable "in between" option—they are convenient and comparably affordable for student parents or any students who are dependent on familial or local resources as they pursue their degrees.

The sociocultural analysis shared in these pages reveals just how students' processes of meaning making are influenced by cultural logics and social institutions that enable or constrain student parents as they navigate complex gender, familial, and educational terrains. When cultural logics fail students, they sometimes reject those logics and seek out alternatives, as we saw with Cynthia and Nicole, who supplanted the logic of human capital and skills with that of credentialing hoops. We also see quite clearly how contemporary cultural logics regarding the purpose of higher education and the social value of caregiving, domestic, or educational labor, as well as student parents' access to key resources, such as child care, financial aid, and academic and emotional support shape their educational journeys.

If student parents are to reap the potential benefits of a college education, however, several key issues need to be addressed. First, to ensure students' access *and* success, colleges must accommodate the unique needs of diverse student populations, including students caring for children and family members, providing them with the child care and parenting resources that they need to thrive and graduate. Ultimately, these student parents show us how we might challenge old logics to make way for new narratives that allow for a more extensive understanding of education and for the possibility of greater gender equality in the home. If we enable them to attain their educational and parenting goals, we are helping them to fulfill their desire to become better students and better mothers and fathers. Second, we need to ensure not only that students can apply to college but that they can afford such an education without encumbering staggering debt. To that end, postsecondary administrators need to work with legislators to ensure adequate funding for public colleges and universities, which are increasingly underfunded and becoming out of reach for too many students. We also need to address the economic reality of a bifurcating job market that is with each passing year offering up more and more positions that do not pay a living wage and in which procuring adequate health care, housing, and child care is becoming increasingly costly. The effects of gendered industries, the demise of labor unions, outsourcing, and changes in technology have collectively produced rampant social inequalities and limit economic opportunity, particularly for those in the middle and at the bottom of the social hierarchy. Finally, we need to acknowledge students' varying expectations regarding the purpose of higher education and to provide viable curricular and degree options that allow for flexibility and personal growth, all while increasing economic and social opportunity. In the sections that follow, I describe these three points in more detail.

Reshaping Gender, Family, and College

While pursuing their educational goals, many of these parents are reconceptualizing what it means to be a mother or father and to value caregiving, household, and educational labor. When student and parent responsibilities collide, these collisions can produce discord or surprisingly harmonic opportunities. In some contexts, student parents perceive no such discordance between their student and parent identities. They are proud to be both students and parents and see these identities as complementary—being a student can make them a better, more informed parent, and being a parent has the potential to make them a better, more focused student. As such, they are challenging the logic of separate spheres and transforming our understanding of college, work, and family.

This is not to say that their responsibilities as students and parents do not at times cause tension in their lives. When resources are tight—child care falls through, bills need to be paid, available time is short—or when support from one's family member or professor is waning, then student parents may experience conflict. However, when students know that their children are well cared for and safe, and when family members help them with household chores or professors at least recognize if not accommodate their needs as parents, they are more likely to feel that their parent and student identities are legitimized and respected. When family and friends understand the value of their educational labor and when professors and college administrators acknowledge the value of their caregiving labor, student parents are less likely to feel disconnected and more likely to weave these identities into a coherent whole.

At school, student parents bring to the classroom life experiences that have the potential to enhance their learning and increase their motivation. Older students, in particular, describe how they are better situated than they were when they were seventeen or eighteen years old to make sense of the historical, political, philosophical, and scientific knowledge presented in the classroom and connect it to their experiences in their families, work places, and communities. And at home, these student parents' college experiences are providing them with opportunities to model parenting and student behaviors that they hope will shape the life course transitions and trajectories of their children. In some cases, their children join them at the dining room table to do homework, while others describe how their learning influences their parenting choices and styles. Just as the women hospital workers interviewed by Garey (1999) engaged in strategies of being that provided a means to weave together their worker and parent identities, these student parents show us how they too are merging their student and parent identities. They see their successes as students being very much connected to their successes as parents.

Additionally, these student parents reveal how the structure and demands of their student lives result in their challenging traditional gender norms and reshaping the dynamics of gendered labor in their households. When heterosexual, partnered mothers return to college, life in their household and for their male partners changes in sometimes dramatic ways. Whether these mothers were formally employed or not before entering college, they are now less likely to be available to cook meals, clean the house, or care for children. Fathers and older children, both sons and daughters, are frequently asked to step up and contribute to more of the household and caregiving labor in the home. Mothers describe how, in asking fathers to increase their share of such labor, they are encouraging their partners to reconceptualize what it means to be a good father and to model good fathering to their children. At the same time, these mothers are redefining what it means to be a good mother, which means for them expanding their cultural understanding of good mothering to include letting dad take on more of the emotion work at home while mom is being a student and engaging in educational labor.

On the other hand, some of these fathers who are going back to school find that their masculinity is challenged as they in some cases relinquish breadwinning roles to focus on their education. Extended family members, and partners in particular, may not be supportive when fathers decide to forgo the short-term economic benefits of a job for the long-term benefits of a college degree. Like the student mothers described earlier in this chapter, these fathers are challenging their partners, family members, and friends to value their educational, caregiving, and household labor in ways that conceptualize masculinity more broadly. They want their work at school and at home to be legitimized and acknowledged as good fathering.

These student parents additionally reveal how organizational cultural shapes and is shaped by social institutions. Carolyn speaks for many student parents when she calls for a deeper "understanding" of caregivers' needs on campus. We can begin to create "understanding" by addressing the ways policies, procedures, and culture function on college campuses and in social service offices, shaping the daily experiences of students who are parents. Because 26 percent of undergraduate students identify as caregivers for children under the age of eighteen, we cannot afford to ignore their needs (Gault et al. 2014). They are a significant and important student demographic that is too often invisible in much discourse about higher education. Through examining these parents' experiences, we are presented with opportunities for change that might result in their feeling more accepted and less ostracized on campus.

These student parents are engaged in the hard work of negotiating cultural change, embracing, rejecting, and modifying cultural logics in ways that best suit their sense of self at a particular moment in time. Further, their processes of reevaluation and reconstruction are fundamentally affected by the cultural logics available to them and of the various structural resources that influence those opportunities and choices. From this research, we gain insight as to how state policy, postsecondary institutions, and individuals are challenging or reinforcing cultural logics and organizational norms within higher education. Most of these student parents publically share their parental status on campus only when their responsibility as a parent comes in conflict with their student identity. Sometimes, upon "outing" themselves as parents, they find that their professors, administrators, and staff respond by providing additional support, as occurred in Dave's case with his athletic coach. Other times they are told that they must adapt to the existing organizational structure as occurred with Lucille, who left the social work program in part due to class scheduling conflicts with her son's school drop-off hours. In both cases, these students, like many other student parents, are very much aware of their outsider status and feel that the overall culture of many college campuses and social service offices does not fully acknowledge their specific needs as parents who are students.

As described earlier, a predominant theme that emerged from my analysis of these stories is students' feeling of displacement. In the welfare office, in the financial aid office and on campuses where child care and the presence of children are nonexistent or minimal, these students are highly cognizant of their "nontraditional" status. If colleges and universities were to provide priority registration, flexible scheduling, sufficient and affordable child care facilities, and study hall or group meeting opportunities for student parents, these institutions would be publicly affirming these mothers' and fathers' parenting and student identities and reaffirming the democratic purpose of our nation's institutions of higher education.

Some universities are already doing this extraordinarily well. The Keys to Degrees Program at Endicott College in Massachusetts, for example, provides comprehensive wraparound services that include family housing, counseling, parenting workshops, academic tutoring, mentoring, and child care for single parents who are pursuing their baccalaureate degrees. Across the country, Portland State University hosts a Resource Center for Students with Children. The center is housed in the Student Union in the middle of campus and provides counseling, peer groups, workshops, academic advising, and information about child care resources on campus, both full-time and subsidized drop-in emergency care. Many student parents actually work in the center, which is funded through student activity fees.

Importantly, both of these college programs provide campus-based child care. However, as funds for public colleges and universities dwindle, campus-based resources are some of the first programs to go, and campus-based child care is no exception. As reported in chapter 3, the number of campus-based child care centers has decreased precipitously since the 2008 recession (Gault et al. 2014). One way to avert this trend would be for the federal government to reinvest in the Child Care Access Means Parents in School Program, which was established during the reauthorization of the Higher Education Act in 1998 and provides grants to colleges and universities to fund child care centers for student parents. Unfortunately, support for this program has been stagnant for most of its twenty years. The CCAMPIS program was defunded by 35 percent in 2003 and remained at the same funding level, on average between $15 and $16 million, for the next fourteen years. In 2017, the secretary of education, Betsy DeVos, included the CCAMPIS program on her list of programs to be eliminated, but in 2018 legislators ensured that the program was not only retained but doubly funded (Dzigbede and Bronstein 2017; Kreighbaum 2018). Although this recent funding move is promising for centers and parents who have long advocated for increased resources for child care, it is clear that the future of this grant program hangs in the balance and remains highly competitive as the demand for affordable child care dramatically outweighs the supply. Policymakers, campus-based child care providers, and parents will be watching.

The unstable funding of campus-based child care is concerning on a number of fronts. On-campus child care centers provide not only important caregiving services for parents but also often serve as an academic and research resource for faculty and students in disciplines as varied as early childhood education, psychology, social work, and nursing. They also have the potential to serve as a central networking site for parents on campus. These centers become places where parents meet and learn about other resources that are available to them on campus or in their communities (Small 2010). Finally, the symbolic role of such centers cannot be underestimated. Seeing children on campus communicates a message to faculty, staff, and students that children and families are valued in the larger campus community.

If student parents are to feel that they belong on campus, thereby increasing their likelihood of returning to school and graduating, faculty, staff, and administrators need to acknowledge and affirm their parental identities. Providing high-quality, flexible, affordable, and dependable child care allows student parents to engage with the campus community and to succeed academically. As outlined earlier, these students are not interested in the online programs available to them that are aggressively marketed to student parents and adult students. Until our social institutions adapt to the complex needs of families and caregivers, we will not fully redress the socioeconomic and gender inequalities that persistently plague our communities (Williams 2000). At the very least, legislators and campus administrators need to advocate for increased and steady funding of the CCAMPIS program and for increased comprehensive child care and drop-in care on their campuses. Ultimately, these student parents' responses highlight the ways institutions and organizations can simultaneously promote academic success and inclusivity, all while communicating symbolically an institution's commitment to supporting their identities as students *and* as parents, improving our campuses for all.

Making College Affordable

It is a fact of our times that funding has declined significantly for the public colleges and universities where these student parents are enrolled. Simultaneously, financial aid covers less of the cost of our nation's public colleges with each passing year. As more and more students are attending college, the proportion of state dollars contributed per student has declined 23 percent since the recession in 2008, and colleges have had to accommodate these cuts through cutting services and increasing tuition (Mitchell, Palacios, and Leachman 2014). All students attending public colleges and universities are hit hard by increasing tuition, but students attending community colleges and regional comprehensive state universities have been hit the hardest. In 2013, nearly 50 percent of the students attending Connecticut's flagship research university took out federal loans as did 60 percent of the students attending one of the state's four regional comprehensive universities. As college tuitions rise, many students, particularly those who work while also relying on loans, are increasingly likely to find themselves deciding how best to use their limited time—studying for an impending exam or sacrificing hours at work, which they need so that they can pay for the next term's tuition.

Those student parents most affected by the diminishing value of financial aid resources are low-income parents, who are disproportionately single parents, racial or ethnic minorities, and women. Restrictive social welfare policies, in particular the decreasing access to child care subsidies or cash assistance through the Temporary Assistance for Needy Families (TANF) program, negatively impact low-income student parents' opportunities, often limiting the kinds of postsecondary education that students who are receiving public assistance can receive. Several of the student parents in this study have incomes low enough to qualify for social welfare programs that provide both cash assistance and funding for child care, but due to these programs' restrictive regulations, case managers denied these students access to cash and child care support because they are pursuing a baccalaureate degree in lieu of pursuing full-time employment.

Additionally, low-income student parents are most likely to be affected by the reduced purchasing power of federal Pell Grants and rising college tuition rates. As public colleges see their resources dwindling, the costs for a college education are passed on to individual students, and low-income parents are increasingly likely to find that they cannot afford to attend college. As described in chapter 2, these grants and loan programs were established to boost college access for low-income students. However, as Desiree's and Lucille's cases make clear, many younger, low-income parents do not qualify for these grants because their family incomes hover just above the poverty line. Also, these grants come nowhere near covering the full costs of a baccalaureate degree, even at state universities. Of the fourteen students in this study who are receiving Pell Grants, thirteen also took out Stafford Loans to subsidize their tuition and educational expenses. During the 2006–2007 academic year, when at least a quarter of these student parents were first interviewed, average annual tuition at the regional public four-year universities was $6,442—the maximum annual Pell Grant available was $4,050. Ten years later, during the 2016–2017 academic year, annual tuition had increased to $9,741, while the maximum annual Pell Grant for that same year was $5,815. Importantly most students do not receive the maximum Pell Grant amount. The average Pell Grant award in 2006–2007 was $2,482 and in 2016–2017 was $3,740, far below the cost of annual tuition for a public university in those same respective years (CCSU 2006, 2017; U.S. Department of Education 2017a).

When we examine the various financial resources that these student parents have taken advantage of, or tried to take advantage of, clear patterns emerge regarding who is most at risk of not completing their degree programs given current financial aid and college cost trends. The job seekers in this student parent sample are much more likely than both the practical explorers and the self-reflective leaners to receive Pell Grants to help finance their education As described in chapter 4, job seekers describe the value of their education primarily in terms of the improved job prospects that a college degree can provide, and they are not strongly connected to their student identities. As a result, financial and familial supports are particularly important resources for these students if they are to remain in school and complete their degrees. Undeniably, low-income job seekers who are taking out loans to finance their education and are tenuously connected to their student identities are most at risk of leaving behind their educational goals, all while acquiring potentially significant debt and no degree. As described earlier, some of those low-income student parents have already been told by social service case managers to give up on college and instead find a job doing "anything" so that they at least qualify for child care benefits. Those student parents in particular perceive that college is not expected of them.

But substantial financial support can make a difference in whether or not job seekers persist and complete their degrees. Just as Pell Grant recipients are more likely to be job seekers, so are GI Bill recipients. Five of the eight student parents who identified as veterans are job seekers, yet these student parents who have access to GI benefits to fund their college education feel that the financial aid systems in place and the campus-based offices that help them to navigate rules defining those benefits fully legitimize their student identities and foment a feeling of belonging in school. Three of these five job seekers—Jim, Lindsey, and Jess—are also taking out loans to cover costs such as rent, child care, or groceries since they are working fewer hours so that they can concentrate on their studies. Despite their weak connection to their student identities and their need to take out additional loans, their GI benefits, including tuition waivers in the state of Connecticut and living stipends, provide them with significant financial resources that keep them connected to their respective universities and in school.

In sum, tuition costs are steadily increasing, and financial aid resources are dwindling. If one does not choose a path in the armed services, lives in a state where tuition waivers are not provided, or is not fortunate enough to have ample family savings in reserve to cover the rising costs of college, then being on campus can feel more like a privilege than a right. To counter those trends, both federal and state governments need to resist trends toward austerity and instead reinvest in their public colleges and universities. Just as Truman's Commission determined back in 1948 that substantial public investment was necessary to promote democracy and increase opportunity, we now need to acknowledge that recent trends toward disinvestment in higher education are contributing to increasing inequality.

To that end, several concrete changes can stem the current tide. First, federal and state social service offices should revise TANF legal guidelines to include long-term educational plans as a viable means of fulfilling program participants' "work participation" requirements. Allowing low-income student parents to use their hours working toward their bachelor's or graduate degrees will then provide them with access to cash benefits and much-needed child care so that they can focus on completing their degrees. Doing so will not only enhance the prospect of improving their family's economic standing but will also provide them with an opportunity to serve as positive role models for their children as they daily demonstrate the value of education.

Maine's Parents as Scholars (PaS) program is already doing this. After welfare reform in 1996, the federal government fundamentally altered the Aid to Families with Dependent Children public assistance program, transforming the funding process from being federally managed into block grants that are internally controlled by each state. In the wake of those legislative changes, Maine developed the PaS program in 1997, using maintenance of effort funds so that low-income parents who had been pursuing their associate's or bachelor's degrees could continue with their education while remaining eligible for TANF benefits. Although successful in graduating thousands of parents over the years, the PaS program has faced several challenges. It has never been able to attract as many student parents as are eligible—the program is capped at two thousand participants per year but has never served more than nine hundred student parents at any one time. Adequately promoting and staffing the PaS program requires additional funding resources, but like many state governments, such resources are scant so many of Maine's leaders have been looking to downsize and not increase the state workforce. Further, because of changes resulting from TANF's reauthorization in 2005, which significantly narrowed eligible work participation activities that states can consider toward their reporting of work participation rates, students enrolled in PaS are not considered by federal funding offices as engaged in qualifying work activities. As a result, Maine has struggled to maintain the necessary work participation levels to continuously receive current block grant levels (Bone 2010). Until the federal government expands its definition of acceptable work participation activities to include all levels of higher education, states will continue to find it difficult to implement programs such as PaS.

In addition to altering welfare laws, states and the federal government need to increase resources for students to ensure that college is affordable and potentially debt-free. States, such as Tennessee and New York, and cities, including San Francisco, are already promising debt-free community college for their residents (Berndtson 2017; Siner 2017). At the time of this writing, nine states had introduced College Promise legislation in response to President Obama's proposal in 2015 that community colleges be tuition free (U.S. Department of Education 2015a). To facilitate free college, the U.S. Department of Education needs to increase Pell Grants, which have not kept up with inflation, so they at the very minimum cover the tuition costs of attending public colleges and universities. Finally, states and the federal government need to invest directly in public colleges and universities to ensure that tuition is more affordable, while maintaining a high quality of education that can compare to private for-profit and nonprofit postsecondary counterparts. Such a commitment to investment in public institutions ensures equal access without sacrificing quality of educational experiences. At various moments in U.S. history, we have committed to maintaining access and affordability of higher education—we are again at such crossroads and must decide whether or not we have the will to change our current course and reverse growing inequality.

Managing Diverse Expectations: Culture and Inequality

In this climate marked by decreasing state funds and increasing tuition and student debt, educational narratives relying on cultural logics that equate the value of college in terms of job outcomes resonate strongly with politicians, voters, and students. Politicians invoke such a narrative when presenting educational initiatives or supporting legislation that emphasize the job skills that higher education can or ought to provide. Despite the prevalence of narrow instrumentalist logics in public discourse, researchers and educational theorists studying U.S. higher education have long challenged the idea that a bachelor's degree provides job-specific skills. A college education may impart some job-specific knowledge and skills, particularly in applied fields such as nursing or engineering, but for most people and many employers a college degree more often signals possession of general knowledge, transferable skills, and status, not job-specific skills. Earning a degree allows one to enter the "club" of college graduates, signaling that one has the self-discipline to complete that degree and that one has acquired wide-ranging knowledge about the world and its processes, systems, cultures, and people. The major one selects is often less important than the prestige of one's college or university and finishing that degree.

It is true that elite colleges and universities are attractive to those who have access to them in part because their retention rates are much higher than those at nonelite universities. To a certain extent that is because those institutions are highly selective and admit only those students who are academically strong and intellectually connected to their student identities to begin with. Students attending elite colleges and universities understand that their degree will be publically and positively recognized and can provide access into circles of students and alumni from that university and from similarly elite educational institutions. Importantly, many students attending elite colleges and universities expect to go on to graduate school for more job specific training and so do not expect a curriculum or undergraduate educational experience narrowly defined by instrumentalist discourse—in fact, most elite institutions explicitly promote their commitment to a broad liberal arts curriculum (Mullen 2010).

However, the student parents interviewed for this study are not attending elite universities, and most are either not cognizant of nor concerned with the prestige of their current institution. Nonetheless, they are very much aware of the status that a college degree can confer in the economic marketplace and in their communities. The students whom I identify as job seekers are primarily concerned with the marketplace value of their college degree. They want and expect a job at the end of their educational journey and will do what they must to earn that degree. Job seekers don't talk at length, or in some cases at all, about their learning and perceive college to be an experience to "get through" in order to increase their economic standing. Cynthia contends that she sees college as "pointless" unless a student is going on to be a professor or a doctor. She continues, "For everyday skills, I don't think it's really necessary." Cynthia is generally correct in her assessment. Most job skills in most work places are attained on the job. However, Cynthia also recognizes that to escape from a life limited by low-wage labor opportunities, she is going to need a credential, not necessarily job-skill training, and so that is why she is continuing to pursue her degree.

Practical explorers likewise expect their educational experience to pay off with a job but are additionally interested in what sociologists refer to as social and cultural capital. Leslie specifically addresses the workplace benefits of acquiring cultural capital when she insists, "Having interesting things to talk about and being well spoken is going to help you in any line of work, whether you're teaching or in business or a public speaker or a professor." But Leslie also describes how earning a degree represents a personal and social accomplishment. She adds, "[Getting a degree] just gives you a sense of I've done something. I've finished. I finally completed something and earned it." Drew also discusses the opportunities to meet diverse people and develop social capital. In describing the value of going to college, he discloses, "You want to meet other people and network yourself. I mean, that's kind of a business thing, but you know, network yourself." For these practical explorers, acquiring a degree that will allow them to embark upon a career after graduation is important. However, these students are additionally motivated by their desire for the rise in status that comes along with being a member of the college "club." They come to value the learning that takes place in a classroom environment because it provides them with an opportunity to become conversant and knowledgeable about a variety of subjects while meeting diverse people as they move up the social ladder.

Finally, self-reflective learners are those students whom Michael Roth, president of Wesleyan University, would want attending his elite liberal arts college. Self-reflective learners are in college to be inspired and informed—they wish to learn more about themselves and others and to be actively involved in civil society. They wish to engage in creative and integrative thought so that they can fully understand their world and participate in it culturally, socially, and politically. Lucille explains how she values education by stressing, "It's your hope that there's a chance for the future. It's not all about just, you know, I got an A. I graduated cum laude, la dee la. Yeah. It's *so* not about that. I've realized that I really don't care what I got in class. I care if I *learned* something." These self-reflective learners are intellectually curious and passionate about expanding their understanding of life. Of all three groups, the self-reflective learners' perspectives are most in line with contemporary advocates of a liberal arts education. They are concerned with the "heart of the matter."

Of all three groups, I was most concerned about the job seekers. These job seekers are on average younger, lower in income, and more likely to be single parents than are the other students in this study and so are more likely at risk of not graduating with a degree. Those job seekers who are older, partnered, economically stable, or possess strong support systems will likely make it through—they tend to choose majors that are more applied or skill specific, such as computer information systems or criminology, and have the supports necessary to make it through to graduation. However, we ought to be concerned about those job seekers who are young, low-income, single parents, and/or lacking in support systems. It is this latter, more vulnerable group that is targeted by recent welfare reform legislation that limits the educational opportunities supported by state and federal programs to short-term or vocational degrees. As McMillan Cottom (2017) reminds us, this latter group is more likely to comprise women, minorities, and minority women, all of whom are often targeted by for-profit colleges offering "risky credentials." This latter group of job seekers is also likely to leave school altogether with no degree and likely some level of debt.

As outlined in chapter 6, job opportunities and the potential for upward economic mobility are constrained by numerous factors, including gendered economic and manufacturing trends, the demise of labor unions, and changes in technology resulting in jobs being eliminated or outsourced. In the face of these trends, earning a vocational or skills-based degree has been put forth by many policymakers as a solution to poverty, but as I reveal in chapter 6, such a solution is narrowly conceived. It is worth noting that two job seekers, Sam and Allie, took that short-term vocational route many years ago, earning associate's degrees in heating, ventilation, air conditioning, and refrigeration (HVACR) and early childhood education, respectively. Jacqueline, another job seeker and a single mom, earned a cosmetology degree back in high school. These student parents were able to obtain jobs upon graduation, but the jobs then available to them proved to be unstable, uninteresting, and/or physically demanding and are no longer what they want. Yes, we will always need plumbers and early childhood educators, but such work is physically demanding, and many entry-level technology jobs quickly change or disappear when a computer can do the job better for less money. Limiting the educational opportunities of low-income parents to a vocational education cannot solve the problems of an economy that is constantly evolving and that disproportionately serves those in its upper tiers. Certainly a vocational education is a viable and even preferable choice for some, but it should not be the only available option.

If we provide free community college as I recommend earlier, and if those community colleges can link with local industries to provide high-quality skills training, then students who prefer such an education can avoid paying tens of thousands of dollars as did Sam when he pursued HVACR certification at an expensive for-profit institution. When community colleges are provided with the necessary resources to respond efficiently to local labor market needs, those students who desire such an education and their surrounding communities can potentially thrive.

Further, we must ensure that the opportunities provided by our public colleges and universities offer flexibility so that individuals can build upon prior credentials, particularly for those graduates of programs that offer job-specific and vocational training. As described in chapter 6, it is not unusual for student parents to move in and out of higher education, and the more that colleges and universities can do to ensure that students are building upon prior knowledge and skills and moving forward, the easier it is for students to reach their educational goals. When policymakers focus merely on providing more short-term vocational or job-training programs, they too often presume that these students will not want to continue on to pursue an associate's or baccalaureate degree, and research has long documented that black, Latinx, and low-income high school students are most likely to be tracked into short-term vocational programs and targeted by for-profit colleges offering job-specific certifications or degrees (Holland and Deluca 2016; McMillan Cottom 2017). As these stories reveal, student parents seek options and should not go into debt while exploring their options.

I acknowledge that none of these solutions confronts the problems caused by the credentialing function of higher education. We can certainly advocate for increased access to debt-free higher education, but so far I have left the credentialing function itself unquestioned. As the practical explorers in particular make clear, the credentialing function of higher education is firmly embedded not only in our economy but in our culture. These practical explorers value the opportunities for personal growth and the exposure to cultural and social capital that a formal college education provides—and they recognize and value the boost in social status that possessing a college degree promises. Researchers have long shown us that there is no getting around the status hierarchies that fundamentally inform our higher education systems and the process of credentialing (Armstrong and Hamilton 2013; Berg 1971; Collins 1979; Mullen 2010). We live in a social world defined by credentialing status inequalities—graduates versus dropouts, Yalies versus state university students, vocational certifications versus academic diplomas. I am convinced that moving beyond the race for numerically more or increasingly selective credentials will require a cultural transformation that is just not possible within the current system of education.

So what can we do? Changing culture is often slow going. Yet there is a way forward, and, although difficult, change is possible: we must start with the economy. As Allie and Joy found out, their credentials in early childhood education did not lead to lucrative jobs in a pink-collar service industry plagued with low wages and few if any health or retirement benefits. Legislators and employers need to ensure that the wages and benefits provided by all jobs will indeed provide a livable wage. Until minimum wages can actually lift a family out of poverty and citizens have access to affordable health care and housing, education alone cannot be expected to solve the problems of increasingly unequal wages and benefits. To that end, we must advocate for increased federal minimum wages and stronger union representation—the Fight for $15 movement, begun in New York City in 2012, provides a pathway for creating change on these fronts.[1] Until we structure an economy that at the very least provides more equitable wages and benefits, it will be impossible to truly redress the inequalities produced by credentialing in the cultural sphere. Only when the economic gaps between those with the most and those with the least are narrowed might the cultural prestige that is associated with possessing a college degree be challenged in the larger social sphere. When students like Cynthia and Nicole, job seekers who are weary (and wary) of jumping through credentialing hoops, can access good-paying jobs without degrees, the value of those credentials will likely lessen. Inequality will not necessarily go away, but we will be closer than we are presently to creating a more just and equitable economy and society.

We must also directly confront another often unspoken cultural reality. As long as powerful positions in society are primarily held by those with elite credentials and as long as college degrees continue to be perceived as social accomplishments deserving of respect, we cannot simply encourage those who do not have access to high-prestige credentials to cease hoping to move up the credentialing ladder. Doing so only preserves those inequalities. Students like Cynthia or Nicole may well be satisfied to forgo higher education as long as their economic needs are met, but those like Leslie, a practical explorer interested in learning more so that she can feel that she has "done something" and believes that "the more education you have, the more respected you are," will likely want to continue with college. As long as a college degree denotes social status, albeit a level of status that varies according to one's local social circles as well as the larger economic and political spheres, we cannot consider solutions to address the rising cost of college that are unidimensional. We cannot focus narrowly on solutions that only conceive of postsecondary education as providing access to jobs. Good jobs are certainly an anticipated and hoped for outcome, but for most students, good jobs are but one of many expected outcomes.

We must acknowledge that students like Rose and Lucille, both self-reflective learners, gain so much more than a credential when they go back to school. Rose now has access to language and ways of meaning making that allow her to understand her husband's gambling addiction and to communicate with others about her religion and culture. Lucille continued on to earn a master's degree in higher education and, at the time of this writing, is working as a director of diversity at a flagship state university, a long way from the grocery store bakery that fired her when she was pregnant with her son. She regularly returns to the state university campus where she received her degrees and participates in community forums about student parenting and, more recently, masculinity and sexual and interpersonal violence. Rose and Lucille have earned more than credentials. Rose's daughter and young sister-in-law and Lucille's two sons are learning along with them how to navigate their student and parent lives. Rose and Lucille are empowered parents with increasingly strong voices, both at home and in their respective communities.

Ultimately, these student parents' narratives reveal that not a single discourse prevails when students begin to talk about why they are in school and what they expect from their college education. Their stories and perspectives bring to light a more nuanced and complex portrait of how culture functions in our lives and influences our understanding of the role of higher education in the twenty-first century. This finding should not be surprising. When we look back at the history, we see that the purpose of higher education has been a subject of debate for hundreds of years. However, in recent decades, instrumentalist discourse that focuses on jobs and the economy has become so central to how the purpose of higher education is conceived of and funded that alternative discourses have become marginalized in the public sphere. We have lost sight that college, like K–12 education, ought to be a public good and not a privatized privilege. Terms from the marketplace—return on investment, the bottom line—more often enter our discussions of higher education than do terms that have traditionally defined a liberal arts education—creativity, critical inquiry, and social responsibility. In such discourse, we see culture at work.

In the words of educator Mike Rose (2012), unless we expand our philosophy of education, "those seeking a second chance will likely receive a barerbones, strictly functional education, one that does not honor the many reasons they return to school and, for that matter, one not suitable for a democratic society" (pp. 185–186). In examining the experiences of student parents, we see how they are embracing, rejecting, and modifying the cultural logics available and useful to them in ways that challenge competing understandings of what it means to be a student or what it means to be a parent at this historical moment. Ultimately, this study sheds light on how culture is not only reproduced but, even more importantly, how it can evolve. When institutional factors such as flexible academic schedules alter one's ability to engage in domestic or caregiving labor at home, an opportunity for cultural change emerges. Change is not promised— the status quo is strong—but change becomes possible. Students who do not feel constrained by finances or by the pressure to become breadwinners may not find economic security to be a defining logic determining their disposition toward education.[2] Again such change is not promised but becomes possible when both institutional and cultural resources align.

ALTHOUGH THE ODDS may at times be against them, the students in this study, who represent a variety of income levels, cultural backgrounds, and family social structures, are continuing to pursue their educational goals. Importantly their experiences reveal how a commitment to reinvesting in public higher education and institutional supports can make their path at school and at home and with loved ones much easier to traverse. For many of these student parents, college can provide a way out of traditional ways of acting, thinking, and being. This is particularly true for the practical explorers and the self-reflective learners described in these pages, who are motivated by more than the promise of a credential—they desire knowledge and self-growth and find that their college learning enriches their understanding of self, their families, and their communities.

These students' varied experiences offer us new ways of understanding their evolving needs and the potential value of higher education. They provide us with understandings that are more comprehensive, creative, and inclusive of all students. Understandings that legitimize caregiving, domestic, and educational labor. Understandings that can produce greater gender equity at home, in our schools, and at work. Understandings that can improve their lives and our world.

APPENDIX

List of Student Parent Participants and Sample Demographics

List of Student Parent Participants and Sample Demographics (n = 40)

Name*	Age	Gender	Self-identified Race or Ethnicity**	Marital Status	# of Children	Age of Children	Highest Level of Degree Attained	Current Degree Program	GPA***	Financial Aid— Grants, Loans, Tax Credits
Job Seekers										
Carolyn	27	female	Hispanic	separated	2	3, 6	—	B.S. Graphic Arts Technology	3.0	Stafford Loan
Cynthia	23	female	Asian	single	1	6	A.A. Liberal Arts	B.A. Psychology	2.9	Pell Grant
Dave	20	male	Latino	cohabiting	1	1	—	B.S. Business Management	2.4	Pell Grant Athletic scholarship
Ed	23	male	white	cohabiting	2	5, 12	—	B.S. Computer Science	4.0	GI Bill
Jackie	31	female	Hispanic	single	1	7	Cert.—Cosmetology A.A. General Studies	B.S. English— Secondary Education	2.7	Pell Grant Stafford Loan
Jaime	26	female	Caucasian	cohabiting	1	1	A.A. Accounting	B.S. Accounting	—	Stafford Loan
Jess	29	female	white	married	2	4, 2	Cert.—Business Travel A.A. Emergency Management	B.S. English— Secondary Education	3.3	GI Bill Stafford Loan Pell Grant
Jim	37	male	white	married	1	5	Cert.—HVACR	B.S. Construction Management	2.5	GI Bill Stafford Loan

Lindsey	26	female	white	divorced	1	1	A.A.—Gen Studies	B.A. Education—History	3.5	GI Bill Pell Grant Stafford/ Perkins Loan
Maribel	26	female	Hispanic/ Peruvian	single	3	9, 3, 1	Cert.—Dental Assisting	B.S. Nursing	—	Pell Grant Stafford Loan
Michelle	28	female	African American	single	1	7	A.A. Criminal Justice	B.A. Criminology	2.6	GI Bill
Myia	21	female	African American	Single	1	5	—	B.A. General Studies	3.7	Pell Grant Stafford Loan
Snow	49	female	Caucasian	divorced	2	19, 13	B.A. Psychology	M.S. School Counseling	4.0	—
Victoria	19	female	Hispanic	cohabiting	1	1	—	B.A. Psychology	3.3	Pell Grant CCSU Scholarship

Practical Explorers

Allie	38	female	Caucasian	married	2	13, 9	A.A. Early Childhood Education	B.A. Criminology	3.9	CCSU Scholarship Stafford Loan
Amber	25	female	white	divorced	1	1	A.A. General Studies	B.A. English	3.8	Stafford Loan
Angie	27	female	Hispanic	married	2	5, 3	—	B.A. Psychology	3.1	Stafford Loan
Charlie	34	male	Hispanic	married	2	14, 12	—	A.A. Computer Information Systems	—	GI Bill

(continued)

List of Student Parent Participants and Sample Demographics (n = 40) (continued)

Name*	Age	Gender	Self-identified Race or Ethnicity**	Marital Status	# of Children	Age of Children	Highest Level of Degree Attained	Current Degree Program	GPA***	Financial Aid—Grants, Loans, Tax Credits
Carol	39	female	Jamaican	married	3	16, 12, 4	A.A. Early Childhood Education	B.A. Elementary Education	—	Stafford Loan
Desiree	20	female	white	single	1	2	—	A.A. Social Work–Dance	3.3	Stafford Loan
Diane	34	female	Hispanic/white	married	3	13, 6, 4	—	B.S. Elementary Education	3.7	Stafford Loan
Drew	23	male	white	cohabiting	1	2	—	B.S. Communication	3.7	—
Elizabeth	31	female	white	married	6	18,17,12, 12,11,2	—	B.S. Accounting	3.4	Stafford Loan Pell Grant
Emma	35	female	black	married	2	6, 3	B.S. Management Information Systems	B.S. Management and Organization	3.8	—
Heather	40	female	Caucasian	married	4	17, 9, 7, 4	A.A. General Studies	B.S. Psychology	3.3	Stafford Loan Scholarship—$500
Heide	22	female	white	cohabiting	1	1		B.S. Psychology	3.8	Pell Grant Misc. scholarships
Jose	45	male	Puerto Rican	married	3	19, 12, 6	—	B.A. History	2.7	Stafford Loan Pell Grant

Leslie	44	female	white	married	2	14, 10	—	A.A. General Studies—Music	4.00	Stafford Loan
Matt	25	male	white	single	1	2	—	B.S. Criminology	3.0	Pell Grant Stafford Loan
Nicole	29	female	white	married	2	5, 3	A.A. General Studies	B.S. Management and Organization	—	Stafford Loan
Raul	41	male	Hispanic	cohabiting	3	14, 13, 1	A.A. Computer Science B.S. Computer Science	M.S. Computer Science	3.3	Stafford Loan Hope Tax Credit
Renee	34	female	white	separated	2	6, 16	A.A. Liberal Arts B.A. History/German	M.A. History	3.7	Stafford Loan Pell Grant Gen. scholarships
Rou	54	male	Caucasian	married	1	4	—	A.A. Human Services	—	
Sam	42	male	white	married	4	11, 10, 8, 7	Cert.—HVACR	A.A. Physical Therapist Assistant	2.6	Stafford Loan

Self-Reflective Learners

Joy	52	female	Caucasian	married	3	19, 17, 13	B.A. Human Dev. and Family Studies M.A. Human Dev.—Early Childhood Education	M.S. School Counseling	4.00	—

(continued)

List of Student Parent Participants and Sample Demographics (n = 40) (continued)

Name*	Age	Gender	Self-identified Race or Ethnicity**	Marital Status	# of Children	Age of Children	Highest Level of Degree Attained	Current Degree Program	GPA***	Financial Aid—Grants, Loans, Tax Credits
Lucille	33	female	African American	married	2	2, 9	—	B.A. Music and B.A. Pre-Social Work	2.50	Pell Grant Stafford Loan
Molly	34	female	Caucasian	married	1	9	—	B.S. Accounting	3.8	—
Philoso	29	male	Sudanese/Dominican	separated	1	2	B.A. Psychology	M.A. Psychology	—	GI Bill
Rose	25	female	Turkish American	married	1	2	—	B.A. Psychology	3.8	Stafford Loan
Sara	29	female	Hispanic/Latina	married	2	3, 2	A.A. Liberal Arts	B.A. Psychology	3.8	Stafford Loan

*Names are pseudonyms selected by the participants to protect their confidentiality and anonymity.

**Participants were asked for written self-descriptions of their race/ethnicity.

***Grade Point Average is a self-reported cumulative estimation.

ACKNOWLEDGMENTS

Each project is a test of patience, perseverance, and trust. First and foremost, this project would not exist if student parents were not willing to voice their struggles, strategies, successes, and frustrations with me. To all the parents who sat down with me and shared your stories, thank you for setting aside precious hours of your day and being willing to be a part of this project. There are some parents, in particular, who inspired me throughout the process of researching and writing this book. Erika Dawson Head, eleven years ago you entered my life and struck me with your determined optimism; your passion for your family and for promoting social justice is incomparable. Leah Glaser, Jacqueline Cobbina-Boivin, Michele Vancour, Tom Bohlke, Rebecca Boncoddo, Talhaht Mannan, and Aimee Pozorski, you have been my ever-steady comrades on campus—we will keep doing what we know is right to improve campus life for parents and their families.

At Central Connecticut State University, I couldn't have done this without the support of the Department of Sociology, the College of Liberal Arts and Sciences, and our valiant union, the Association of American University Professors. I relied extensively on AAUP Research Grants that supported the key work of interviewing, transcribing, researching, and writing. I am union proud and appreciative and thank current leaders for recognizing that these work–life–family issues are labor issues and for supporting current childcare and paid leave initiatives on our college and university campuses.

Friends and colleagues reviewed some insufferably rough drafts over the years—I thank Wendy Simonds and Mary Erdmans for inspiring me to be courageous and "set loose my inner writer." John O'Connor, you have the uncanny skill of asking just the right questions and challenging me to think outside my comfort zone, which helped to propel the analysis forward. Long conversations while hiking in Sunol with Michael Doyle helped me sort through ideas as we considered the challenges of teaching and wrestled with my project's themes and theories. I am also indebted to the close readings and responses provided by a number of anonymous readers and by Lisa Nunn, who steered me in directions that ultimately strengthened this project's current form while cheering me on at every turn. Melanie Daglian was indispensable in helping me to transcribe these interviews at a moment's notice. And, of course, I couldn't have completed this project successfully without my editor at Rutgers University Press, Lisa Banning, who seamlessly guided me through the publishing process, and my production editor, John Donohue, an expert in detail and style.

Christine Steiner, I remember strolling with you around the campus of Chabot Community College soon after you had decided to go back to school—now with a bachelor's degree in political science and over fifty years of public housing experience, your influence is recognized and lauded by city and county leaders across the United States. You inspire others, particularly your two daughters, with your tenacity, energy, and strength—thank you Mom. Michael Pearson, you have long reassured me with your patience, your endurance, and your devotion to family. Whether rescuing me when stranded in the Central Valley or following my adventures cross country, you have trusted my decisions and supported me at every turn as we journey this thing called life. Thank you, Dad.

Deb Pearson, your perceptive takes on people and their motivations keep my mind in constant motion—and when I am lulled into complacency, you always know the right time to shake up my roots. Seneca and Danielle, you likely didn't even know it, but your very being has shaped all of my work. Do you know how lucky you are? I know how lucky I am. Scott Ellis, you're my game partner in every sense of the word—you worked with me as I struggled with ideas early in the morning and late at night. You read every section multiple times, and when I was drowning in history or others' research, you encouraged me to "go back to the data." I did. I listened to you in the way that you listened to me, and all of our life adventures are better because of that—thank you my luv.

NOTES

CHAPTER 1   "WE'RE NOT LIVING IN THE OLD SCHOOL ANYMORE"

1. More information about these programs can be found on their respective websites: Smith College's Ada Comstock Program, https://www.smith.edu/admission-aid/how-apply/ada-comstock-scholars; Tufts University's REAL Program, https://students.tufts.edu/academic-advice-and-support/real-program; Endicott College's Keys to Degrees Program, https://www.endicott.edu/student-life/student-services/student-affairs/keys-to-degrees.
2. Some fathers—particularly those who are married, reside with the family, and are biologically related to their children—benefit in regard to real wages, an effect referred to in the literature as a "fatherhood premium" (Hodges and Budig 2010; Killewald 2012). Women instead are more likely than fathers to experience a "motherhood wage penalty," thereby limiting their lifetime earnings (Budig and England 2001).
3. Bourdieu further defines *habitus* as "the universalizing mediation which causes an individual agent's practices, without either explicit reason or signifying intent, to be nonetheless 'sensible' and 'reasonable'" (1977: 79).
4. Swidler fleshes out these ideas in *Talk of Love: How Culture Matters* (2001), in which she examines how people use culture to make sense of their romantic relationships, a meaning-making process that simultaneously explains and guides their actions in the context of those relationships. She not only explores how contexts, codes, and institutions influence the tools available to social actors but also examines variations in the quality of their tools and knowledge of how to use those tools.
5. Swidler (2001) explicitly acknowledges the similarity of Bourdieu's (1977) "habitus" to "strategies of action," but maintains that she sees "learning such cultured capacities as a much more active, open, and continuous process than Bourdieu seems to do" (247n11).
6. Garey's (1999) analysis is grounded in symbolic interactionist theories of the self, which emerged from the work of sociologists, including George Herbert Mead (1934/1962), Herbert Blumer (1969), Erving Goffman (1959), and Arlie Hochschild (1979). Symbolic interactionist theories presume the self to be in a constant state of construction and negotiation. Although strongly influenced by norms and roles, individuals are creating at every moment a sense of self through their actions and beliefs that reify or challenge those societal frames.
7. Blair-Loy (2003) similarly explores how some of the mothers in her sample, "the mavericks," challenge traditional schemas, engaging in strategies of action that serve to reshape those schemas of devotion to work and home incrementally over time as cultural norms and institutional resources evolve. These mavericks pursued both work and family life, refusing to forgo one or the other in pursuit of their devotion to work

or their devotion to home. In pursuing both work and family, these mavericks reveal the constraining power of gendered schemas of devotion to work and home and the emotional and moral conflicts they face. However, they also forge new understandings of gender as they challenge what it means to be a successful mother and employer.

8. Like Swidler, I turn to Ronald Jepperson's (1991) definition of institutions: "An institution is then a social pattern that reveals a particular reproduction process. When departures from the pattern are counteracted in a regulated fashion, by repetitively activated, socially constructed, controls—that is by some set of rewards and sanctions—we refer to a pattern as institutionalized" (p. 145).

CHAPTER 2   THE AMERICAN DREAM?

1. For a comprehensive overview of the history of higher education in the United States, see Thelin's (2004) *A History of American Higher Education*.

2. Such an intent is clearly revealed in the preamble of the colonial era charter for what later became Brown University: "Institutions for liberal Education are highly beneficial to Society . . . preserving in the Community a Succession of Men duly qualified for discharging the Offices of Life with usefulness and reputation" (qtd. in Thelin 2004: 37).

3. Postsecondary schools serving women reflected a variety of interests and "institutional names, including 'college,' 'academy,' 'female seminary,' and 'literary institute'" (Thelin 2004: 83).

4. Such changes were evidenced in the New York's People's College and the New York Agricultural College, the latter of which subsequently became Cornell University (Rudolph 1962).

5. Frederick Rudolph (1962) notes the strengthening connections between an emerging culture of consumerism, capitalism, science, and higher education. Over time, Rudolph contends, "what sold agricultural education to the American farmer . . . was evidence that scientific agriculture paid in larger crops, higher income, and a better chance to enjoy higher living standards—in other words, an opportunity to make frequent use of the Montgomery Ward or Sears Roebuck catalogue" (260–261).

6. Morrill's initial legislative efforts were rebuffed by then–sitting president James Buchanan, but later, in the midst of the Civil War, Morrill found both a new president and a political moment that were favorable toward his educational proposals. The overall influence of the Morrill Acts, at least their immediate effect on changing the face of higher education, has been deemed questionable at best. At the time, Morrill and other politicians were just as likely concerned with determining how to judiciously parcel out and use government-owned land, particularly in the still very open West, as they were with advancing higher education. Further, the funds earned from state sales of federal lands were too often squandered and not used to establish public state schools but instead supported the agricultural arms of established and well-connected institutions such as Cornell, Yale, and Dartmouth (Thelin 2004: 77–78). Nevertheless, the Morrill Acts established a model of the university that has prevailed to this day and paved a pathway allowing for the creation of a public system of colleges and universities.

7. See Mettler (2014) and McMillan Cottom (2017) for comprehensive analyses of the relationship between for-profit higher educational institutions and rising social inequalities in the United States in recent years.

8. See for example Aronowitz (2000); Berg (1971); and Collins (1979).

9. The term *human capital* is attributed to Theodore Schultz (1961), and human capital theory has come to be identified with the work of Schultz's student Gary Becker (1964) and Jacob Mincer (1974).

10. These changes to welfare programs were also facilitated by a discourse of "undeservingness" that permeated discussions of the poor and of the various public assistance programs developed to provide aid to low-income individuals and families. See for example Abramovitz (2000); Katz (1989); and Reese (2005) for comprehensive historical overviews of discourse that relies on themes of deservingness to frame opposition to social welfare programs targeting low-income populations in the United States.

11. See Michael Roth's (2014) *Beyond the University: Why Liberal Education Matters* for a review of these debates as presented by a number of U.S. intellectuals, including Thomas Jefferson, Benjamin Franklin, Booker T. Washington, W.E.B. Du Bois, Ralph Waldo Emerson, Jane Addams, William James, and John Dewey.

CHAPTER 3   "I'M JUST LOOKING FOR SOME KIND OF UNDERSTANDING"

1. See for example Armstrong, Hamilton, and Sweeney (2006); Binder and Wood (2013); McDonough (1997); Nunn (2014); Pascarella and Terenzini (2004); Stephens et al. (2012); Stuber (2011); and Tinto (1993).

2. In analyzing these retention rates, one must also consider that the student bodies at many selective colleges and universities are very different from the student bodies at those public institutions that are less selective. Students at more selective institutions are more likely than their counterparts in less selective institutions to be academically and culturally prepared for the rigor required in college. They are more likely to be of traditional college-going age, to have parents who graduated from college, and to have fewer external familial commitments. They are also less likely to work outside the classroom and live off campus, which increases their opportunity to socially and academically integrate, factors that are significantly related to retention (Mullen 2010; Tinto 1993).

3. The concept "return on investment" is most often measured in starting salaries and potential earnings. It is used by web-based tools hosted by the U.S. Department of Education ("College Scoreboard") and *The Chronicle of Higher Education* ("College Reality Check"), both of which allow individuals to compare colleges across a variety of factors (Carlson 2013).

4. As Pierre Bourdieu initially conceptualized the term, to have knowledge of elite culture is to possess a particular form of social power, which he referred to as cultural capital. Bourdieu and Passeron introduced the concept of cultural capital as it related to the formal educational system in *Reproduction in Education, Culture, and Society* (1977). Bourdieu continued to develop this concept in his comprehensive analysis *Distinction: A Social Critique of the Judgment of Taste* (1984) and in the essay "The Forms of Capital" published in the *Handbook of Theory and Research for the Sociology of Education* (1986). In the latter work, Bourdieu (1986) refined his definition of cultural capital to include three types: embodied, objectified, and institutionalized. *Embodied cultural capital* refers to competencies and skills, whereas *objectified cultural capital* refers to objects whose meaning is most fully understood using those embodied competencies or skills. A rosette on a young man's lapel, for example, only has meaning for those who understand its social significance as a marker of one's lineage or membership in a socially elite organization. Finally, *institutionalized cultural capital* refers to the

credentials one may possess and the value accorded to those credentials within the context of social exchanges.

5. Stuber theoretically frames her analysis of culture using Bourdieu's (1977, 1984) concept of habitus, innovatively and convincingly demonstrating how organizations themselves possess a habitus that reflects dispositions and patterns of action that ultimately reproduce social inequalities.

6. Although the advertised tuition costs for the liberal arts college was $32,000 at the time of Stuber's study, the average financial aid award was $20,000, which combined both merit and needs-based aid. Such large financial aid awards are quite typical at many selective liberal arts colleges, which maintain substantial endowments in order to draw potential students, especially those who might not qualify for needs-based aid. At the state flagship university, average in-state tuition was $11,000 and tuition for out-of-state residents was $16,000. The average financial aid award for the state students was $5,500 and included only needs-based aid.

7. In recent years, members of the House of Representatives have introduced a number of bills that would improve access to college for U.S. veterans. Representative Jeff Miller of Florida introduced HR 357, The GI Bill Tuition Fairness Act of 2013, during the 113th session of Congress, which would require states to charge veterans in-state tuition rates, allowing them to bypass states' residency requirements. Because the GI Bill will only cover posted in-state tuition costs, many veterans living in states with strict residency requirements must pay the difference between in-state and out-of-state tuition rates, which prohibits many veterans from attending college. HR 357 never made it past committee status in 2013 (House Committee on Veterans' Affairs 2013).

8. For more information about how 1996 welfare reform affected regulations for biological and nonbiological parents, who are married or unmarried, see the U.S. Department of Health and Human Services 2009 report *Cohabitation and Marriage Rules in State TANF Programs.*

9. Because case managers assess clients individually, they are afforded limited levels of discretion when interpreting and implementing state and federal regulations. For an overview of case managers' varying perspectives on regulations regarding postsecondary education in the wake of welfare reform in 1996, see Pearson (2007).

10. For more information about TANF legislation and rules, see U.S. Congress (1996) and U.S. Department of Health and Human Services (2006, 2009).

11. The 2009 American Recovery and Reinvestment Act also expanded the Hope Tax Credit, implemented in 1998, which provides tax credits for select expenses related to a college education including tuition, books, and course materials.

12. For overviews of state-level spending cuts and their effects on the functioning of U.S. public colleges and universities see Suzanne Mettler's (2014) study *Degrees of Inequality: How the Politics of Higher Education Sabotaged the American Dream*; Michael Mitchell, Michael Leachman, and Kathleen Masterson's (2017) report for the Center on Budget and Policy Priorities, *A Lost Decade in Higher Education Funding*; and the U.S Government Accountability Office's (2014) report *Higher Education: State Funding Trends and Policies and Affordability.*

13. Small (2010) innovatively analyzes how child care centers located in an urban setting provide forms of social capital to parents, particularly low-income parents, as a result of their organizational structure. Central to Small's analysis is the idea that individuals are organizationally embedded actors whose opportunities are influenced to some degree by the organizations in which they function. Small uses the

term *brokerage* to describe a "general process by which an organization connects an individual to another individual, to another organization, or to the resources they contain" (p. 19). In this way, child care centers are an integral organization linking parents to various relevant resource providers.

14. See for example Armstrong and Hamilton (2013); Pascarella and Terenzini (1991); Stuber (2011); Tinto (1993).

CHAPTER 4   WHAT STUDENTS WANT AND WHY

1. See chapter 3, note 4 of this volume for a detailed explanation of cultural capital.

2. In "The Forms of Capital," Bourdieu (1986) fleshed out yet another dimension of interactional power, social capital, which he defined as "the aggregate of the actual or potential resources which are linked to possession of a durable network of more or less institutionalized relationships of mutual acquaintance and recognition" (p. 248). Such capital refers to the social networks in which one moves that, in conjunction with one's economic and cultural capital, can facilitate social mobility or, as is more often the case, social stasis. Together these various forms of capital help us to understand the complex functioning of power in our social exchanges, which more often than not serves to reproduce social and cultural inequalities.

3. Vincent Tinto (1988, 1993) and Alexander W. Astin (1984, 1993) have long documented the influence of various individual and institutional variables—including students' personal commitments and goals and their access to institutional resources—that collectively shape their academic and social integration on college campuses. Academic and social integration in turn are correlated with students' satisfaction and likelihood of completing their degree.

CHAPTER 5   WEAVING EXISTING AND NEW IDENTITIES AT HOME

1. The following analyses presume that gender—unlike an individual's biological sex, which is primarily determined in reference to biological differences—is socially constructed and achieved. West and Zimmerman's (1987, 2009) theoretical formulation of "doing gender" draws on symbolic interactionist theories and presumes that gender and our social comprehension of gender are primarily located within the context of interaction. As such, gender as a dimension of one's sense of self is constantly being constructed via action and interaction and is validated (or not) by others by way of their appraisal and evaluation.

2. Building upon and extending our understanding of these processes of meaning making, both Michele Lamont (1992) and Mary Blair-Loy (2003) have produced a particularly compelling body of research that examines the moral and emotional dimensions of cultural logics and schemas that influence meaning making and strategies of being. These researchers argue for a renewed attention to moral signals and the ways that cultural schemas serve as "institutionalized and partially internalized models for cognition, morality, and emotion" (Blair-Loy 2003: 175).

3. Barbara Risman (1998), in her book *Gender Vertigo*, contends that gender "is not manifested just in our personalities, our cultural rules, or other institutions," but is a "structural property of society" and is "deeply embedded as a basis for stratification, differentiating opportunities and constraints" (p. 28). For one, diverse cultural and structural forces contribute to women being more likely than men to forgo employment opportunities in order to care for young or ailing family members (Jones 2012;

Moe and Shandy 2010; Williams and Boushey 2010). A lack of adequately affordable child care, nursing care, and family leave resources makes such decisions necessary in the first place. That women more often take on these roles than do men is in part a result of gendered norms that are rooted in both history and the cultural belief that women are more nurturing and family oriented than are men. However, even heterosexual parents who actively challenge gendered norms frequently find themselves deciding to have the mother rather than the father stay home due to historical gendered income differentials in the workplace. Risman argues that "even when individual women and men do *not* desire to live gendered lives or to support male dominance, they often find themselves compelled to do so by the logic of gendered choices" (p. 29). For an excellent overview of recent research that examines how the "logic of gendered choices" contributes to the construction and maintenance of gendered inequalities see Cecilia Ridgeway's (2011) *Framed by Gender: How Gender Persists in the Modern World*. In chapter 5, Ridgeway specifically examines research that reviews how gender operates as an organizing principle in the home, shaping micro- and macro-level inequalities.

4. Arlie Hochschild and Anne Machung (1989) coined the term "second shift," which refers to the household and caregiving labor disproportionately borne by women.

5. Mary Blair-Loy (2003) provides a comprehensive analysis of these morally infused cultural processes as they shape women's lives in her insightful exploration of devotion to work and devotion to family schemas.

6. Arlie Hochschild (1979) conceptualizes "emotion work" as "the act of trying to change in degree or quality an emotion or feeling" (p. 561). Such work is a central component of many feminized occupations, which involve high levels of human interaction. She most famously examined flight attendants and bill collectors in her 1983 book *The Managed Heart: Commercialization of Human Feeling*, in which she elaborates on this concept as it is connected to the labor economy.

7. Freeman (2017) similarly found in her qualitative study exploring the experiences of low-income single mothers enrolled in an antipoverty program that mothers frequently described their own educational experiences as tied to and connected to those of their children. Their parenting and student roles merged as they saw their children as necessary motivation for their educational pursuits and saw their own work in the program as necessary to improve their family's social standing, including role-modeling the value of education in the context of day-to-day family life.

8. Garey (1999) refers to an individual's assets as well as the economic, social, and political structures that shape an individual's access to assets as "resource constellations." These constellations are shaped by income, wealth and class background, education, occupational field, job security and seniority, marital relationship, family support, race/ethnic privilege, public support programs, neighborhood context, transportation, family size, and physical health (pp. 52–55).

9. Gerson (2010) likewise found that the vast majority of students whom she surveyed, nearly 80 percent of the women and nearly 70 percent of the men, desired an egalitarian relationship in which both partners would share paid work and family responsibilities (p. 106).

CHAPTER 6   FALSE PROMISES?

1. Classic educational studies that examine the varied ways that schooling organizations are complicit in the reproduction of social inequalities include Apple (1982), Bowles

and Gintis (1976), Cookson and Persell (1985), MacLeod (1987), Spring (1976), and Willis (1977). Two more recent studies that examine the ways that secondary school environments shape students' transition to college include McDonough (1997) and Nunn (2014).

2. On the other hand, many elite nonprofit colleges and universities have historically focused nearly exclusively on providing exactly the kind of education that self-reflective learners desire. As reported in 2012, Rebecca Chopp, president of Swarthmore College, argues, "The case for the liberal arts, in my opinion, needs to be reframed to suggest not only how well we serve individual students but also how we act as a counterforce against a culture that is commodifying knowledge and projecting a view of community and anthropology that is reductionist and dangerous" (Kiley 2012). Of course, colleges and universities like Swarthmore rely on strong alumni networks to ensure students' access to internships and postgraduation job opportunities—they continue to "sell" to students access to these social networks, while simultaneously promoting an educational vision that prioritizes personal empowerment over economic security.

3. These scholars' ideas can be traced historically to Weber's ([1958] 2003) theories of status and stratification (see Brown 2001 for a comprehensive analysis of these connections) and Gramsci's [1928] 1971 analysis of schools and the production of cultural hegemony. In *The Higher Learning*, Veblen [1918] 1993 also issued a vitriolic critique of the university systems emerging and expanding at the beginning of the twentieth century. Veblen was particularly concerned about the infiltration of business language and values in the halls of academia, which he believed ought to be a refuge from industrial interests.

4. See for example Becker (1964), Mincer (1974), and Schultz (1961).

5. Not all colleges or programs will necessarily facilitate such movement. For example, very few students who are accepted into and then attend high-prestige universities or who enroll in highly competitive programs are likely to leave those institutions or programs without a degree, and so the openings available for students desiring to transfer in will be limited. The level of competition for access to those programs and institutions will determine the level of movement into and out of those programs and institutions.

6. In fact, many contemporary commentators covering the state of education in the twenty-first century emphasize the value of creative thinking that can result from an education that is varied in regard to subject matter and that challenges students to forge connections across disciplines. In 2014, Thomas Friedman, editorial writer for the *New York Times*, interviewed Lazlo Bock, chief hiring officer at Google, about the value of a liberal arts education in the high-tech world. Bock responded that such an education continues to be "phenomenally important," and then clarified his point with an example: "Ten years ago behavioral economics was rarely referenced. But [then] you apply social science to economics and suddenly there's this whole new field. I think a lot about how the most interesting things are happening at the intersection of two fields."

7. According to Autor and Dorn (2013), job growth is highest in fields requiring "abstract tasks," such as problem solving and creativity, that define traditionally high-paid positions in engineering, management, medicine, and science. Job growth is also high in fields that require "situational adaptability" and "in-person interaction," which are skills required in a variety of low-paid service-sector jobs, such as food services, retail, or security. Many jobs that previously provided middle-class wages that were

defined by "routine tasks," such as organizing or manipulating objects or information, have been replaced by technology—factory workers and bookkeepers are but two examples of the types of jobs that have decreased in number due to a combination of sourcing out their labor to other countries or replacing their labor with technology.

8. See for example Mettler (2014) and the U.S. Senate Health, Education, Labor and Pensions Committee (2012). For a comprehensive overview of how for-profit institutions fill a gap in our educational landscape via the provision of "risky credentials" see McMillan Cottom (2017).

9. For more information about New York's Excelsior Scholarship Program see https://www.ny.gov/programs/tuition-free-degree-program-excelsior-scholarship.

10. Welfare reform debates in the late 1990s very frequently focused on individuals and perceptions of deservingness (see, for example, Abramovitz 2000; Katz 1989; Reese 2005). In response to public perceptions that welfare participants lacked a desirable work ethic that would allow them to succeed economically, policies were put into place that required welfare participants to pursue jobs in order to continue receiving cash and child care assistance. Many critics and researchers highlighted the long-term career limitations of putting low-income parents, most of them women, in primarily low-wage jobs (Shaw et al. 2006). Nonetheless, these new welfare policies served the employment needs of many businesses and companies reliant on low-wage labor. The strands of public discourse surrounding welfare that emphasized the importance of participants' working tended to overwhelm competing framings highlighting the exploitation of welfare participants by businesses and companies offering low wages (Reese 2005).

CHAPTER 7   "IT'S A MARATHON, NOT A SPRINT"

1. See https://fightfor15.org/.
2. Similar dynamics emerge in Mullen's (2010) examination of students attending Yale University. The privileged women Yale students interviewed by Mullen were more likely than their men counterparts to select their majors based on their intellectual interests and passions. Men on the other hand, were more likely to consider the status of the major in the context of the university or their anticipated jobs.

REFERENCES

Abramovitz, Mimi. 2000. *Under Attack, Fighting Back: Women and Welfare in the United States.* New York: Monthly Review Press.

American Association of Community Colleges (AACC). 2016. *Fast Facts: February 2016.* http://www.aacc.nche.edu/AboutCC/Pages/fastfactsfactsheet.aspx.

Apple, Michael W. 1982. *Education and Power.* London: Routledge and Kegan Paul.

Armstrong, Elizabeth A., and Laura T. Hamilton. 2013. *Paying for the Party: How College Maintains Inequality.* Cambridge, Mass.: Harvard University Press.

Armstrong, Elizabeth A., Laura T. Hamilton, and Brian Sweeney. 2006. "Sexual Assault on Campus: A Multilevel, Integrative Approach to Party Rape." *Social Problems* 53, no. 4: 483–499.

Aronowitz, Stanley. 2000. *The Knowledge Factory.* Boston: Beacon Press.

Astin, Alexander W. 1984. "Student Involvement: A Developmental Theory for Higher Education." *Journal of College Student Personnel* 25, no. 4: 297–308.

Astin, Alexander W. 1993. *What Matters in College? Four Critical Years Revisited.* San Francisco: Jossey-Bass.

Aud, Susan, William Hussar, Frank Johnson, Grace Kena, Erin Roth, Eileen Manning, Xiaolei Wang, and Jijun Zhang. 2012. *The Condition of Education 2012* (NCES 2012-045). Washington, D.C.: U.S. Department of Education, National Center for Education Statistics. https://nces.ed.gov/pubs2012/2012045.pdf.

Autor, David H., and David Dorn. 2013. "How Technology Wrecks the Middle Class." *New York Times,* August 24. http://opinionator.blogs.nytimes.com/2013/08/24/how-technology-wrecks-the-middle-class/.

Autor, David H., Lawrence F. Katz, and Melissa S. Kearney. 2006. "The Polarization of the U.S. Labor Market." Working Paper 11986. Cambridge, Mass.: National Bureau of Economic Research.

Bain, Ken. 2004. *What the Best College Teachers Do.* Cambridge, Mass.: Harvard University Press.

Barr, Margaret J., and Mary K. Dessler. 2000. *The Handbook of Student Affairs Administration.* San Francisco: Jossey-Bass.

Baum, Sandra, and Jennifer Ma. 2013. *Trends in College Pricing 2013.* The College Board. https://trends.collegeboard.org/sites/default/files/college-pricing-2013-full-report-140108.pdf.

Bauman, Dan. 2018. "Is Student Debt Big Enough to Hold Back the Economy? What the Research Says." *Chronicle of Higher Education,* March 1. https://www.chronicle.com/article/Is-Student-Debt-Big-Enough-to/242719.

Baumann, Roland M. 2010. *Constructing Black Education at Oberlin College: A Documentary History.* Athens: Ohio University Press.

Becker, Gary. 1964. *Human Capital: A Theoretical and Empirical Analysis, with Special Reference to Education*. Chicago: University of Chicago Press.

Berg, Ivar. 1971. *Education and Jobs: The Great Training Robbery*. Boston: Beacon Press.

Berndtson, Dave. 2017. "San Francisco Becomes First City to Offer Free Community College Tuition to All Its Residents." *PBS NewsHour*, February 8. http://www.pbs.org/newshour /rundown/san-francisco-becomes-first-city-offer-free-community-college-tuition -residents/.

Bianchi, Suzanne M., Melissa A. Milkie, Liana C. Sayer, and John P. Robinson. 2000. "Is Anyone Doing the Housework? Trends in the Gender Division of Household Labor." *Social Forces* 79: 191–228.

Bianchi, Suzanne M., John P. Robinson, and Melissa A. Milkie. 2006. *Changing Rhythms of American Family Life*. New York: Russell Sage Foundation.

Bills, David B., and David K. Brown. 2011. "Introduction: New Directions in Educational Credentialism." *Research in Social Stratification and Mobility* 29: 1–4.

Binder, Amy J., and Kate Wood. 2013. *Becoming Right: How Campuses Shape Young Conservatives*. Princeton, N.J.: Princeton University Press.

Bivens, Josh, Elise Gould, Lawrence Mishel, and Heidi Shierholz. 2014. *Raising America's Pay: Why It's Our Central Economic Policy Challenge*. Briefing Paper no. 378. Washington, D.C.: Economic Policy Institute.

Blair-Loy, Mary. 2003. *Competing Devotions: Career and Family among Women Executives*. Cambridge, Mass.: Harvard University Press.

Blumer, Herbert. 1969. *Symbolic Interactionism: Perspective and Method*. Englewood Cliffs, N.J.: Prentice-Hall.

Bone, Josh. 2010. *TANF Education and Training: Parents as Scholars Program*. Center for Postsecondary and Economic Success. Washington, D.C.: Center for Law and Social Policy. http://www.clasp.org/resources-and-publications/files/PaS.pdf.

Bound, John, Michael F. Lovenheim, and Sarah Turner. 2010. "Increasing Time to Baccalaureate Degree in the United States." NBER Working Paper No. 15892. Cambridge, Mass.: National Bureau of Economic Research.

Bourdieu, Pierre. 1973. "Cultural Reproduction and Social Reproduction." In *Knowledge, Education, and Cultural Change: Papers in the Sociology of Education*, edited by Richard K. Brown, 71–84. London: Tavistock.

Bourdieu, Pierre. 1977. *Outline of a Theory of Practice*. Translated by Richard Nice. Cambridge: Cambridge University Press.

Bourdieu, Pierre. 1984. *Distinction: A Social Critique of the Judgment of Taste*. Translated by Richard Nice. Cambridge: Cambridge University Press.

Bourdieu, Pierre. 1986. "The Forms of Capital." In *Handbook of Theory and Research for the Sociology of Education*, edited by John G., Richardson, 241–258. Westport, Conn.: Greenwood Press.

Bourdieu, Pierre, and Jean-Claude Passeron. 1977. *Reproduction in Education, Society, and Culture*. Translated by Richard Nice. London: Sage.

Bowles, Samuel, and Herbert Gintis. 1976. *Schooling in Capitalist America: Educational Reform of Economic Life*. London: Routledge and Kegan Paul.

Brint, Steven. 2002. *The Future of the City of Intellect: The Changing American University*. Palo Alto, Calif.: Stanford University Press.

Brint, Steven. 2017. *Schools and Societies*. 3rd ed. Palo Alto, Calif.: Stanford University Press.

Brown, David K. 2001. "The Social Sources of Educational Credentialism: Status Cultures, Labor Markets, and Organizations." *Sociology of Education* 74: 19–34.

Budig, Michele J., and Paula England. 2001. "The Wage for Motherhood." *American Sociological Review* 66, no. 2: 204–225.

Bush, George W. 2007. "President Bush Signs College Cost Reduction and Access Act." Washington D.C.: The White House. http://georgewbush-whitehouse.archives.gov/news /releases/2007/09/print/20070927-3.html.

Carlson, Scott. 2013. "Is College Worth It? Two New Reports Say Yes (Mostly)." *Chronicle of Higher Education*, November 4. http://chronicle.com/blogs/bottomline/is-college-worth -it-two-new-reports-say-yes-mostly.

Central Connecticut State University (CCSU). 2006. "At a Glance." http://docs.ccsu.edu/oira /institutionalData/fastfacts/Fast_Facts_Fall_2006.pdf.

Central Connecticut State University (CCSU). 2008. "College Portrait of Undergraduate Education: CCSU 2007." http://web.ccsu.edu/admission/pdfs/CCSU_FactsFigures.pdf.

Central Connecticut State University (CCSU). 2011. "At a Glance." http://docs.ccsu.edu/oira /institutionalData/fastfacts/Fast_Facts_Fall_2011.pdf.

Central Connecticut State University (CCSU). 2017. "At a Glance." http://docs.ccsu.edu/oira /institutionalData/fastfacts/Fast_Facts_Fall_2016.pdf.

Charles, Maria, and David B. Grusky. 2004. *Occupational Ghettos: The Worldwide Segregation of Women and Men*. Palo Alto, Calif.: Stanford University Press.

Choy, Susan. 2002. *Nontraditional Undergraduates*. Washington D.C.: National Center for Education Statistics.

Christopher, Karen. 2012. "Extensive Mothering: Employed Mothers' Constructions of the Good Mother." *Gender & Society* 26, no. 1: 73–96.

Cohen, Arthur N., and Carrie B. Kisker. 2010. *The Shaping of American Higher Education: Emergence and Growth of the Contemporary System*. 2nd ed. San Francisco: Jossey-Bass.

College Board. 2014. *Trends in Higher Education: Federal Pell Grant Awards in Current and Constant Dollars over Time*. http://trends.collegeboard.org/student-aid/figures-tables/fed -aid-federal-pell-grant-awards-current-and-constant-dollars-over-time.

Collins, Randall. 1979. *The Credential Society: An Historical Sociology of Education and Stratification*. New York: Academic Press.

Commission on the Humanities and Social Sciences (CHSS). 2013. *The Heart of the Matter*. Cambridge, Mass.: American Academy of Arts and Sciences. https://www.humanities commission.org/_pdf/hss_report.pdf.

Connecticut Office of Early Childhood (COEC). 2017. "Quality Improvement: Workforce Development." http://www.ct.gov/oec/cwp/view.asp?a=4541&q=535848.

Connor, Michael E., and Joseph L. White. 2006. *Black Fathers: An Invisible Presence in America*. Mahwah, N.J.: Lawrence Erlbaum Associates.

Constable, Kevin. 2017. "Tuition Hikes Blunt CSCU Budget Gap." *Connecticut Mirror*, March 29. https://ctmirror.org/2017/03/29/tuition-hikes-blunt-cscu-budget-gap/.

Cookson, Peter W., Jr., and Caroline Hodges Persell. 1985. *Preparing for Power: America's Elite Boarding Schools*. New York: Basic Books.

Delbanco, Andrew. 2012. *College: What It Is, Was, and Should Be*. Princeton, N.J.: Princeton University Press.

Deming, David, Claudia Goldin, and Lawrence Katz. 2013. "For-Profit Colleges." *The Future of Children* 23, no. 1: 137–163.

Desrochers, Donna M., and Rita J. Kirshstein. 2012. *College Spending in a Turbulent Decade: Findings from the Delta Cost Project*. A Delta Data Update, 2000–2010. Washington, D.C.: American Institute for Research.

DiMaggio, Paul. 1997. "Culture and Cognition." *Annual Review of Sociology* 23: 263–287.

Doucet, Andrea. 2006. *Do Men Mother? Fathering, Care, and Domestic Responsibility*. Toronto: University of Toronto Press.

Douglas, Susan, and Meredith W. Michaels. 2004. *The Mommy Myth: The Idealization of Motherhood and How It Has Undermined Women*. New York: Free Press.

Dumais, Susan A. 2002. "Cultural Capital, Gender, and School Success: The Role of Habitus." *Sociology of Education* 75, no. 1: 44–68.

Duncan, Greg K., and Richard J. Murnane, eds. 2011. *Whither Opportunity? Rising Inequality, Schools, and Children's Life Chances*. New York: Russell Sage.

Duncan, Simon, and Rosalind Edwards. 1999. *Lone Mothers, Paid Work and Gendered Moral Rationalities*. New York: St. Martin's Press.

Duquaine-Watson, Jillian. 2017. *Mothering by Degrees: Single Mothers and the Pursuit of Postsecondary Education*. New Brunswick, N.J.: Rutgers University Press.

Dzigbede, Komla, and Laura Bronstein. 2017. "Trump's Education Budget Could Spell Disaster for Poor Children." *Business Insider*, June 4. http://www.businessinsider.com/the-trump-devos-education-plan-could-have-long-lasting-implications-for-poor-children-2017-6.

England, Paula. 1982. "The Failure of Human Capital Theory to Explain Occupational Sex Segregation." *Journal of Human Resources* 17, no. 3: 358–370.

England, Paula. 2010. "The Gender Revolution: Uneven and Stalled." *Gender & Society* 24, no. 2: 149–166.

England, Paula, and Su Li. 2006. "Desegregation Stalled: The Changing Gender Composition of College Majors, 1971–2002." *Gender & Society* 20, no. 5: 657–677.

England, Paula, and Anjula Srivastava. 2013. "Educational Differences in US Parents' Time Spent in Child Care: The Role of Culture and Cross-Spouse Influence." *Social Science Research* 42: 971–988.

Freeman, Amanda. 2017. "Moving 'Up and Out' Together: Exploring the Mother–Child Bond in Low-Income, Single-Mother-Headed Families." *Journal of Marriage and Family* 79, no. 3: 675–689.

Friedman, Thomas L. 2014. "How to Get a Job at Google, Part 2." *New York Times*, April 19. https://www.nytimes.com/2014/04/20/opinion/sunday/friedman-how-to-get-a-job-at-google-part-2.html.

Friedman, Zack. 2017 "Student Loan Debt in 2017: A $1.3 Trillion Crisis." *Forbes*, February 21. https://www.forbes.com/sites/zackfriedman/2017/02/21/student-loan-debt-statistics-2017/#65e1b4e45dab.

Garey, Anita Ilta. 1999. *Weaving Work and Motherhood*. Philadelphia: Temple University Press.

Gault, Barbara, Lindsey Reichlin, Elizabeth Reynolds, and Meghan Froehner. 2014. "Campus Child Care Declining Even as Growing Numbers of Parents Attend College." Institute for Women's Policy Research: Fact Sheet #C425. Washington D.C.: IWPR.

Gerson, Kathleen. 1985. *Hard Choices: How Women Decide About Work, Career, and Motherhood*. Berkeley: University of California Press.

Gerson, Kathleen. 1993. *No Man's Land: Men's Changing Commitments to Family and Work*. New York: Basic Books.

Gerson, Kathleen. 2002. "Moral Dilemmas, Moral Strategies, and the Transformation of Gender: Lessons from Two Generations of Work and Family Change." *Gender & Society* 16, no. 1: 8–28.

Gerson, Kathleen. 2010. *The Unfinished Revolution: Coming of Age in a New Era of Gender, Work and Family*. New York: Oxford University Press.

Goffman, Erving. 1959. *The Presentation of Self in Everyday Life*. New York: Anchor Books.

Goldin, Claudia, and Lawrence F. Katz. 2007. "Long-Run Changes in the U.S. Wage Structure: Narrowing, Widening, Polarizing." *Brookings Papers on Economic Activity* 2: 135–165.

Goldin, Claudia, and Lawrence F. Katz. 2009. "The Future of Inequality." *Milken Institute Review* 3: 26–33.

Goldin, Claudia, Lawrence F. Katz, and Ilyana Kuziemko. 2006. "The Homecoming of American College Women: The Reversal of the College Gender Gap." *Journal of Economic Perspectives* 20, no. 4: 133–156.

Goldrick-Rab, Sara. 2016. *Paying the Price: College Costs, Financial Aid, and the Betrayal of the American Dream*. Chicago: University of Chicago Press.

Goldrick-Rab, Sara, and Kia Sorenson. 2011. "Unmarried Parents in College: Pathways to Success." Fast Focus, Paper No. 9-2011. Madison: Institute for Research on Poverty, University of Wisconsin–Madison.

Grall, Timothy. 2009. "Custodial Mothers and Fathers and Their Child Support: 2007." Current Population Reports, P60-237. Washington, D.C.: U.S. Census Bureau. http://www.census.gov/prod/2009pubs/p60-237.pdf.

Gramsci, Antonio. [1928] 1971. *Selections from the Prison Notebooks*. New York: International Publishers.

Green, Erica L. 2018. "DeVos Ends Obama-Era Safeguards Aimed at Abuses by For-Profit Colleges." *New York Times*, August 10. https://www.nytimes.com/2018/08/10/us/politics/betsy-devos-for-profit-colleges.html.

Greenberg, Milton. 1997. *The G.I. Bill: The Law That Changed America*. New York: Lickle Publishing.

Grubb, Warner Norton. 1999. *Honored But Invisible: An Inside Look at Teaching in Community Colleges*. New York: Routledge.

Hamer, Jennifer. 2001. *What It Means to Be Daddy: Fatherhood for Black Men Living Away from Their Children*. New York: Columbia University Press.

Hamrick, Florence A., Nancy J. Evans, and John H. Schuh. 2002. *Foundations of Student Affairs Practice: How Philosophy, Theory, and Research Strengthen Educational Outcomes*. San Francisco, Calif.: Jossey-Bass.

Harper, Shannon, and Barbara Reskin. 2005. "Affirmative Action at School and on the Job." *Annual Review of Sociology* 31: 357–379.

Haynie, Devon. 2014. "U.S. News Releases Ranking of Best Online Programs in 2014." *Huffington Post*, January 8. https://www.huffingtonpost.com/2014/01/08/us-news-best-online-programs-ranking-2014_n_4557085.html.

Hays, Sharon. 1994. "Structure and Agency and the Sticky Problem of Culture." *Sociological Theory* 12, no. 1: 57–72.

Hays, Sharon. 1996. *Cultural Contradictions of Motherhood*. New Haven, Conn.: Yale University Press.

Hays, Sharon. 2003. *Flat Broke with Children: Women in the Age of Welfare Reform*. Oxford: Oxford University Press.

Hochschild, Arlie. 1979. "Emotion Work, Feeling Rules, and Social Structure." *American Journal of Sociology* 85, no. 3: 551–575.

Hochschild, Arlie, with Anne Machung. 1989. *The Second Shift: Working Parents and the Revolution at Home*. New York: Viking Penguin.

Hochschild, Arlie Russell. 1983. *The Managed Heart: Commercialization of Human Feeling*. Berkeley: University of California Press.

Hodges, Melissa J., and Michelle J. Budig. 2010. "Who Gets the Daddy Bonus? Organizational Hegemonic Masculinity and the Impact of Fatherhood on Earnings." *Gender & Society* 24, no. 6: 717–745.

Holland, Megan M., and Stefanie DeLuca. 2016. "Why Wait Years to Become Something? Low-Income African American Youth and the Costly Career Search in For-Profit Trade Schools." *Sociology of Education* 89, no. 4: 261–278.

House Committee on Veterans' Affairs. 2013. "H.R. 357, G.I. Bill Tuition Fairness Act of 2013." https://veterans.house.gov/legislation/gi-bill-tuition-fairness-act-of-2013.htm.

Immerwahr, John. 2004. *Public Attitudes on Higher Education: A Trend Analysis, 1993 to 2003.* San Jose, Calif.: National Center for Public Policy & Higher Education.

Institute of Medicine and National Research Council (IM/NRC). 2015. "Transforming the Workforce for Children Birth through Age 8: A Unifying Foundation." Washington, D.C.: National Academies Press.

Jacobs, Jerry A. 1996. "Gender Inequality and Higher Education." *Annual Review of Sociology* 22: 153–185.

Jepperson, Ronald L. 1991. "Institutions, Institutional Effects, and Institutionalism." In *The New Institutionalism in Organizational Analysis*, edited by Walter W. Powell and Paul J. DiMaggio, 143–163. Chicago: University of Chicago Press.

Jones, Bernie D. 2012. *Women Who Opt Out: The Debate over Working Mothers and Work—Family Balance.* New York: New York University Press.

Katz, Michael P. 1989. *The Undeserving Poor: From the War on Poverty to the War on Welfare.* New York: Pantheon Books.

Kerr, Clark. 1963. *The Uses of the University.* Cambridge, Mass.: Harvard University Press.

Kiley, Kevin. 2012. "Making the Case." *Inside Higher Ed*, November 19. https://www.inside highered.com/news/2012/11/19/liberal-arts-colleges-rethink-their-messaging-face -criticism.

Killewald, Alexandra. 2012. "A Reconsideration of the Fatherhood Premium: Marriage, Coresidence, Biology, and Fathers' Wages." *American Sociological Review* 78, no. 1: 96–116.

Kobosco, Katie. 2017. "Rhode Island Just Made Community College Free." *CNN Money*, August 4. http://money.cnn.com/2017/08/03/pf/college/rhode-island-tuition-free-college /index.html.

Kreighbaum, Andrew. 2018. "New Boost for Student Research and Aid." *Inside Higher Ed*, March 22. https://www.insidehighered.com/news/2018/03/22/omnibus-spending-pack age-boosts-student-aid-while-restricting-devos-priorities.

Lamont, Michele. 1992. *Money, Morals, Manners: The Culture of the French and the American Upper-Middle Class.* Chicago: University of Chicago Press.

Lareau, Annette. 2003. *Unequal Childhoods: Class, Race, and Family Life.* Berkeley: University of California Press.

Lazerson, Marvin. 1998. "The Disappointments of Success: Higher Education after World War II." *Annals of the American Academy of Political and Social Science* 559, no. 1: 64–76.

Long, Dallas. 2012. "The Foundations of Student Affairs: A Guide to the Profession." In *Environments for Student Growth and Development: Librarians and Student Affairs in Collaboration*, edited by Lisa Janicke Hinchliffe and Melissa Autumn Wong, 1–39. Chicago: Association of College & Research Libraries.

Lucas, Christopher J. 2006. *American Higher Education: A History.* 2nd ed. New York: Palgrave Macmillan.

Lyness, Karen S., Janet C. Gornick, Pamela Stone, and Angela R. Grotto. 2012. "It's All about Control over Schedule and Hours in Cross-National Context." *American Sociological Review* 77, no. 6: 1023–1049.

MacLeod, Jay. 1987. *Ain't No Making It: Leveled Aspirations in a Low-Income Neighborhood.* Boulder, Colo.: Westview Press.

McDonough, Patricia M. 1997. *Choosing Colleges: How Social Class and Schools Structure Opportunity*. Albany: State University of New York Press.

McFarland, Joel, Bill Hussar, Xiaolie Wang, Jijun Zhang, Ke Wang, Amy Rathbun, Amy Barmer, Emily Forrest Cataldi, and Farrah Bullock Mann. 2018. *The Condition of Education 2018* (NCES 2018-144). Washington, D.C.: National Center for Education Statistics. https://nces.ed.gov/pubsearch/pubsinfo. asp?pubid=2018144.

McMillan Cottom, Tressie. 2017. *Lower Ed: The Troubling Rise of For-Profit Colleges in the New Economy*. New York: New Press.

McPherson, Michael S., and Lawrence S. Bacow. 2015. "Online Higher Education: Beyond the Hype Cycle." *Journal of Economic Perspectives* 29, no. 4: 135–153.

Mead, George H. [1934] 1962. *Mind, Self, and Society: From the Standpoint of a Social Behaviorist*. Edited by Charles W. Morris. Chicago: University of Chicago Press.

Mettler, Suzanne. 2014. *Degrees of Inequality: How the Politics of Higher Education Sabotaged the American Dream*. New York: Basic Books.

Miller, Kevin, Barbara Gault, and Abby Thorman. 2011. *Improving Child Care Access to Promote Postsecondary Success among Low-Income Parents*. Washington D.C.: Institute for Women's Policy Research.

Mills, C. Wright. 1959. *The Sociological Imagination*. New York: Oxford University Press.

Mincer, Jacob. 1974. *Schooling, Experience, and Earnings*. New York: Columbia University Press.

Mitchell, Michael, and Michael Leachman. 2015. *Years of Cuts Still Threaten to Put College Out of Reach for College Students*. Washington D.C.: Center on Budget and Policy Priorities, May 13. http://www.cbpp.org/sites/default/files/atoms/files/5-13-15sfp.pdf.

Mitchell, Michael, Michael Leachman, and Kathleen Masterson. 2017. *A Lost Decade in Higher Education Funding: State Cuts Have Driven Up Tuition and Reduced Quality*. Washington D.C.: Center on Budget and Policy Priorities, August 23. https://www.cbpp.org /research/state-budget-and-tax/a-lost-decade-in-higher-education-funding.

Mitchell, Michael, Vincent Palacios, and Michael Leachman. 2014. "States Are Still Funding Higher Education below Pre-Recession Levels." Washington D.C.: Center on Budget and Policy Priorities. http://www.cbpp.org/cms/?fa=view&id=4135.

Moe, Karine, and Dianna Shandy. 2010. *Glass Ceilings and 100-Hour Couples: What the Opt-Out Phenomenon Can Teach Us about Work and Family*. Athens: University of Georgia Press.

Moen, Phyllis, and Yan Yu. 2000. "Effective Work/Life Strategies: Working Couples, Work Conditions, Gender, and Life Quality." *Social Problems* 47, no. 3: 291–326.

Morest, Vanessa Smith. 2013. "From Access to Opportunity: The Evolving Social Roles of Community Colleges." *The American Sociologist* 44: 319–328.

Morrill, Justin S. 1862. "Agricultural Colleges: Speech of Hon. Justin S. Morrill, of Vermont in the House of Representatives, June 6 1862." s.l.: s.n.

Mullen, Ann L. 2010. *Degrees of Inequality: Culture, Class and Gender in American Higher Education*. Baltimore, Md.: Johns Hopkins University Press.

National Center for Education Statistics (NCES). 2011. *Digest of Education Statistics, 2010*. Washington D.C.: U.S. Department of Education. https://nces.ed.gov/pubs2011/2011015.pdf.

National Center for Education Statistics (NCES). 2014. *Integrated Postsecondary Education System*. Washington D.C.: U.S. Department of Education. https://nces.ed.gov/ipeds/use -the-data.

National Center for Education Statistics (NCES). 2015a. *Demographic and Enrollment Characteristics of Nontraditional Undergraduates: 2011–12* (NCES 2015-025). Washington D.C.: U.S. Department of Education. https://nces.ed.gov/pubs2015/2015025.pdf.

National Center for Education Statistics (NCES). 2015b. *Trends in Pell Grant Receipt and the Characteristics of Pell Grant Recipients: Selected Years 1999–2000 to 2011–12* (NCES

2015-601). Washington D.C.: Department of Education, September. https://nces.ed
.gov/pubsearch/pubsinfo.asp?pubid=2015601.

National Center for Education Statistics (NCES). 2016. *Digest of Education Statistics, 2015* (NCES
2016-014). Washington D.C.: U.S. Department of Education. https://nces.ed.gov/pro
grams/digest/d15/.

National Center for Education Statistics (NCES). 2017. *Digest of Education Statistics, 2016* (NCES
2017-014). Washington D.C.: U.S. Department of Education. https://nces.ed.gov/pro
grams/digest/d16/.

National Center for Education Statistics (NCES). 2018. *Digest of Education Statistics, 2017* (NCES
2017-144). Washington D.C.: U.S. Department of Education. https://nces.ed.gov/programs
/digest/d17/.

Noll, Elizabeth, Lindsey Reichlin, and Barbara Gault. 2017. *College Students with Children:
National and Regional Profiles.* Washington D.C.: Institute for Women's Policy Research.
https://iwpr.org/wp-content/uploads/2017/02/C451-5.pdf.

Nomaguchi, Kei, and Wendy Johnson. 2016. "Parenting Stress among Low-Income and
Working-Class Fathers: The Role of Employment." *Journal of Family Issues* 37, no. 11:
1535–1557.

Nunn, Lisa M. 2014. *Defining Student Success: The Role of School and Culture.* New Brunswick,
N.J.: Rutgers University Press.

Obama, Barack H. 2009. "Remarks by the President on Higher Education." Washington,
D.C.: The White House. http://www.whitehouse.gov/the_press_office/Remarks-by-the
-President-on-Higher-Education/.

Obama, Barack H. 2014. *State of the Union Address.* Washington, D.C.: The White House.
http://www.whitehouse.gov/the-press-office/2014/01/28/president-barack-obamas
-state-union-address.

O'Brien, Matt. 2017. "Tuition-Free College a Partial Win for Rhode Island Governor." *U.S. News
& World Report,* June 23. https://www.usnews.com/news/best-states/rhode-island/arti
cles/2017-06-23/tuition-free-college-a-partial-win-for-rhode-island-governor.

OECD. 2015. *Education at a Glance 2015: OECD Indicators.* Paris: OECD Publishing. https://doi
.org/10.1787/eag-2015-en.

Oliff, Phil, Vincent Palacios, Ingrid Johnson, and Michael Leachman. 2013. "Recent Deep
State Higher Education Cuts May Harm Student Economy for Years to Come." Center
on Budget and Policy Priorities, March 19. Washington, D.C.: Center on Budget and Policy Priorities.

Padavic, Irene, and Barbara Reskin. 2002. *Women and Men at Work.* 2nd ed. Thousand Oaks,
Calif.: Pine Forge Press.

Pascarella, Ernest T., and Patrick T. Terenzini. 1991. *How College Affects Students: Findings and
Insights from Twenty Years of Research.* San Francisco, Calif.: Jossey-Bass.

Pearson, A. Fiona. 2007. "The New Welfare Trap: Case Managers, College Education and
TANF Policy." *Gender & Society* 21, no. 5: 723–748.

Pearson, A. Fiona. 2010. "The Erosion of College Access for Low-Income Mothers." In
21st Century Motherhood: Experience, Identity, Policy and Agency, edited by Andrea
O'Reilly, 216–233. New York: Columbia University Press.

President's Commission on Higher Education. 1948. *Higher Education for American Democracy.* 5 vols. New York: Harper & Brothers.

Reese, Ellen. 2005. *Backlash against Welfare Mothers: Past and Present.* Berkeley: University of
California Press.

Ridgeway, Cecilia. 2011. *Framed by Gender: How Gender Inequality Persists in the Modern World.*
New York: Oxford University Press.

Risman, Barbara. 1998. *Gender Vertigo: American Families in Transition.* New Haven, Conn.: Yale University Press.

Roberts, Dorothy. 1997. *Killing the Black Body: Race, Reproduction, and the Meaning of Liberty.* New York: Vintage Books.

Rondini, Ashley C. 2016. "Healing the Hidden Injuries of Class? Redemption Narratives, Aspirational Proxies, and Parents of Low-Income, First-Generation College Students." *Sociological Forum* 31, no. 1: 96–116.

Rose, Mike. 2012. *Back to School: Why Everyone Deserves a Second Chance at Education.* New York: New Press.

Ross, Terris, Grace Kena, Amy Rathbun, Angelina Kewl Ramani, Jijun Zhang, Paul Kristapovich, and Eileen Manning. 2012. *Higher Education: Gaps in Access and Persistence Study* (NCES 2012-046), U.S. Department of Education, National Center for Education Statistics. Washington D.C.: Government Printing Office.

Roth, Michael. 2014. *Beyond the University: Why a Liberal Education Matters.* New Haven, Conn.: Yale University Press.

Ruddick, Sara. 1989. *Maternal Thinking: Towards a Politics of Peace.* Boston: Beacon Press.

Rudolph, Frederick. 1962. *The American College and University: A History.* New York: Alfred A. Knopf.

Sadker, David, Myra Sadker, and Karen R. Zittleman. 2009. "Opening the Schoolhouse Door." In *Still Failing at Fairness: How Gender Bias Cheats Girls and Boys in School and What We Can Do about It,* 29–62. New York: Scribner.

Schmidt, Erik P. 2018. "Postsecondary Enrollment before and since the Great Recession." In *Current Population Reports,* P20-580. Washington, D.C.: U.S. Census Bureau. https://www.census.gov/content/dam/Census/library/publications/2018/demo/P20-580.pdf.

Schultz, Theodore. 1961. "Investment in Human Capital." *American Economic Review* 51: 1–17.

Selingo, Jeffrey J. 2013. *College (Un)Bound: The Future of Higher Education and What It Means for Students.* Boston: New Harvest, Houghton Mifflin Harcourt.

Sewell, William H. 1992. "A Theory of Structure, Duality, Agency, and Transformation." *American Journal of Sociology* 98: 1–29.

Shaw, Kathleen M., Sara Goldrick-Rab, Christopher Mazzeo, and Jerry A. Jacobs. 2006. *Putting Poor People to Work: How the Work First Idea Eroded College Access for the Poor.* New York: Russell Sage Foundation.

Siner, Emily. 2017. "As Free Community College Becomes Tennessee Law, Schools Will Cater More to Adult Students." Nashville Public Radio, May 24. http://nashvillepublicradio.org/post/free-community-college-becomes-tennessee-law-schools-will-cater-more-adult-students#stream/0.

Small, Mario Luis. 2010. *Unanticipated Gains: Origins of Network Inequality in Everyday Life.* Oxford: Oxford University Press.

Spring, Joel H. 1976. *The Sorting Machine.* New York: David McKay.

Staklis, Sandra, Vera Bersudskaya, and Laura Horn. 2011. *Students Attending For-Profit Postsecondary Institutions: Demographics, Enrollment Characteristics, and Six-Year Outcomes.* Washington D.C.: National Center for Education Statistics. http://nces.ed.gov/pubs2012/2012173.pdf.

Stephens, Nicole M., Stephanie A. Fryberg, Hazel Rose Markus, Camille S. Johnson, and Rebecca Covarrubias. 2012. "Unseen Disadvantage: How American Universities Focus on Independence Undermines the Academic Performance of First-Generation College Students." *Journal of Personality and Social Psychology* 102, no. 6: 1178–1197.

Stuber, Jenny M. 2011. *Inside the College Gates: How Class and Culture Matter in Higher Education.* Lanham, Md.: Lexington Books.

Swidler, Ann. 1986. "Culture in Action: Symbols and Strategies." *American Sociological Review* 51: 273–286.

Swidler, Ann. 2001. *Talk of Love: How Culture Matters.* Chicago: University of Chicago Press.

Taylor, Paul, Kim Parker, Richard Fry, D'Vera Cohn, Wendy Wang, Gabriel Velasco, and Daniel Dockterman. 2011. *Is College Worth It? College Presidents, Public Assess Value, Quality and Mission of Higher Education.* Washington D.C.: Pew Research Center, May 15. http://www.pewsocialtrends.org/2011/05/15/is-college-worth-it/.

Thelin, John R. 2004. *A History of American Higher Education.* Baltimore, Md.: Johns Hopkins University Press.

Tinto, Vincent. 1988. "Stages of Student Departure: Reflections on the Longitudinal Character of Student Leaving." *Journal of Higher Education* 59, no. 4: 438–455.

Tinto, Vincent. 1993. *Leaving College: Rethinking the Causes and Cures of Student Attrition.* 2nd ed. Chicago: University of Chicago Press.

Tuchman, Gaye. 2009. *Wannabe U: Inside the Corporate University.* Chicago: University of Chicago Press.

U.S. Census Bureau. 2018. *Poverty Thresholds.* https://www.census.gov/data/tables/time-series/demo/income-poverty/historical-poverty-thresholds.html.

U.S. Congress. 1862. *Morrill Act.* Public Law 37-108, Enrolled Acts and Resolutions of Congress, 1789–1996; Record Group 11. Washington, D.C.: General Records of the United States Government; National Archives. http://www.ourdocuments.gov.

U.S. Congress. 1996. *Personal Responsibility and Work Opportunity Reconciliation Act of 1996.* Public Law 104-193. H.R. 3734. http://thomas.loc.gov.

U.S. Department of Education. 2014. *Child Care Access Means Parents in School Program.* http://www2.ed.gov/programs/campisp/index.html.

U.S. Department of Education. 2015a. "America's College Promise Playbook." https://www2.ed.gov/documents/press-releases/college-promise-playbook.pdf.

U.S. Department of Education. 2015b. "Fact Sheet: Obama Administration Increases Accountability for Low-Performing For-Profit Institutions." July 15. https://www.ed.gov/news/press-releases/fact-sheet-obama-administration-increases-accountability-low-performing-profit-institutions.

U.S. Department of Education. 2016. "Education Department Proposes New Regulations to Protect Students and Taxpayers from Predatory Institutions." June 13. https://www.ed.gov/news/press-releases/education-department-proposes-new-regulations-protect-students-and-taxpayers-predatory-institutions.

U.S. Department of Education. 2017a. "Programs: Federal Pell Grant Program." https://www2.ed.gov/programs/fpg/funding.html.

U.S. Department of Education. 2017b. "Secretary DeVos Announces Regulatory Reset to Protect Students, Taxpayers, Higher Education Institutions." June 14. https://www.ed.gov/news/press-releases/secretary-devos-announces-regulatory-reset-protect-students-taxpayers-higher-ed-institutions.

U.S. Department of Health and Human Services. 2006. *Reauthorization of the Temporary Assistance for Needy Families (TANF) Program: Interim Final Rule.* Washington, D.C.: U.S. Government Printing Office.

U.S. Department of Health and Human Services. 2009. *Cohabitation and Marriage Rules in State TANF Programs.* https://aspe.hhs.gov/basic-report/cohabitation-and-marriage-rules-state-tanf-programs.

U.S Department of Labor. Bureau of Labor Statistics. 2018a. Occupational Employment and Wages, May 2017. https://www.bls.gov/oes/2017/may/oes399011.htm#st.

U.S. Department of Labor. Bureau of Labor Statistics. 2018b. *Occupational Outlook Handbook.* https://www.bls.gov/ooh/.

U.S. Department of Veterans Affairs. 2012. *The GI Bill's History.* http://www.gibill.va.gov /benefits/history_timeline/index.html.

U.S. Department of Veterans Affairs. 2013. "One Million Now Benefit from Post-9/11 GI Bill." November 8. Washington, D.C.: Office of Public Affairs and Media Relations. https:// www.va.gov/opa/pressrel/pressrelease.cfm?id=2490.

U.S. Department of Veterans Affairs. 2015. *2015 Economic Opportunity Report.* Washington, D.C.: U.S. Department of Veteran Affairs. http://www.benefits.va.gov/benefits/docs/vet eraneconomicopportunityreport2015.pdf.

U.S. Government Accountability Office. 2014. *Higher Education: State Funding Trends and Policies and Affordability.* Report to the Chairman, Committee on Health, Education, Labor, and Pensions, United States Senate, GAO 15-151. Washington, D.C.: GAO. http:// www.gao.gov/assets/670/667557.pdf.

U.S. Senate, Health, Education, Labor and Pensions Committee. 2012. *For Profit Higher Education: The Failure to Safeguard the Federal Investment and Ensure Student Success.* Majority Committee Staff Report and Accompanying Minority Committee Staff Views. Washington, D.C.: U.S. Senate, July 30. https://www.help.senate.gov/imo/media/for _profit_report/PartI-PartIII-SelectedAppendixes.pdf.

Veblen, Thorstein. [1918] 1993. *The Higher Learning in America.* New Brunswick, N.J.: Transaction Publishers.

Weber, Max. [1958] 2003. *The Protestant Ethic and the Spirit of Capitalism.* Translated by Talcott Parsons. Mineola, N.Y.: Dover Publications.

Wei, Christina Chang, and Horn, Laura. 2009. *A Profile of Successful Pell Grant Recipients: Time to Bachelor's Degree and Early Graduate School Enrollment* (NCES 2009-156). Washington D.C.: National Center for Education Statistics. https://nces.ed.gov/pubs2009/2009156.pdf.

Wells, Ryan S., and Cassie M. Lynch. 2012. "Delayed College Entry and the Socioeconomic Gap: Examining the Roles of Student Plans, Family Income, Parental Education and Parental Occupation." *Journal of Higher Education* 83, no. 5: 671–697.

West, Candace, and Don H. Zimmerman. 1987. "Doing Gender." *Gender & Society* 1, no. 2: 125–151.

West, Candace, and Don H. Zimmerman. 2009. "Accounting for Doing Gender." *Gender & Society* 23, no. 1: 112–122.

Whitebook, Marcy, Deborah Philips, and Carollee Howes. 2014. *Worthy Work, STILL Unlivable Wages: The Early Childhood Workforce 25 Years after the National Child Care Staffing Study.* Berkeley, Calif.: Center for the Study of Child Care Employment. http://cscce .berkeley.edu/files/2014/ReportFINAL.pdf.

Williams, Joan. 2000. *Unbending Gender: Why Families and Work Conflict and What to Do about It.* Oxford: Oxford University Press.

Williams, Joan C., and Heather Boushey. 2010. *The Three Faces of Work-Family Conflict: The Poor, the Professionals and the Missing Middle.* Center for American Progress/Center for Work Life Law—University of California, Hastings College of the Law. https://cdn .americanprogress.org/wp-content/uploads/issues/2010/01/pdf/threefaces.pdf.

Willis, Paul. 1977. *Learning to Labor: How Working Class Kids Get Working Class Jobs.* New York: Columbia University Press.

Zakaria, Fareed. 2015. *In Defense of a Liberal Education.* New York: W. W. Norton & Company.

Zornick, George. 2017. "Bernie Sanders Just Introduced His Free College Tuition Plan." *The Nation*, April 3. https://www.thenation.com/article/bernie-sanders-just-introduced-his -free-college-tuition-plan/.

INDEX

ABOUT THE AUTHOR

A. FIONA PEARSON is a professor of sociology at Central Connecticut State University in New Britain.